Duels At Dawn

Essays, 2010-11

by David R. Roell

Astrology Classics
Bel Air

The photo of Vivian Robson, pg. 139, supplied by Philip Graves.
Celebrity photos courtesy Wikimedia Commons.
Cover photos of the author taken by the author himself,
except for the lower one on the front cover, which was taken by his mother.

ISBN: 978 1 933303 49 9

Published by
Astrology Classics

The publication division of
The Astrology Center of America
207 Victory Lane, Bel Air MD 21014

On the net at www.**AstroAmerica.com**

✤ Table of Contents

✤Table **of Contents**, *by subject*

✤Introduction

YOU have economic hard times to thank for this book. I am by profession a bookseller. In 2007, Margaret Cahill, at the Wessex Astrologer, suggested a newsletter as a way of enhancing book sales. I think she had monthly specials, promo sheets and upcoming new titles in mind, but I was too dense for that. Instead I wrote on topics of my own fancy.

The first two years, 2007-9, when the newsletter appeared monthly were, well, dreadful. The week that Venus went retrograde in March, 2009, with the stock market stabilizing after months of plunging, I shifted from a monthly single-page newsletter, to a weekly three-pager.

I followed a strict three-page format for a couple of years. Most of the worth-while essays were compiled in my first book, *Skeet Shooting for Astrologers*.

Two years later in March, 2011, with the economy ever more bleak and myself running out of ideas, I started writing celebrity delineations and in the process broke out of a rigid format. The delineation of Jon Stewart, of the Daily Show, was the first of these. Retrograde Venus has turned up in a surprising number of the charts I've written about, given its rarity, among them, the chart for the Republican Party, as well as the charts for Rep. Ron Paul, Mayor Michael Bloomberg, Jon Stewart, and some others. No, my Venus is not retrograde.

What follows is in order of publication, in part as I think organizing by topic makes for a boring block of reading. The book starts with the last of the 2-column essays from the original 3-page weekly.

Meanwhile the economy is now in the fifth year of straight decline. Things are getting desperate. I do wish the people in charge of the country would just send us all envelopes stuffed with cash. (They seem incapable of actually governing.) I can live on barter just as well as money, but when that happens there will be no authors, there will be no books, there will be no commerce. Money has its uses.

David R. Roell

June 22, 2012

✤Legend

Signs		Planets	
0° ♈	Aries	☉	Sun
30° ♉	Taurus	☽	Moon
60° ♊	Gemini	☿	Mercury
90° ♋	Cancer	♀	Venus
120° ♌	Leo	♂	Mars
150° ♍	Virgo	♃	Jupiter
180° ♎	Libra	♄	Saturn
210° ♏	Scorpio	♅	Uranus
240° ♐	Sagittarius	♆	Neptune
270° ♑	Capricorn	♇	Pluto
300° ♒	Aquarius	☊	Node (north)
330° ♓	Pisces	⚷	Chiron

✤Houses versus Signs, *part 1*

Vivian Robson is the finest modern astrologer I have ever found, but I was surprised that even he lumped houses and signs together. Maybe I expect too much, or maybe I'm the only one who knows.

I've mentioned houses and signs before, but I've just realized that up to now I've never shown you a straight house to sign comparison. So here are the first five pairings:

Aries vs: the First House: ARIES is impulsive, aggressive, impatient, eager, thrusting, gotta be first, doesn't remember yesterday, doesn't care about tomorrow, let's do it NOW, I'm in a rush! and is otherwise Martial in every way it can be.

THE FIRST HOUSE is how other folks see you. Not how you see yourself (your view of yourself is your Moon by sign and house). Whatever sign is on your ascendant owns the place and expresses itself as it sees fit. "The first house is like Aries"–? Ever meet an aggressive Pisces rising? No, I haven't either.

Taurus vs: the Second House: TAURUS just wants TO BE. Preferably he prefers his being to be pretty, but he won't bother himself overmuch if it isn't. Some describe him as tending to inertia. Some others note a tendency to greed.

THE SECOND HOUSE contains your possessions. Whatever it is you value, and the means by which you get—or lose—them. The house is not inherently greedy or acquisitive, active or passive, it does not favor the pretty over the dull, it does not invariably collect merely for itself. All of these traits, and many more, are given to it by the various combinations of signs and planets.

Gemini vs: the Third House: GEMINI is quick-witted, fleet of foot, restless, nervous, two-faced (a trait they are sometimes unaware of), never at peace, with, as Robson himself pointed out, a certain cruel streak. Robson had a stellium in Gemini, he should know.

THE THIRD HOUSE is said to be many things: Early childhood, gram-

1

mar school, brothers and sisters, short trips, the nearby environment, etc. Taken together, this is Daily Life. Is Gemini daily life? No. It's too busy to notice. A nicely placed Moon in Leo in the third and you're the town big shot. A badly placed Saturn and you may flee for more distant climes.

Cancer vs: the Fourth House: CANCER is intensely personal. Takes life personally. The first to laugh at the joke, the first to cry. They are very sensitive, as a result, they make good diplomats or housewives.

THE FOURTH HOUSE are where your roots are, presuming you have any. It tells us what kind of home you have: Where, when, how expensive, how furnished, etc. It's your father (not, as some think, your mother), it's the end of the matter, including how you will end up in life, for better or worse.

Leo vs: The Fifth House: LEO is proud, the leader, the authority, the one in charge, the boss, the king. He brooks no rivals. He wants to be generous and larger than life and oftentimes actually is. And he can be petty and mean, a tyrant. But he is always the Leo, he never takes a day off, he knows nothing else.

THE FIFTH HOUSE has been compared to theatre. So let's combine that with romance, another 5th house specialty, and see what we get.

Males are vaudevillians. They live out of a trunk. They are perpetually on the road, going from engagement to engagement: A nomad's life. A new day, a new town, a new audience. They dream of settling down, but when the curtain rises, there is stage fright, a fear of entrapment, a desire to escape.

Females are the audience. (Theatre requires an audience.) They are avid theatergoers. They talk about the new shows among themselves, they read the reviews, they are impressed by marquee blandishments ("Limited Engagement!" "Greatest Show on Earth!" "Command Performance!" "One Night Only!" "Held Over!") — aka pick-up lines, if you haven't got the drift by now. She makes her choice, she buys a ticket, she goes to the show, she is eager, she wants to be entertained. She expects the actor to play to her alone. The actor can find the audience's demands daunting and may lapse into well-worn schtick. On the one hand he yearns for a standing ovation and a long term contract. On the other, deep inside there will always be the lure of the road, and, for his audience, the perpetual fear the show may slip out of town. This is Leonine to the extent that when the actor is on stage, he must command it, but that is a small part of the theatre overall. The lure of the road is a vagabond's life, the Sagittarian way. For the woman it is a matter of choice and possession, even if fleeting. The fifth house is complex. Success is when the two find balance. — *October 26, 2010*

✤Houses versus Signs, *part 2*

AFTER the first installment two weeks ago, someone from Australia — I think it was — emailed to say they've been treating houses and signs as separate entities since forever. I was encouraged. If this distinction could be taught right from the beginning, we'd all be better astrologers. But to repeat:

Houses are departments of life. Signs are traits and/or abilities. Signs are applied to houses by means of the planets that rule the signs, or are physically domiciled in the house in question. To wit:

Houses are raw materials.

Signs are tools.

Planets are workers. Two examples:

First: The raw material is paper. The tool is paste. The worker is 6 years old. The result: A mess. Second: The raw material is paper. The tool is paste. The worker is a bookbinder. The result: A bound book. Change only one of the three variables and you get an entirely different outcome. But note this carefully: You must specify all three to get any result at all. A house by itself, a sign by itself, a planet by itself, is meaningless.

Once this concept is clear you will never again read books on house delineations, as you will find them crude and useless.

I covered the first five houses two weeks ago. Here are Six through Nine:

Virgo versus the Sixth House: Virgo is analytical. It is precise. It loves details. I love these people more than any other, because they have a truth and honesty that no other sign can match.

The Sixth House is about health. It used to be about your servants, but modern times turned it about and it now shows you as a servant, i.e., your job. The 6th is about the food you eat. The element on the cusp tells us more. Earth, you eat starch. Water, you love sauces. Fire, you like spicy. Air, your sense of smell is acute. If the water sign is Scorpio, it's booze: aspects to Mars tell us if you're a drunk or a teetotaler. A Jupiter-

Moon conjunction in this house, in an earth or water sign, can make you quite large. And the 6th is the house of the army.

Libra verses the Seventh House: I think of Libra as the "what if" sign. What if we considered the alternative? Libra stops us from plunging straight ahead. It makes us consider alternatives. It likes harmony, it likes balance, and, paradoxically, it will fight to get it — the old "harmony through conflict" conundrum.

Which almost never applies to the 7th house. The seventh house is about The Other. Your spouse, your business partner, any peer. Whether they oppose you or love you or support you or block your every turn depends on the sign on the cusp, the sign and house of its ruler, and any planets that may be in the house itself. When the Sun, Moon, or ruler of the ascendant are here, you NEED a partner and if at all possible are rarely without one. You should ALWAYS consider your 7th house as your partner's 1st (turn the chart) and read the turned chart as if it were your partner's chart, as that's the relationship that you inherently attract, over and over again.

Scorpio versus the Eighth House: Scorpio is intense. Which might just be all that it is. Black and White. Why is it driven to sex? Because sex, not money, not friendship, not blood ties per se, is the ultimate relationship between two people. Whatever Scorpio does to you, he has previously done to himself.

The Eighth house are the things your partner brings to you. Their money, if a business partner. Their body, if a lover. The sign on the cusp will tell you the conditions they will attach to your use of it. The right sort of progressed aspect to the 8th cusp in a correctly timed chart shows the moment of your death. (Don't try this at home, it's lots more complicated than it looks.) Death and the trappings of death account for the psychic and occult connotations of this house, though I personally have a hard time conceptualizing exactly why.

Sagittarius versus the Ninth House: Sagittarius is a seeker. Someone on a quest. It is therefore oblivious to others, as Charles Carter once noted. Sagittarians make for bores on one hand, and Valley Girls on the other. It likes grand concepts. It has no patience for details.

The Ninth House is about what is foreign to you. Facts and figures you don't quite understand. Strangers who speak a strange language, including that of the law and courts. Travel to strange and unknown places. Things that are rare and unusual. Dreams are in this house (NOT the 12th, as the psychobabblists imagine), because dreams are things that are not part of your everyday reality. — *November 9, 2010*

❖Houses versus Signs, *part 3*

READERS will note I have simple ideas of the signs of the zodiac. I note if they are cardinal (active), fixed (stubborn) or mutable (helpless), I note if they are fiery (dynamic), airy (intellectual), wet (emotional) or earthy (practical, or inert). I do not bother myself with much more. Linda Goodman delineated people in terms of their sun signs. She was a master and should be studied. I am working in other areas.

For planets, I use simple keywords. **SUN:** Life. The focal point. Spirit. Energy. Men, in general. **MOON:** What is customary, cheap, common. What comes and goes. Women, in general. **MERCURY:** Communication. Wit. Intelligence. Speed. Youth. Duality. What adapts. **VENUS:** Harmony. Balance. Beauty. Females, especially young ones. Pulchritude. What is pleasant. **MARS:** Aggression. Energy. War. Testosterone. Raw male energy. **JUPITER:** Magnification, expansiveness. **SATURN:** Age, restriction, blackness, NO and NOT, denial. **URANUS** is mostly effective when angular, as I am otherwise often unable to find it. **NEPTUNE** is deceit. More than that he does not deserve. **PLUTO:** Revulsion. **NORTH NODE:** A Niagara of incoming, uncontrolled energy. **SOUTH NODE:** An energy drain, a vampire.

Capricorn vs: The 10th House: Capricorn is often well-polished, if a bit shopworn. An old classic. Willing to work hard for little reward. Often timid.

The tenth house, and especially the MC itself, is where you stand, stark naked, at high noon in the public square. How will you fare? What will you do? These questions are answered by the sign on the cusp. I have Aquarius there. This is the "who, me?" position, as Aquarius is the first to deny himself and look elsewhere for others. William Lilly said that Mercury, Venus or Mars in the 10th gave profession. Which they do. Communication (Mercury), the Arts (Venus), or soldiery or the physical trades (Mars). Lech, an old friend, was born with Mercury retrograde in the 10th. He was quite shy, up until the year his Mercury went direct by

5

progression. Whereupon, to his great surprise, he became a public speaker, finding he enjoyed it immensely.

The 10th is NOT "career" and NOT "fame." Off the top of my head, I'd say that fame is bestowed by planets in cardinal signs in angular houses, one of which is the 10th, of course. But I do not think the presence of a planet in the 10th will make you famous, nor a lack of a planet there will prohibit you. Like most things astrological, there are many solutions to the same problem. Learn to read dynamically and the chart will tell you all about itself. You will be constantly surprised by the variety of the human condition.

Aquarius vs: the Eleventh House: Aquarius is the Not-Self. He who repudiates himself. He who studies the entire world except himself. He who delights in being different, merely for its own sake. As all other signs think of themselves first, the Aquarian is a refreshing contrast, but that doesn't make him better. Just different.

The Eleventh House is the house of friends. People you know socially, not romantically. The cute young thing who says, "Can't we just be friends" wants you out of her 5th and into her 11th. Which is precisely where you don't want her to put you, her 11th being the opposite of what you were hoping for. The ability to turn friends into romantic partners is not, alas, shown by a good aspect between the rulers of 5 and 11, as I have them in tight sextile. The 11th is also the house of ideals, the things you believe in, beliefs that are a part of you. Note carefully the distinction with the 9th. The 9th concerns things which are greater than you, things that are strange to you, things which, at best, you merely aspire to. The 11th is personal.

Pisces vs: The Twelfth House: Pisces is formless and shapeless, a muddle, a mess. It is also universal and all-encompassing. In its brief moments of coherence, it can stagger you with a beauty and power beyond anything you can imagine.

The twelfth house can be confinement and seclusion. It can be life as a cog in a large institution, such as the army. It can be things which, while known to you, are generally unknown to others. The Hindus put lovemaking in this house for that reason: This house concerns what you do in private, not in public. Unoccupied, this house rules what is secret, even to you. Occupied, it shows what you cannot express to the world, despite all efforts. In horary astrology, this house rules lions, tigers and bears, also horses, in other words, all large animals. Any zookeepers with big 12ths out there? — *November 16, 2012*

✤Houses versus Signs, *part 4*

THE December/January issue of *The Mountain Astrologer* arrived this week. In it, the article, *Before the Client Arrives*, by Lenea van Horn. How to prepare yourself. So far as making a general character study of your clients, the rules on pg. 68 are a useful start. So far as preparing you for that client, not so much.

Clients don't come and pay your fee to hear the story of their life. At least, the clients you want to cultivate don't. They come with specific needs, often quite immediate ones. Which, given the "occult nature" of "astrology," they think you "already know." If you launch into a carefully rehearsed Great Life Script, they will, most of them, quietly hear you out, pay your fee, and then leave and not come back. This is so pervasive, and astrologers themselves so thick-headed, that entire books have been written about how to get the most out of such a strange encounter.

Yet the client's initial hopes were not misplaced. Astrology is full of magic. There is a traditional means whereby we may know what is troubling the man. It was used extensively by Evangeline Adams, and would have been used by William Lilly, if anyone in his day had natal charts:

You note the time the client enters your office, you determine the precise degree rising in the east at that moment, you find that degree in the client's natal chart. The house that contains that degree is what he came to see you about.

In most cases, that house will have a planet in it, because houses with planets in them are the important ones. If by chance there is no planet in that house, then you are to go to the planet which rules the sign on the cusp. The problem with the house in question (where the degree of the moment can be found) will be controlled by the house and sign of the planet which rules it.

For example, if someone should arrive and the ascendant of that moment fall in his seventh house (his spouse or partner), but there be no planet in that house, such as with my chart, we are to go immediately to the

7

ruler, which in my case is in the 11th.

What this house rules, in this case, my 11th, immediately becomes important. We need more than the usual natal cookbook delineations. We find them in a good book on horary. I'm supposed to be a great genius, but I quite often stick my nose in a book. I have so many around me. I suggest you do likewise. My first choice would be Anthony Louis. My second choice, only because of the typeface, would be Ivy. After that, Lilly and Derek Appleby and John Frawley, etc. All first rate.

The query, "what's going on with Dave's wife" immediately goes in two directions, but now that I have the subject narrowed down, Dave himself will lead me.

On the one hand, it could be that she's taken up with a friend of mine, as my friends are shown by my 11th house. With the ruler of my 7th in that house, I get my friends from my wife, I have few of my own (true). If this is the case, then as Dave has come to see me, I consider that Dave suspects some plot against him. Dave's progressions, and the transits activating them, will tell me if he has anything to fear. A simple matter.

On the other hand, to my spouse, my 11th house is her 5th (turn the chart). Her 5th represents her casual romantic affairs. In blunt terms, infidelity. Combining both possibilities, I consider that if Dave's wife has been unfaithful, she would have taken up with someone well-known to Dave himself. A friend, in other words. In this matter the astrologer must pay close attention to the sex of the signs in question. If the gender of the 7th house sign is the same as the gender of the sign containing the ruler, then Dave's wife is most likely being catty with one of her girlfriends. I confirm this by noting progressed and transiting *applying* aspects to Dave's Venus and Mars, including the all-important lunar aspects formed on the day itself. If these are benign, then Dave has nothing to worry about. If, on the other hand, retrograde Venus is applying to Dave's Mars, then he is well and truly cuckolded. This is a classic rule, and rarely wrong, but *it only applies to properly asked horary questions.* **NOT** a simple transit.

Yes, yes, yes. Plot those outer planet transits. Tell Dave what the next five years will bring him. Emphasize his cycles. Watch Dave's eyes glaze over. Or, by distinguishing between planets and signs and using the clock on the wall, find his problem and answer his question. He'll be happy when you do. The entire session will take half an hour, with time left over for follow-ups. *"Next client!"* — *November 23, 2010*

✤ Angles and Aspects

A FEW weeks ago in talking about houses and signs, I gave the example of the seventh house ruler domiciled in the first house, that it was a partner or spouse who was eternally underfoot. A woman wrote and offered her own chart. In it, I found the ruler of the first opposed by the ruler of the seventh, the planets physically located on the 6th and 12th house cusps. That's not "underfoot." That's "combat."

Which made me think. What about aspects between the rulers of the angles in a chart? The angles are the places in a chart that are most exposed to the world, therefore aspects among those rulers will be large factors in our lives. An obvious observation, don't you think?

So I thought I'd try it out on my self. The ruler of my ascendant is Mercury in the 9th. It's tightly sextile the ruler of my 7th, which is Jupiter in Aries in 11. Ergo, my partners are friends (11) with whom I enjoy a great many (Jupiter) intellectual (9th) conversations (Mercury). It has always been an easy process (sextile).

Okay. How about ruler of the ascendant and ruler of the midheaven? That would be Mercury with Saturn in Libra. They're trine, which, other factors being equal, means it's easy for me to be serious (Saturn) and to work professionally. Is that the same as being famous or well-known? Well, no. Not quite. Saturn is retrograde. He is—literally—facing away. I have never been concerned about my "reputation".

Ruler of the 10th house—Saturn—is also trine the ruler of the 4th house, which is the Sun in Aquarius in 9. Which means my preference is to work at home. This is actually the best of a bad deal, since Saturn, being retrograde, doesn't care if I'm actually in public, while the debilitated Sun would just as well hide at home.

Ruler of the ascendant—Mercury—widely conjunct the ruler of the 4th—the Sun. I'd just as soon invite you all over, where we could all sit around and have stimulating intellectual conversations (9th house Sun). But, as the Sun is debilitated, that never seems to happen.

9

Ruler of the 4th house—Sun—is widely sextile to the ruler of the 7th —Jupiter. When you're trying to sort out conflicting influences in a chart, this one's neat. The Sun-Jupiter sextile is subordinate to the Jupiter-Mercury sextile, and for two reasons. One, Jupiter-Mercury is a lot tighter. Two, Mercury is much stronger in Aquarius than the Sun. Result: My wife will largely leave us alone, and, preferably, would rather we not invade the house as a whole.

Here's where it gets fun. The ruler of the 7th house—Jupiter—is opposite the ruler of the 10th: Saturn. This means my wife merely tolerates what I do for a living. Doesn't really understand it. This was true of everyone I ever dated. If I were to suddenly drop dead, this business would probably not survive a month. That's just the way it is.

But there's more. Did you ever wonder if a business partnership was right for you? **Look for an aspect between the ruler of your 7th (partnerships), and the ruler of your 10th, profession.** If they're in trine or sextile, you'll have an easy time of it. If they're in square, you'll fight. If they're opposed, the two of you will eventually split. Conjunctions are variable, and you should always consider the relative strength of the ruler of the 10th (your profession) and the strength of the ruler of the 7th (your partner) as to who will be stronger. If there is no aspect nor disposition, then a professional partnership will probably never arise.

Now expand the idea. Ruler of the 10th—profession—in aspect to the ruler of the 3rd: partnership with a brother or sister. In my case, ruler of the 3rd is moving away from a wide sextile to the ruler of the 10th—Saturn. Ruler of the 3rd is also in the third, which means I know them only too well!

How about Father and Son, or in my case, Daughter? Ruler of the 10th house—Saturn—is in the 5th house. So far, so good, but as the ruler is retrograde, she won't be the one to think of it. Yet the cusp of the 5th is ruled by Mercury, which is in a good sextile to Saturn, which means she might eventually. Or, since there's a strong 9th house flavor, she might use daddy to establish herself abroad. Will your son follow in his daddy's footsteps? Now you have the means to find out!

One would expect her mother to look on disapprovingly as we've already established that Jupiter opposes the business in general, but as my daughter's mother/aka my wife, is favorably placed in other ways, the opposition would not be severe. For those of you who like what I do (being a bookseller), I just have to hang in there long enough to leave the biz to my daughter, who is now ten. — *December 14, 2010*

♣Mangling Hellenistic Astrology

ON Friday I was asked if I knew of Chris Brennan and Zodiacal Releasings. Turns out, once I'd hummed a few bars it came back to me, but I had never checked out the score. These releasings have to do with the Aphasis, which is described in Vettius Valens. Starting at birth, you go sign by sign. Each sign has a certain number of years, which are counted, starting at birth. When the time allotted for one sign ends, you are "released" into the next.

Googling, I quickly turned up *Zodiacal Releasing 1.48,* by Curtis Manwaring. My preliminary instructions said, Use the Sun for day births, the Moon for night births. Since the output is in signs, I presumed that meant to use the Sun's sign. So I used Aquarius.

To date, I have had three releasings (*Aphasis*): Aquarius to Pisces, Pisces to Aries, and Aries to Taurus. The first date was within two weeks of getting kicked out of London, a life changing event. The second date was within a week of deciding to leave New York, move to California, and start what became this business, another life changing event. The third date, two years ago, was two weeks prior to my much-delayed marriage, an elected event *(thanks, Debbi!).*

That's impressive.

Damn impressive.

But then I found it wasn't right. Manwaring's software has a default of Leo, and by now the sources I was Googling were implying that day births are Leo, and night births are Cancer. I'm a day birth, so I tried Leo. The dates were garbage.

But then I read that what was really meant was to use the sign of the Part of Fortune (for some things), and the sign of the Part of Spirit (or Daemon: *Al Biruni*) for other things. These two Parts are related, as one is the reflection of the other, with the Ascendant/Descendant as the mirror. As I'm a full moon birth, both of these are in Sagittarius. I tried that. The dates were meaningless.

11

By now I was just plain puzzled, so I also tried the Ascendant, which is Gemini. Those dates, also, were gibberish.

I needed someone else to try, so I tried the wife. She was a day birth (early Taurus), so I tried that. She said she doesn't remember dates, and while that's common, the results should be plainly obvious, so when she didn't recognize anything, I had an inspiration. What if the Sun was for boys and the Moon was for girls? Elizabeth's Moon is in Libra, so I tried that. There was one releasing. The date was within two months of leaving academia and moving to Santa Fe. Another life-changing event.

But the texts I was reading all had to do with Time Lords. Time Lords are Firdaria, which is *Abu Ma'shar*. So I found an on-line Firdaria and went at it. Gave it my date of birth. The results were completely different from *Aphasis*, which establishes the two systems as fundamentally different. But the Fidaria results were, again, garbage.

Which, by the way, was the same sort of disappointing results I had always gotten with Vimshottari Dashas. Which is why, to answer an earlier question, I don't feature Vedic astrology in this newsletter: I don't understand it. I can't make it work. The dasha dates look like gibberish to me.

This made me all the more curious as to what was actually being translated, if it was being translated, and understood, correctly. I haven't the space to bore you with the details, but it seems to me that both the translators, as well as many of the exponents of Hellenistic astrology, have previous backgrounds as psychological astrologers. While I bless the very soul of astro psychobabble, it is a foggy discipline at best. Could it be that, lacking the ability to read charts precisely, the Hellenistic crowd has transferred their earlier psychological fuzziness into their Hellenistic studies, wholesale? That they are, in other words, simply not demanding enough? If so, they are caught in a most delicious trap. Hellenistic astrology is full of the most intricate details. Lacking clear comprehension (go look at the translations, for heaven's sake!), are astrologers spinning their wheels? Just as we had, previously, with Dane Rudhyar and his likes?

So I would like to hear from those of you old enough to know. Try the *Aphasia*, try *Fidaria*. With either of them, with whatever methods you use, do you get dates that are of immediate relevance, Yes or No? —
December 21, 2010

♯Chuck and Dave and Firdaria

LAST week GJ took my challenge to explain Firdaria to me. She proposed the chart of Prince Charles, heir to the British throne. Charles was born November 14, 1948, at 9:14 pm GMT, in London. His chart has 5 degrees Leo rising. Entering his data (night birth), GJ told me that Charles is now very depressed that things are not going well in his life, having entered his Mercury Firdaria on November 14, 2010, little more than a month ago. I said forecasting Charlie's psychological state was silly, whereupon we snarled and spat on each other. This, by the way, is how astrologers greet one another. Dogs sniff each others' butts, astrologers, like cats, claw each others' eyes out. Always have, always will. Now you know.

If Firdaria is so hot, I said, explain his marriage to Diana Spencer on July 29, 1981, during his Mars period. Which GJ did.

The marriage was in order to produce an heir to the throne. Mars rules Chuck's 5th house of children (Scorpio) and is, in fact, domiciled in the 5th (in Sagittarius). (Chart, pg. 58.) Mars rules his MC (Aries), which means that producing a child is necessary for his public standing—which is true. In a night chart, Mars is the triplicity ruler of all water signs, which reinforces its nominal rulership of Scorpio. GJ also points out that Scorpio was on the 7th house of his November 1980 solar return, meaning his problem with children could be solved, at some point during the year, via marriage. 1980 was a nine year for profections (advance the chart 30° a year), highlighting Charles' 9th house. Charles' 9th is empty, but its ruler, Jupiter, is natally in his 5th, which is, again, children.

This may scream "children", but none of these, not the Firdaria, not the return, not the profection, timed the wedding, on July 29, nearly three-fourths of the way into the return/ profection. Nor did any of it have much to say about the bride, Lady Diana. Marriage first, children later is how it's supposed to go.

I had more prepared, but then I started thinking about my own Firdarias. My Mercury is in the 9th and during my Mercury Firdar, from

13

age 18 to 31, I travelled internationally. My Moon is in the 3rd. During my Moon Firdar, from age 31 to 41, I travelled domestically. Heck, I kept on travelling during my Saturn Firdar, despite the fact that Saturn is in my 5th. This was also the time I dated the most. I'd been dating since my Mercury period and went on dating during my Moon period, and then it came to me: The Firdar highlights the house the planet is domiciled in. NOT the one it rules, or at least, not primarily. And if it does anything with triplicity rulers, well, I can't find it in my chart.

I am a day birth, so I started with the Sun Firdar. My Sun is in the 9th. Guess what? My daddy (Sun) dragged us around from town to town in Kansas when I was growing up. To a small child, that's as much a 9th house affair as an adult emigrating to a foreign land. I attended half a dozen different schools before I graduated high school, which is also 9th.

And it made no difference that in Mercury I travelled for myself, or that in Moon I travelled with a partner, or that I kept travelling while in Saturn.

What about the houses the Firdar planet rules? In Chuck's case, Mars rules the house it was in, as well as his MC. During his Mars period, November 1980—November 1987, his feud with Lady Di nearly destroyed the monarchy as a whole. That's Mars whacking the MC. Once started, it went on through his north node, south node, and most of his Sun Firdars. Just as, once I started travelling, I kept on travelling, even when the Firdar had me kissing the girl next door.

How about my dad? My Sun rules my 4th house. Which is *my* family, not his. As a five year old, I didn't have a family. I have an army of younger siblings. What did daddy's meanderings mean to them? Ken, a night birth, a year after me: 12th house Moon, the first nine years were invisible. Followed by 11 years of a 10th house Saturn: By the end of the Firdar, he had become prominent at an early age. Even though he was moved about, just as I was, Brother Ken did not "experience" travel at all. Sister Barbara was a day birth a year later. First house Sun, her first eight years of daddy's wanderings hit her full in the face. Rashomon! The events were the same. The Firdar's stories were all different.

What do we know about Firdaria? First: It emphasizes the house the planet is in. Second: It builds during its course. Third: Events begun during the period will continue after it ends. Fourth: There is some tendency to influence the houses the planet rules. Fifth: You can't use it for timing. Sixth: You can't predict all that it may bring: Mars brought Charles combat with his 7th house. — *December 28, 2010*

♣A Eclipse and an (Astrological) Election:
A post-mortem

LAST Tuesday's solar eclipse wasn't much, as eclipses go. The Moon was off to the left of the Earth, its penumbra barely clipped the Earth's western limb. Which is a fancy way of saying the west coast of Europe woke up to a sunrise that was partially eclipsed, the node being 11 degrees distant. Rule of thumb: The closer an eclipse is to the node, the more total it is.

Yves Smith, at *Naked Capitalism*, chose that moment to file her petition, "*Citizens call for tough regulation of mortgage servicers.*" In America, home mortgages have been sold to investors. Banks, now termed "servicers", collect the monthly payments and pass them on to the investors. Since we're all now broke, banks-cum-servicers are making ends meet by foreclosing for trivial reasons, kicking the residents out, selling the property for whatever they can get, thereby rendering people homeless on one hand, and stiffing the investors on the other. It has gone on for more than two years and so far has been ignored by federal, state and local authorities. This is not good and most likely illegal. Criminally. And yes, some (though not all) of these home owners were behind, but homelessness as a penalty for minor mortgage arrears is as cruel as amputation for purse snatching. I've been homeless.

So Yves Smith and friends circulated a petition, collected 12,000 signatures, and to my dismay, electronically submitted it to the US government officials, including Timothy Geithner, Ben Bernanke, Mary Shapiro, Sheila Bair, Ed DeMarco and John Walsh, early last Tuesday morning. During the eclipse itself. (Yves is active in the wee hours before dawn.)

Since this was clearly an elected event, and as we're A*s*t*r*o*l*o*g*e*r*s, let's have a look at it. We will use the eclipse chart, set for Yves's locale of New York: January 4, 2011, 4:03 am EST. I get a chart with 29 Scorpio rising.

The chart is radical and can be judged, as we find the Moon, which rules the common people (the governed), in Capricorn, the sign of government.

15

Which is not good, as the Moon in Capricorn is debilitated and hence, weak. Eclipsed, it is by definition combust the Sun, which is to say, burnt up. In such circumstances we would not expect the People's Voice to be heard.

I went to Robson for the details, chapter 3, *The Moon in Electional Astrology.* Do not elect for the new moon, Robson says. Avoid doing things with the Moon in debility. As for the outcome of an elected event, judge by the first aspect the Moon makes after the election.

For a moment, I was hopeful. Yves means well, and has a notable book to her credit: *Econned,* on the economic collapse of 2008. The Moon's first aspect would save the day.

But it didn't.

The Moon's first aspect after the eclipse, occurring well after I saw her post, was at 10:00 am EST: *square to Saturn.* Saturn, ruler of Capricorn, enemy of the Moon, is the symbol of government itself.

Given the Moon's already weakened state, Saturn's square made the immediate conclusion, that Yves's petition, with its thousands of signatures, was Dead On Arrival.

Squares indicate stress, but what sort, exactly? Was Saturn-as-government unable to help? Good intentions but powerless to act? Or was the government contemptuous, but unwilling to speak openly (which would be the opposition, as oppositions are always overt)? I decided to look at terms.

At 16 Capricorn, the Moon was in terms of Mercury. It wants to talk, but, debilitated, it can't. Saturn at 16 Libra was in terms of Venus: Wants to help but can't (the square gets in the way). With faces, Saturn's face is Saturn. No means no. The Moon's face is Mars: Don't tempt me, I might hurt you.

Such was the Moon's first aspect after the eclipse. The second aspect? Conjunct Mars. Which is to say, underlying the petition is the People's Rage. Lots of rage—Mars is powerful in Capricorn. Government indifference to homeowner distress is dangerous. Mars is the ruler of the eclipse chart, but with 29 degrees Scorpio ascending, the chart as a whole has no room to maneuver. It is boxed.

That the first two aspects the Moon made after the eclipse were with malefics shows how sour the eclipse was. The very next day, Morgan R., an 81 year old Wiccan, rang to ask about the upcoming super conjunction in Aries, in May: Mercury, Venus, Mars, Jupiter, Uranus, with the Moon on the 1st and 2nd of the month. All opposed by Saturn and squared by Pluto. Find them all in the Equinox chart (March 20, 2011, 7:21 pm EDT, Washington), with Moon a day past full and Aries on the 7th. Get set for fireworks. — *January 11, 2011. The Occupy movement started in September.*

♣Ophiuchus, the "13th Sign"

THIS *past week a group of homeless astronomers in Minneapolis suckered the local paper, the* Tribune, *into running the old lie about Ophiuchus being the "13th sign of the zodiac." Which got picked up by* KSTP, *the local TV station, and then by* CNN, The Christian Science Monitor, The Huffington Post *and everyone else. Somebody in nearby Baltimore made a YouTube video in which he blamed the Astrology Center of America (that's us, folks) and told viewers to call our number. Which he gave. It promptly went viral and I got lots of angry phone calls, before I got Google to remove it for violating my privacy.*

In response I sent the following to the Tribune. *I would be most surprised if it was printed:—*

REGRET to report the article was wrong in all respects. The tropical zodiac is based on the Earth-Sun relationship. Not on stars.

Zero Aries is defined as the Vernal Equinox.

Zero Cancer is the Summer Solstice.

Zero Libra is the Autumnal Equinox.

Zero Capricorn is the Winter Solstice.

All based on declination, not longitude.

This was expounded by Ptolemy in his *Tetrabiblos*, c. 140 AD, but it wasn't his idea. It had already been in use for some time prior. Please note that in Ptolemy's day, the Sidereal and Tropical zodiacs were, to a casual eye, identical.

There is a zodiac based on star positions, with Aldebaran as fiducial (marker). That is the Sidereal Zodiac, in use in India. It is a radically different system that cannot be compared to the Western Tropical Zodiac.

As none of the signs are based on stars (not in the Tropical system, nor the Sidereal), use of this or that constellation is symbolic. Not actual. And always has been. In the classical system there are 12 signs and seven planets. Extrapolated from these are not only the calendar, but the seven

17

day week and the 24 hour day. Seriously adding or subtracting pieces would literally collapse human time-keeping. Sure you wanna do that?

Nor is the tropical system static. Because the Earth does not have a perfectly circular orbit, some seasons are longer than others, and over the centuries, the dates of the Earth's perihelion and aphelion change. In 1838, perihelion was on January 2. In 2020, perihelion will be on January 5 (precise times are available). (Source: *Tables of Planetary Phenomena 3rd edition*, Michelsen/ Pottenger, Starcrafts Publishing, 2007.) The tropical zodiac reflects this. The sidereal zodiac does not.

Which means some signs of the zodiac are actually longer in time than others. Which means that a degree in the tropical zodiac is accurate, whereas a degree in the sidereal zodiac is merely the annualized mean. From shortest "degree" to longest "degree," the difference over a year amounts to roughly 30 seconds of arc. Tropical shows this. Sidereal cannot.

You can take the entire solar system, Sun, planets, moons, aster-oids, you can drop them into a distant galaxy far, far away, and the tropical zodiac will still be exactly accurate, since it will still be based on the Earth-Sun relationship. Which is fundamental. The Sidereal zodiac is relative. ALL Sidereal zodiacs (there are, let me see, the Fagan-Bradley, Lahiri, Krishnamurti, Raman, Shill-Ponde and three or four others) are based on the Tropical Zodiac. The fudge factor they all use is called the Ayanamsa. Which is a variable that is subtracted from Tropical positions.

Any self-respecting astronomer KNOWS THIS, as it is nothing but the Earth's own orbital mechanics. You cannot send a space probe to the Moon, much less Venus or Mars, unless you have mastered these essen-tials. The Jet Propulsion Lab in Pasadena has.

There are a group of astronomers who trot this story out every three or four years or so. I heard it three years ago at a local high school in Edgewood, MD. I heard it back in the mid-1990's, I heard it back in the late 1980's. It probably goes a lot further back, because it's guaranteed the astronomers behind it have learned nothing. Nor do they want to.

In recycling this erroneous story, you have done a disservice to your readers as well as launched a near panic in many quarters, as the phone calls I got on the 13th, here in Maryland, will prove.

I am,

David R. Roell

I run the Astrology Center of America, where we keep track of things like this, in order to spare the ignorant their embarrassment. — *January 18, 2011. I subsequently developed the first comprehensive theory of astrology.*

✣The Orbit of the Moon is not what you think.

THIS week the AFA sent me a copy of their newest book, *Black Moon Lilith*, by M. Kelly Hunter. Isn't she the one that wrote that other book? You mean, *Living Lilith, Four Dimensions of the Cosmic Feminine*? Yes. Same one. And only a couple of years ago, too.

Hunter's new book focuses on the empty second center of the Moon's elliptical orbit around the Earth. This is in keeping with Kepler's laws, that all orbits are in fact eccentric and have two focal points. The Earth, or the Earth/Moon barycenter, is one. The empty second point is Hunter's Black Moon, aka the Biblical Lilith. More or less.

So I went looking for this second focal point. And I discovered something interesting. The Moon, in fact, does not orbit the Earth. Never did. Never will. *Can't.*

The Earth and Moon are, in fact, dual planets who weave in and out of each other's orbital paths, in the process creating the illusion that one "goes around" the other. From New Moon to New Moon, the Earth/Moon pair travels one-thirteenth of the Earth's orbit around the Sun. One-thirteenth of the orbit is approximately 45 million miles. The "Moon's orbit around the Earth" has a diameter of approximately 500,000 miles. Dividing one into the other, we discover the Moon fails to actually orbit the Earth by a factor of 90. Which means the Moon would have to make nearly 1200 orbits in a year to actually orbit the Earth. It manages only 13.

Which sort of wrecks Hunter's Black Moon premise. Well, maybe not. There is still an empty focal point, only we need to look further afield. The Moon's empty focal point is in fact the same as the Earth's empty focal point. Given the Earth's orbital eccentricity, it can be found a little to the left of the Sun, some 93 million miles away. Sorry about that. — *January 25, 2011*

✤ Astrology and Medicine

I was furious, and then ashamed, of the lies that Parke Kunkle told the world two weeks ago. Are Astrologers so stupid, so intellectually flabby, that we permit this nonsense? We talk of 13th planets and dark moons and depth psychology and just plain *make stuff up* and is it any wonder that people take us at our word and think we are fools? It is time to get serious. It is time to show the world Astrology.

By use of Astrology, you may know what ailments you will be subject to. By use of Astrology, you may know your prognosis once you become ill. By use of Astrology you may know the means of your passing. By use of Astrology—and this only if you are very, very careful—you may know the date of your death.

Medicine without astrology is inconceivable. Doctors who do not construct the charts of their patients are no better than blind men stumbling about in a hurricane. It's not that I wonder how doctors treat their patients without the use of astrology, it's that I am frankly amazed that doctors, shorn of astrology, are of any use whatever.

Some of you will disagree and point to this or that doctor, this or that hospital, this or that technique. I agree there are exceptions to this bleak picture. I only ask, How long did it take for the doctor to arrive at the proper diagnosis? How long to chance upon the proper treatment? Any doctor who stays in contact with his patient for years on end will do a dang fine job, but what if you don't have such a doctor? What if it's an emergency? What if you've been generally healthy for years and years? What if you're one of the millions of Americans who have no health insurance? What if you're one of the tens of millions whose health insurance is, unknown to you, actually worthless?

Do you suppose all doctors are like Gregory House? Have you actually watched that show? *House* is 50 minutes of patient-endangering, cost-soaring WILD GUESSES before the solution is magically pulled from a hat. It is, in fact, the *Physician's Desk Reference* run backwards.

20

ASTROLOGY is Knowledge. Astrology is Power. Learn to read your chart and you will never again be at the mercy of doctors, good or bad. So let's start.

Your natal chart is the key to your personal ailments and diseases. What will afflict you. Will you be generally healthy? Will you be generally unhealthy? Here are the starting points:

•Sun sign.
•Moon sign.
•Ascendant and planets conjunct.
•The chart ruler and its sign.
•Aspects these make to each other.
•Aspects from the benefics.
•Aspects from the malefics.

In my chart I have Sun and Moon opposed, from Aquarius (blood) to Leo (heart). I consequently have a very stressed heart. I had elevated blood pressure and heart palpitations in my 20's. By my early 50's these had become dangerous and I now take better care of myself.

But what about my colon? Colon problems are common. A close friend has colitis? Should I be concerned?

No. I should not. I have Mars in Scorpio, which rules the colon. My intestines, like my Mars, are strong.

How about diabetes? Some members of my family suffer from that. Carter gives the formula. In brief, planets at 17° Cancer-Capricorn produce diabetes. I don't have that.

How about epilepsy? Generally if you have it, you know, but what about your newborn? Will he or she have it? The formula, in brief, is an afflicted Mercury in no aspect to the Moon, but you should study the classical rules carefully, as there are tricks.

Jupiter or Venus, in good aspect to the ascendant or its ruler, make for good health. Saturn in hard aspect makes for poor health. Mars in hard aspect can make for a life of fevers or debilitating injuries.

In my case, Jupiter sextile both ascendant and chart ruler, the chart ruler trine the ascendant, Saturn trine both the ruler and the ascendant, my health has been, despite my grumbling, surprisingly good, and this despite a debilitated Sun in hard aspect to Pluto.

Learn Astro-Medicine and become your family's physician. Be their first line of defense. Know in advance what the possibilities are. I will have more next week, but the subject is vast and I cannot cover it in detail. Here are two books to start: Carter's *Encyclopaedia of Psychological Astrology*, for specific degree areas, and Robson's *Student's Text-Book*, for ailments specific to individual signs. Both will reward study. — *January 25, 2011*

✠ Astro Med

ASTROLOGER Paul Robles (not his real name) of Los Angeles (not quite his real address) had an AHA! moment last week. He has a brother born September 25, 1963, at 6:06 am EST at 39N, 87W. Paul read last week's newsletter and emailed, *"The moon was the giveaway for the blindness, being at 25 Sag (and angular, too, tho that wasn't mentioned). I'm not a good astro-diagnostician, but what about his chart makes all this so extreme? I mean, lots of folks have moon in the degrees mentioned without blindness, and lots of people have asc. ruler Merc conj. Pluto in the 12th... without the degree of affliction* [also almost totally deaf as well as autistic] *he shows. Insights from Mr. Astrodoc?*

ASTRODOC replies that angularity has a lot to do with it (makes it worse), and that his left eye should be worse than his right, since the Moon rules the left eye in males.

<u>Deafness:</u> Combining Robson, Carter and Sepharial: Mercury afflicted in the 12th, afflicted from the 6th (Saturn rules the 6th and while in the "5th", is in the sign of the 6th, Aquarius). Carter expressly identifies Virgo rising as a factor in deafness, also semi-squares to malefics (Mars is 47 degrees away). I note that Mercury, while in Virgo, is retrograde (weak), which makes it unable to carry out its duties as chart ruler. It is also an example of a failed dispositor, as it disposes of the two malefics, Pluto and Uranus, both of which are in Virgo and in the 12th. That these two are not technically conjunct Mercury is a saving grace. (Retrogrades matter!)

Carter quotes Lilly that malefics in the terms of Mercury cause deafness: Saturn at 17 Aquarius is in terms of Mercury. Uranus at 7 Virgo is also in terms of Mercury. Carter is skeptical of Lilly, but in this case, Lilly is right.

Autism is defined as a neural development disorder, which is squarely Mercurial. Of insanity, Carter says Mars in a water sign in the 3rd, which is the case here. Under mental deficiency, he notes 22 degrees of mutables (Mercury in this case) are often involved. Set the chart 10 minutes earlier and he would have 22 mutable on all four angles.

Such is an astrological analysis of a tragedy. The individual in question grew up to be a computer troubleshooter for the defense department. Richer than his astro-brother! — *February 1, 2011*

♱George Washington's Chart

JUST in on Friday, Thomas Canfield's new book on Eris, *Yankee Doodle Discord, A walk with planet Eris through USA history.* Canfield's premise is that Eris is a little bit like Uranus and a little bit like Neptune: Trines and sextiles mess you up, squares and oppositions are good, the conjunction is a mess. A *"Frenemy."* After brief preliminaries, he gets down to 21 chapters of chart examples.

So I picked one at random: Chapter 4, on George Washington. Eris dead conjunct Mars in Scorpio, in the 7th, meant that George was an oaf as a commander.

But I saw something else. Scorpio on the cusp of the 7th, Mars in Scorpio in the 7th, that's Martha Washington. The usual interpretation is that she's the ever watchful, ever-ready-to-pounce eagle, soaring high above. Or the common scorpion, ready to attack without warning. She also has rights in George's 12th house, as it has Aries on the cusp. The 12th holds the skeletons in George's life, those private things he didn't want disturbed. Which, in George's case, Martha had free access to, to do with as she pleased. Which can be quite extremely painful to George. So is this an accurate representation of Martha? No. *Wiki* says they loved each other madly. So much for 10 am LMT.

Flipping 10 *am* to 10 *pm* (a common mistake) gives a much better chart. Adding twelve hours changes George's Venus from Pisces to Aries and puts it on the 6th. With Libra rising, ruler in Aries in 6, his army (6th house) loved him. 10 pm makes Mars in 2 the final dispositor. I like. A commander who is fair (Libra rising), but determined and hard working (Venus/Saturn conjunct in 6) and ruthless (Mars) to get what he wants (2nd). Leo on the MC, a leader, but the ruler in the 5th in Pisces, he'd rather be home enjoying himself. The Moon in Capricorn late in 3, he can travel by instinct if he has to, but would rather not (Moon debilitated). This has possibilities: **George Washington, February 22, 1732, 10 pm, Wakefield, VA** (Gregorian calendar). *Dave's rectification.* What is hard about rectification? — *February 8, 2011*

✤Basic Medical Chart Analysis

TO everything there is a season, which in this case means the twelve signs rule parts of the body. Here is the usual list:

Aries: Head

Taurus: Throat

Gemini: Arms and lungs

Cancer: Breasts, stomach

Leo: Heart

Virgo: Intestines

Libra: Kidneys

Scorpio: Genitals and anus

Sagittarius: Hips, thighs

Capricorn: Knees, skin, bones

Aquarius: Ankles, circulation/blood

Pisces: Feet

Note carefully: **This is a generalization.** Taurus rules the lower jaw, for example, just as Aries rules the upper jaw. For detailed rulerships, get *Cornell.* Also note the table on pgs. 119-120 of *Christian Astrology, Book 1*, where rulerships of planets in the signs are given. Here, for example, are the various rulerships given to Aries:

Sun in Aries: *Thighs*

Moon in Aries: *Knees, head*

Mercury in Aries: *Genitals, legs*

Venus in Aries: *Kidneys, feet*

Mars in Aries: *Belly, head*

Jupiter in Aries: *Neck, throat, heart, belly*

Saturn in Aries: *Breast, arms*

Note that Lilly's rulerships refer to **horary charts**.

What this means: Your principal medical areas of interest will be the signs of the Sun, Moon, Ascendant and its ruler. If these are strong, well-placed and well-aspected, then you most likely will not suffer problems from them. My Gemini ascendant, for example, is well-aspected and its ruler, Mercury, is well placed as well as well-aspected. Consequently, when I once slammed a knife into the crux between the thumb and index finger of my right hand, and, so far as I can tell, severed a ligament or a nerve (all ruled by Gemini/Mercury), I suffered no loss in either finger. This puzzled the doctors in New York, who spent an hour looking at it, asking me to wiggle my finger. Which I did. I almost had to beg them to stitch me up. (Don't try this at home, I was at work at the time!)

On the other hand, as I've mentioned before, Sun in Aquarius (its debility), opposite Moon in Leo means I have a rather delicate heart/circulatory system. In general, hard aspects to Ascendant, Sun, Moon and chart ruler make for weakness and problems, whereas good aspects from benefics (Venus and Jupiter) make for strength.

The next step is to look for specific problems. For the most part, these are cataloged in two priceless books: Robson's *Student's Text-Book of Astrology*, and Carter's *Encyclopaedia of Psychological Astrology*, which also contains a handy table in the back. We owe both books to Robson, as I suspect Carter did his out of envy. I am serializing both in the newsletter at the moment, but you should have them in your library.

Thus, on pg. 168 of Carter, I read that afflictions in 19° of Leo-Aquarius cause spinal curvature. That's where my Moon is and, yes, my spine is bent and I am slightly stooped. If this were angular, if there were hard aspects from malefics, I would be a hunchback.

Carter and Robson between them cover most of the traditional ailments. What about the new modern ones? AIDS for example? Astrological analysis shows these to be new names for traditional problems. AIDS, for example, works out to be a form of cancer.

Also note the sign on the cusp of the 6th house, the house of its ruler, and any planets in the 6th, as these are traditional trouble spots. Robson delineates the ruler of the 6th through the twelve houses, which I will summarize:

1st: Much ill health.
2nd: Spends much money on health.
3rd: Sick while travelling.
4th: Hereditary ailments.
5th: From pleasure —or childbearing.
6th: Overwork.
7th: Through marriage or women.
8th: Is often near death.
9th: Sick while travelling abroad.
10th: Sick from business or promotion.
11th: Disappointments lead to illness.
12th: Confinement, as in an asylum.

Sun or Moon or the chart ruler in the 6th can lead to general ill-health. Also note aspects between the chart ruler and the ruler of the 6th, as that relationship will reveal much. This can be extended to the rulers of the 8th, 12th and 4th, all of which have to do with health, one way or another, and all of which are brought forward when in aspect to the chart ruler, Sun or Moon.

All of this, and more, are what we are predisposed to suffer. Those of you who read charts for a living could well enhance your reputations by studying your clients' charts to learn the ailments they are subject to. — *February 8, 2011*

Robert Blaschke

On Monday one of my suppliers said it was discontinuing Robert Blaschke's books. I was surprised, I asked why. Request of the publisher, they said. That didn't sound right, so I looked up Earthwalk's phone number and left a message. A few minutes later, Mr. Blaschke's wife phoned back. She said,

Robert Blaschke passed away at 7:18 pm, January 18, 2011, in Santa Monica, CA, his birthplace. I knew the end was near. I did not want to believe the day had come.

He is a great loss. There are so few among us who are genuinely creative and vital, who have new and refreshing points of view. Astrology is such an old science, we badly need our Blaschkes!

I cannot honestly say I knew him. He came to Maryland a few years ago and made a point of taking me to lunch. I was curious about his books. He said he had seven planned. He told me what the remaining two were. I, of course, forgot. According to his wife, the sixth book was to be on triple conjunctions. Because he kept setting himself ever greater goals, the books became harder and harder to research and write, and the time between them became greater as well. In this, his books reminded me of the symphonies of Jean Sibelius, the great Finnish composer, each of which were greater than the previous.

His books will remain in print, hopefully for many years to come. In the stress of his passing, his wife was confused as to how to continue with his work, Earth Walk Astrology, and mumbled the wrong thing to his distributor. This has now been sorted out.

Robert Blaschke had a most interesting chart (November 15, 1953, 1.37 am, Santa Monica, CA). When sufficient time has passed, I may delineate it. — *February 15, 2011*

27

✤The Decumbiture Chart

THE decumbiture chart is as old as the natal chart. Before the advent of modern natal astrology, it was often the only chart the medical astrologer had. And while the natal chart itself is essential, medieval medical astrologers were unanimous that the decumbiture chart, by itself, was a comprehensive guide to diagnosis and treatment.

As the name implies, Decumbiture is cast for the moment when you're so sick you take to your bed, but unlike modern usage, you're not just a bit under the weather and having a sick day. A decumbiture is a form of horary, and the question it seeks to answer is if you will ever rise from it. In other words, **Decumbiture is a matter of life and death.** In modern speech, Decumbiture is when the ambulance comes. If this time was lost, then the astrologer would cast a chart for the moment the patient's urine was presented to him. Blagrave termed the urine the *"excrement of the blood"* and said he could often foretell the state of the urine (in a sealed container) merely by glancing at the decumbiture.

Blagrave says the rising sign of the decumbiture must describe the patient himself. By implication this means Blagrave would change the sign on the ascendant until it did. He presumably based this on the patient's physical appearance and perhaps on his station in life.

The ascendant and the Moon were the key factors. If they were both in cardinal signs, the ailment would soon be over. If they were in fixed, the ailment would be long in duration, if in mutables, it would come and go.

The nature of the ailment was shown by hard aspects (conjunction, square, opposition) to the Moon from Saturn/Mercury, or Mars/Sun, where Mercury and the Sun are secondary. Explicit delineations were customarily given for Moon to Mars, and Moon to Saturn aspects, through each of the twelve signs, but the exact nature of the delineations varied from astrologer to astrologer.

Thus, writing in 1647, Lilly's 24 delineations included five in which

28

he thought the patient would die. By contrast, Blagrave's delineation of these same 24 aspects (Moon to Mars, Moon to Saturn, through the twelve signs), forecasts death not once. I deduce from this that Blagrave was the better healer, though one should remember that Lilly took up medicine later in life and might have improved his skills thereby.

Here is an example. **Moon in Aries**, conjunct, square or opposed to Mars:

Lilly: If the Moon next after her separation from the Malevolent beams or aspect of Mars do also apply to the conjunction or opposition of Saturn, and she decreasing in light and slow in motion, there's small hopes of life; let the sick prepare for God.

Blagrave: ... then the sick shall be tormented with continual Fevers, with little or no rest or quietness, a continued extreme thirst, and dryness of the tongue and breast, an inflammation of the Liver, tending to a Phrensie, high and inordinate Pulses. . . . If Venus be stronger than Mars, then cooling remedies will be suitable; however 'twil be necessary to let blood.

Times of crisis occur when the transiting Moon squares, opposes and then squares its position in the decumbiture. If at any of those times she makes hard aspects to malefics, the patient's condition worsens, or he dies. On the other hand, if at the time of the decumbiture there is a helpful aspect from a benefic (Venus or Jupiter), the sick, though he may suffer, will recover. He also recovers if, at the critical times of the squares and opposition, the benefics cast favorable rays to the Moon. (This applies as well to the Moon's semi-squares to itself.) A waxing Moon (new to full) conveys strength and hope. A waning Moon is a sign of weakness. Know these simple rules about decumbiture and the transiting Moon, and you will know, in advance, when your loved one will recover, or relapse.

If the malady lasts for a full lunar month, it is said to be chronic, whereupon the Sun replaces the Moon as an indicator.

It was not my conscious intention to publish medieval medical texts, but it seems I have. All of these are excellent and worthy of your attention:

Christian Astrology books 1 and 2, by William Lilly, 1647.

The Astrological Practice of Physick, by Joseph Blagrave, 1671.

The Astrological Judgment and Practice of Physick, by Richard Saunders, 1677. This is a most excellent book. Ben Franklin thought highly of it.

Astrological Judgment of Diseases from the Decumbiture of the Sick, by Nicholas Culpeper, 1655.

Encyclopaedia of Medical Astrology, by Cornell. Study this one last. When you understand Blagrave, you will understand Cornell. — *February 22, 2011*

Jon Stewart, The Daily Show

Jonathan Stuart Leibowitz, better known to most of us as the host of the Daily Show, was born on November 28, 1962, in New York City or New Jersey, as I have seen three different birth places given. This is of no importance, since his birth time is unknown. Rather than whine that Lois Rodden isn't here to give us his birth time, let's see what we can do with it.

In rectifying a chart we are not looking for events that we can tag to the ascendant, since we can be misled by any number of false positives. A more certain route is to sum up the man and then see how his chart might fit.

Stewart (he changed the spelling) is glib and witty and extremely bright. Of the twelve signs, that's Gemini, but Stewart has no planets in Gemini. Instead, he has Sun, Moon and Mercury in Sagittarius. And a planet in Leo, and one in Scorpio and one in Aquarius and one in Pisces. This is a Sag kid.

Sagittarius???? That's eager enthusiasm. Well, okay. Which of the twelve houses does Stewart seem the most enthusiastic about? The first? Sag rising? Eager to experience life and everything in it? That's not what I see on the Daily Show.

How about the second? I want money and things and I want a lot of both and I don't care from where? Well, no. That's not Stewart.

The 4th? I wanna live abroad? Stewart's never really left New York. Nope.

The 5th? Girls girls girls? Sorry, no cigar.

The 7th? I am my wife's cheerful slave?

The 10th? Look at me! Look at me! Stewart bombed hosting the Academy Awards, remember?

How about Sun-Moon-Mercury in the third? The third is brothers and sisters, errands, grade-school education. Long ago I summed the third up as daily life. Daily life — Daily Show? Strong third house types are BMOC's (Big Men on Campus, which is an old term). The Big Shot.

30

Stewart certainly is one.

The third house is associated with Gemini. If Stewart has Sun-Moon-Mercury in the "wrong sign" on the third, would that make for someone who saw daily life from the opposite end of the spectrum? A contrarian view? Glib? Compulsively funny?

Okay. Let's take that for a start. Sag on 3 makes for Libra rising. Quick! Turn to the books with pictures. Howard Duff has kind of a good profile, except the guy looks a lot heavier.

Judith Hill has a portrait that looks kind of Jon-ish, except it's kind of feminine (a lot of Judith's pictures are that way). Anrias, in the frontis-piece of his book, nails Stewart. First decanate of Libra rising.

Libra rising, that puts Capricorn on 4. Which is the house of daddy. A Capricorn daddy can be kind of hard on a kid. Reading his *Wiki* page, I learn that Stewart's parents divorced when he was eleven. Stewart's Saturn is in Aquarius. Technically it's in his 4th, but with a 2 am chart, it's actually in Stewart's 5th, as the 5th has Aquarius on the cusp. Planets which fall outside the house, but have the same sign as the cusp, are "running to get into it," to coin a phrase. Ruling the 4th house from the 5th, note that Stewart's 5th house is the second house of daddy. Which is daddy's money. Note also the south node nearby. Judith Hill tells me the south node is like a cosmic drain. Could it be that Stewart's daddy refused to provide for Stewart? Gave him no money/love? Had no money/love to give? Is this why Stewart broke off relations with him, long ago?

The 2 am rectification puts Mars in Leo in the 11th. For the sake of argument, we will say that Mars in 11 represents the Daily Show's correspondents. Many of them have said, perhaps only in jest, that Stewart abuses them. On the show they often berate him. Mars is warfare, Leo is Stewart (Leo is always an individual), the 11th house is associates. Associates beat up on the Leo, the Leo beats up the associates.

But there is more. That Mars rules Stewart's Venus, in the second, in Scorpio. Which ties correspondents to Stewart's money. Many of them, in fact, have done quite well from the Daily Show, which Stewart himself produces. Many of the correspondents stayed long enough to make a name for themselves and then split for greener pastures. Is this Martian aggressiveness combined with retrograde Venusian stinginess?

Retrograde, debilitated Venus in Scorpio as chart ruler? I'm still puzzling that. I don't see any of the other eleven signs doing as well on the ascendant. I would hazard that retrograde Venus in Scorpio ruling a Libran ascendant is an intense (Scorpio) feeling that "nobody loves me" (the retrograde). According to Wiki, as a child Stewart experienced anti-Semitic bullying. For that to end up in *Wiki* 40 years later is evidence just how intense the bullying was. Judging by his chart, it might be more accurate to say that Stewart was bullied and that the bullies used his Jewishness as their excuse. It's also true that, Mars ruling Venus from the 11th, that "everybody bullies Jon." Everybody bullied Jon when he was a kid. They piled on. His correspondents still do today. For his part, on his show Stewart often lampoons media bullies — Fox News among them — for abusing their audiences. Which climaxed with an October 15, 2004 appearance on CNN's *Crossfire*, where he begged the hosts to "stop hurting America" and called them "partisan hacks." On his show he frequently targets hypersensitive Israelis and Jews, as if to say, *I had it tough, but you, not so much.*

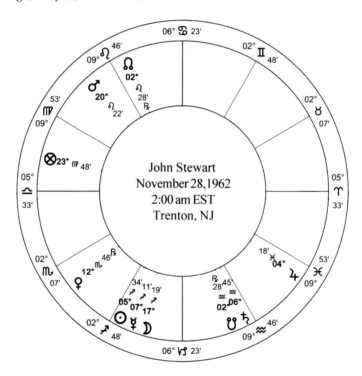

Elsewhere, I note the north node in Leo in the 11th, which is to say that Stewart has profited from his associations, aggressively, as Mars is there as well. Moon in Sag rules the 10th house cusp (Cancer), which is getting up the nerve to stand up in front of the crowd and talk (3rd house) to them. Reading *Wiki*, I find Stewart has a history of late-late-late night appearances, first at live comedy clubs, and then on TV. He's still late night. The Daily Show airs at 11 pm Eastern. Judging by the Oscars, he's clearly not comfortable in front of big crowds at times of day when everyone might be watching.

Stewart married for the first time in 2000, age 37. This is late. Ruler of the 7th, Mars, is in Leo in the 11th. Ruler of 7 in 11 is mistaking friends for lovers. As Mars is trine the 7th, this might work, except that lovers are not friends and friends are not lovers, which tends to make the relationships break down, which delays marriage.

Marriage is also delayed when few planets are in water signs, the signs of fertility. In Stewart's case, Sun, Moon, Mercury and Mars are all in Fire, the least fertile signs. The sign on the 5th, of children, is aloof, indifferent, childless Aquarius. Of the critical planets, Venus alone, in Scorpio, is fertile, except, retrograde, it's not paying attention and so lets opportunities slip, and, debilitated, is not in the mood anyway. Consequently, Stewart's two children arrived late: A boy in 2004 (age 41), and a girl in 2006 (age 43). I would be surprised if he has a third.

To sum up, it seems that Jon Stewart had a long, lonely childhood, without a father and with few friends. He has grown into an adult who blusters a thinly disguised rage at the world. A world that, right now, needs a lot more people raging at it. His fame is not an accident. He is a man of his time. *— March 8, 2011*

✤The Japanese Earthquake

THE quake hit at 2:46 pm, Japan time (GMT + 9:00 = JST), on Friday, March 11, 2011, some miles east of Sendai, Japan. I have a chart with 16♌27 rising, with a midheaven of 8♉18. The exact time is speculative, since the quake seems to have lasted approximately ten minutes.

An overview. Leo rising, chart ruler Sun in Pisces in the 8th — the house of death — with malefics Mars and Uranus with it, this is a chart of death on a massive, universal, Piscean scale. Pisces, a water sign, tells us that most of the deaths will be by water, not shifting earth: The tsunami. A great, great tragedy.

B.V. Raman, in *Astrology in Predicting Weather and Earthquakes*, says to note the angles of the eclipse chart, as well as the angles of the preceding solar eclipse. That solar eclipse was January 4, 2011, at 6:03 pm JST, Tokyo. The rulers of the angles in the eclipse chart are identical to the rulers of the angles in the earthquake chart: Sun, Saturn, Venus, Mars. In the eclipse chart Mars rules the Aries MC. In the earthquake chart Mars rules the Scorpio 4th, of endings. It is as if the eclipse Mars was a guillotine that fell, MC to IC, in the earthquake chart.

In the quake chart, Sun and Mars are conjunct in Pisces the 8th house. Pisces is ruled by Jupiter. At the eclipse, Jupiter was 27 Pisces, but when the quake came, it was at 10 Aries.

Marjorie Orr and others have pointed out that in the quake chart, the Sun (20 ♓) was at the Mars (13♓) - Uranus (30♓) midpoint. Which Ebertin says is a sudden adjustment to new circumstances. Witte says, sudden injury to the body.

This wouldn't seem to be relevant as it isn't angular, nor is it on the midpoint of the Asc/MC (27♓), but then you note that Jupiter was exactly at 27♓ at the eclipse. And that in the earthquake, the Sun (20♓) - Jupiter (10♈) midpoint is Uranus, at 30♓. Which puts Uranus (30♓) at the midpoint of quake [Asc/MC midpoint (27♓)] and Mercury (3♈). You may further note the midpoint of Neptune (26♒) and the Jupiter/

34

Uranus conjunction at 27♓ in the eclipse chart was exactly Mars in the earthquake - 13♓. These are a lot of links between the solar eclipse and the earthquake, all in a very small space.

An anonymous blogger found the fixed star Scheat at 29♓ 32, conjunct Uranus. Among its attributes are murder, suicide and drowning. When with Uranus, Robson says, death through drowning or by water, especially if in 1st, 6th, 8th or 10th houses. The final death toll has yet to been established.

Judith Hill tells me to look at the previous lunar eclipse, in addition to the solar. That eclipse was on December 21, 2010, at 5.13 pm JST. It was at 29 Gemini/Sagittarius and very nearly angular, as the chart, set for Tokyo, has 9 degrees Cancer rising. In the lunar eclipse chart we find the Twenty-nines. In that chart Uranus is at 29♓, the nodes are at 28♐ Ⅱ. Kronos, one of the Transneptunians, is at 29♐. Apollon, another of the Transneps, is at 28♎. (*Old New York trick:* In disaster charts, always check the Transneptunians, as they're very often in hard aspect.) Neptune is at 29♒.

The Moon had just left 29 Taurus for the "safety" of 0 Gemini 15 minutes before the eclipse struck. Moon in Gemini is the "Japanese Moon," as a Moon in Gemini turns up in various national charts. I had analyzed the 29's a week earlier to answer a private query as to the Christchurch earthquake. I wanted the Sendai earthquake to be different, rather than caused by many of the same factors as the one in New Zealand.

Judith tells me that each region of the world has its own earthquake signature, this from research she did in the 1980's. She tells me she thought the Sendai quake to be a week early, as she was expecting a major quake on or around or shortly after the full moon on March 19th, which, at 29♍ is exactly square to December's lunar eclipse.

OR that there's another big earthquake still to come. There's been enough loss of life. Let's hope she's wrong.

In the quake chart Saturn is retrograde in Libra in the 3rd. This is the local (3rd house) guy (Libra) who was looking the other way (retrograde). Saturn in Libra is in mutual reception with Venus, in Aquarius, which ties the 3rd house, with Saturn in it, to the 6th, with Venus. Soldiers — 6th house — were quickly mobilized by the government (Saturn) to help the locals — 3rd house. They were warmly greeted: Venus.

Which leads us to Jupiter, the ruler of 8th house Pisces, is in Aries in the 9th. It and Mars are in mutual reception, which welds the 8th house and the 9th house together: Foreign onlookers to the national tragedy.

The news media: Expanding on that, if we consider the third to be "local news", then the 9th is the international press. The local Saturn opposes the international Jupiter. While Saturn is well-placed in Libra to

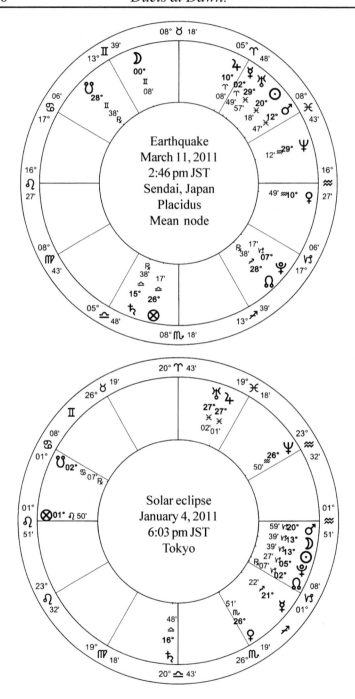

Earthquake
March 11, 2011
2:46 pm JST
Sendai, Japan
Placidus
Mean node

Solar eclipse
January 4, 2011
6:03 pm JST
Tokyo

dig out the story, as it is retrograde I deduce the Japanese media probably won't tell much. It will be left to the international press.

The nuclear power plants. One of the few modern rulerships I like (fear is a better word) is Pluto for nuclear energy. When Pluto was discovered on February 18, 1930, Saturn was at 9 Capricorn, Mars was at 9 Aquarius, Uranus at 9 Aries.

When Hiroshima was bombed, August 6, 1945, 8:16 am JST, the south node was at 9 Capricorn, Mars was at 9 Gemini, Pluto was at 9 Leo.

Look again at the lunar eclipse in Tokyo: 9 Cancer rising. Now look at the earthquake chart. MC at 8 Taurus, 8th house at 8 Pisces, Pluto at 7 Capricorn, Venus at 10 Aquarius, Jupiter at 10 Aries. Will the 7's and 8's and 10's smear the Sendai earthquake into a nuclear disaster as well as a watery one? I really don't know. I pray not!

The next day, March 12, 2011 at 3:36 pm, one of the reactors at Fukushima exploded. The Japanese Moon was then at 13 Gemini, exactly squaring Mars at 13 Pisces.

Note also that Uranus has turned the corner and is now in Aries, which makes the nuclear problem entirely different from the quake itself.

In the quake chart, Pluto in Capricorn, representing the poisonous reactors, is "running to get into" (*Dave's term*) the 6th house, where it will deliver its poison to Japanese workers (in this case, soldiers) and impair the nation's health generally, which are both ruled by the 6th. Hopefully the runaway reactors will be brought under control before things get out of hand.

In the quake chart, the Moon is conjunct Alcyone. It is the chief of the Pleiades. With the Moon, Robson says, *Injuries to the face, sickness, misfortune, wounds, stabs, disgrace, imprisonment, blindness*, etc.

The MC is conjunct Hamal. Robson: *It causes violence, brutishness, cruelty and premeditated crime*. Three fixed stars prominent in a chart are rare.

There is much more that could be said about the quake, many more charts that could be included. — *March 15, 2011. The local/international media, the nuclear disaster, turned out much as I had feared.*

❖Elizabeth Taylor

I WAS asked yesterday how to put a chart reading together. How to make all the pieces fit, how to get an overall picture?

My method is to find the key way into the chart. Some personality quirk, some habit the person has that makes me think of some astrological factor or other.

This week I want to delineate the late Elizabeth Taylor. I thought it would be easy, that I could take her chart off the shelf and it would be laid out for me, but no such luck!

Dame Elizabeth Rosemond Taylor was born on February 27, 1932, in London (more or less), at 2:00 am, 2:15 am, 2:30 am, 7:56 pm and 8:00 pm. After this ordeal, her mother, Sara Southern Taylor (1895-1994) had no further children. Could you blame her?

Some of these charts have Libra rising. Some have Sagittarius rising. Astrologically, she was said to be defined by a precise Venus-Uranus conjunction in Aries, but in the 2:00 am-ish charts it falls in the fourth, not the 5th. In the 8 pm-ish charts, it falls in the 7th. If Taylor had Venus-Uranus in the 7th, she would be defined by her marriages, as in *who* is she with now and what is *he* doing? Seventh house charts are not about oneself, but rather, about the partner. Seventh house people *need* partners. When their partner changes, they change, often in fundamental ways. I have observed this to be true even when the sign on the cusp of the 7th is fixed.

This *Libra rising chart* puts the Mars-Sun-Mercury triple conjunction in Pisces late in the 5th. By my rules, where the sign on the cusp of a house takes in — or wants to take in — all the planets of the same sign, those planets are in the 6th. Mars in 6 is a workaholic. Sun in 6 would be a tyrant on the set (e.g., at work), Mercury in 6 is efficient and tidy, or would be, but in Pisces is debilitated and so would be efficiently slovenly.

The Libra chart puts Saturn in Aquarius in the 5th. Which would make her icy cold romantically, with the loss of at least one child, if she bore any at all. Taylor in fact bore four children and was a grandmother at age 39. Finally we consider the illustrations in *Anrias* and conclude that Elizabeth Taylor does not look like Jon Stewart. Now we consider the Sagittarius chart.

At 2:00, 2:15 and 2:30 am, Liz Taylor had Sagittarius rising. Venus-Uranus now falls in the 4th, which is a home that is dynamic (Aries), quirky (Uranus) but beautiful in a masculine sense (Venus, debilitated). As is true of all debilitated planets, Venus wanted to radiate to the opposite house, the 10th, to the public. In the Sag chart the conjunction itself does not seem to be all that significant, but note that Venus is disposed by Mars in Pisces, a sign in which Venus has considerable strength. Venus-Mars mutual receptions are a sign of sex appeal. Sex appeal happens whenever the boy planet (Mars) teams up with the girl planet (Venus), not by aspect, but by rulership. Aspects make dispositors stronger, and along the lines of the aspect itself, for better or worse.

In the third house of the Sag chart we find the triple conjunction of Mars, Sun and Mercury, all in Pisces. As all three of these are personal planets we would be justified in considering a disorganized and messy (Piscean) third house to be the main focus of Taylor's life. Just as one is known by his sun and ascendant signs, one is also known by his or her dominant house. For Liz Taylor, it seems to be the third. Since we suspect Taylor to have Sag rising, we check again with Anrias, who confirms. (Rectification is never, ever, completely settled. At this point we would try to spot transiting Saturn hitting the angles, to see if the native reacts accordingly.)

Immediately we see the ruler of the 7th, Gemini, is in the third (Mercury), and that both are mutable, which is to say, unable to control the events around them. In Mercury's case, it doesn't want to control, it wants to oscillate among them, but as it's debilitated in Pisces, it won't do a very good job of it. Now we see that Taylor's Mercury is exactly conjunct her Sun, which means the Sun was driving it as if the Sun was Mercury. To me Taylor's Sun-Mercury conjunction is more interesting than her Venus-Uranus.

Sun-Mercury puts emphasis on the houses that Mercury rules, which were the 7th and 9th. Now we begin to understand her marriages. She wanted men who were witty and versatile, verbal and intelligent. They were also, unfortunately, mercurial and changeable, fleet of foot, so just as quickly gone from her life. In true double-bodied sign fashion (both Gemini and Pisces are double-bodied), she married the same man twice (Burton). And as is true of empty houses generally, the marriages were secondary to her busy life — the 3rd house.

Whenever we see Mercury debilitated, and the Mercury signs prominent in one or other of the relationship houses, questions of sexual orientation arise, but here we must finesse carefully. You express yourself sexually through the 5th and 8th houses. Taylor had Taurus on the 5th, ruled by a hot-headed, impulsive Venus in Aries. That's not gay. She has Cancer on the 8th, ruled by the Moon in intense Scorpio. That's not gay, either. Not by a long shot.

But Gemini on the 7th, ruled by a debilitated Mercury, describes her husbands as men who could very well be bisexual. According to what I read on *Wiki*, Burton tried homosexuality, and allegedly attempted to seduce Eddie Fisher, another of Taylor's husbands. Early in her life Taylor was associated with Montgomery Clift, who was bisexual. Towards the end of her life she was associated with Michael Jackson, whose sexuality was murky, but, true to Gemini, definitely childlike.

Pluto on the 8th house cusp means one of the husbands would die. (Michael Todd. *Tod* is the German word for death, by the way.) As Taylor's Scorpio Moon rules Pluto, Todd's death hit her very, very hard. As did the deaths of Clift and Jackson, both of whom she considered more than just friends. Moon in Scorpio in the 11th, friendship was intensely personal to Taylor. Friends were never just "friends."

Jupiter, retrograde in Leo, is in her 8th house. The 2:15 am chart has Leo/Aquarius intercepted between the second and the 8th. Capricorn on the second, Taylor earned her money, and while Saturn-Jupiter opposed can indicate bankruptcy, I get the impression that the wideness of the orb, Jupiter being retrograde, both planets intercepted, and a great big fuss going on in the 3rd, 7th and 9th, Taylor was never really aware of her money. It is said she gave heavily to AIDS research, which was doubtless because of Gemini on the 7th house cusp and the many close friends she had in the gay community.

Note the Sun-Mercury conjunction lands, by Mercury's rulership, squarely on Taylor's Virgo 9th house, of religion. Mercury, like Venus, is debilitated by sign, and would rather have been in the house opposite, the 9th. Age 27, Taylor converted from Christian Science, to Judaism. The opposition with Neptune in Virgo meant this was not well understood by others, and, with the south node lurking nearby, kept her religion secondary to her career as an actress.

You will note that thespians often have a lot of mutables in their charts. This leaves them with a weak sense of their own identity, which makes it easy for them to abandon themselves and take on other characters. Carter notes actors have strong 12th houses, but Mars-Sun-Mercury in Pisces in 3 will do nicely.

Elizabeth Taylor is gone now, and we have only the memory. — *March 29, 2011*

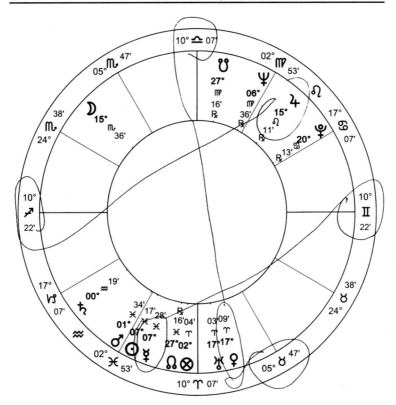

Elizabeth Taylor
February 27, 1932
2:15 am, GMT
London

✦Time Twins

TIME-twins are two unrelated people born more or less on the same day. It's been said that such people share broadly similar lives, but of the people whom I have met, or heard of, born on the same day as myself, I have to disagree.

I am a full-moon birth. All full moon births are defined by their Sun-Moon oppositions. Figure out the houses those two are in, and you have the chart in front of you. In my case, as a wandering, rootless intellect, I have Sun and Moon in 9 and 3. One day in the 8th grade, the teacher brightly read from a book that out of any 30 people, two of them will have the same birthday. By which was meant, the same month and day.

As the class had about 30 students, we all named off our birthdays. Mine was the same as Cindy F.'s, and we were, as expected, the only pair. As we were in the same class, that meant we were also born the same year.

So where do you suppose Cindy's Sun and Moon were? Well, her father ran the town's funeral home. We delivered their daily newspaper. The two-story house still stands. They lived upstairs. Dead bodies were downstairs. Sounds like 2 and 8 to me: Money from the dead. Unlike me, Cindy was precocious. Got pregnant in high school, dropped out, came back with a new name and graduated with her class. That's still 2 and 8. I wasn't there for it. Nine and three, ever restless, I had already moved on. She has now retired from her father's business, a pillar of the community.

Then there was a Native American I briefly met in California. He was born in Oklahoma, was a day laborer and had been in and out of jail. Sounds like Sun and Moon in 6 and 12 to me.

And a third, born the same day, month and year as myself. He has run a small Asian nation for some years. Where are his Sun and Moon? His birth time is not published, but I would guess 4 and 10. For a long time I thought I was 4 and 10, but I don't run a country. I publish books. Some say the man is autocratic and a dictator, but that went with the day itself. Ask Cindy, next time you see her. Or read any of my imperious book reviews, or consider what life is like when you're on the other end of things, like the day-laborer, in and out of jail.

We study Time Twins to enhance our chart reading skills, because house placement, not signs and not aspects, determine the actual person.
— *April 5, 2011*

♣Johnny Cash MAN IN BLACK

TIME-twins are unrelated souls who are born more or less the same day, month and year. They are said to have largely identical lives and be worthy of our study. But are their lives similar?

There are many pairs of notable people born on the same day, or very nearly so. By definition, all their planets, including their Moons, are in the same exact signs and make the same exact aspects. The differences between them are, therefore, purely a matter of house placement. Their charts are the most practical studies in delineation.

John R. "Johnny" Cash was born February 26,1932, at 7:30 am CST, in Kingsland, Arkansas. 23 Pisces rises. The time is per Rodden, who says, "from memory", but the Cancer-Scorpio sketch of Pisces from *Anrias* is a dead ringer. Which is a good start.

His time twin? **Elizabeth Taylor**, born (approximately) 17 hours, 45 minutes later.

Cash, like Taylor, had a tight Venus-Uranus conjunction, but Cash, unlike Taylor, had only two marriages, both of long duration. We may therefore surmise that a mere aspect is not sufficient to create facts on the ground. Those of you who use aspects as your primary means of delineation should take note.

Given Sag rising and a cluster in Pisces in the 3rd, Taylor's life was a perpetual whirlwind of activity. That same cluster fell in Cash's 12th house. What does the 12th rule? **Prison**. Cash had several minor brushes with the law and spent a few nights in county jails, but was never a prisoner. If you want to be fancy, his identification with prisoners would seem to stem from Mercury in Pisces in 12, hemmed in between Mars and the Sun, and opposite to Neptune, in the 6th.

Robson says Mercury debilitated in 12 makes one deaf. Cash was not, but, speaking of myself as one with a "funny" sense of hearing, I am certain the acuity his Mercury found in the 12th shaped his singing style.

Note the debilitated Mercury wants to be in Virgo, where it finds

43

Neptune, exactly opposed. For Elizabeth Taylor, the Mercury-Neptune opposition drew her away from her Christian upbringing and converted her to Judaism. For Johnny Cash, the same aspect, now from 12 to 6, produced a lifetime's addiction to drugs of all sorts. Yes, the opposition made both Cash and Taylor sensitive to the thoughts and feelings of others, but so far as I am aware, it did not make either person notably deceitful, in other words, their careers were not based on telling fibs. You cannot read charts with your nose stuck in an astrological cookbook!

Cash's "blackness" can be traced to his exact Moon-Mercury trine. His Moon is in Scorpio, the sign of darkness, and in the 8th house, the place of death. The intensity and the darkness flowed out of him, the Moon not only trine Mercury, but the Sun as well. Many of Cash's songs were about death. I still remember a song, *25 Minutes to Go*, about a man about to be hung, counting down the minutes until his life ended, yet I have not heard it in more than 40 years.

Chart ruler for both Taylor and Cash was Jupiter, retrograde in Leo. She with Sag rising, he with Pisces. By sign Jupiter was opposed by Saturn. In Taylor's chart, the opposition, from houses 2 to 8, made her rich, seemingly despite herself. In Cash's chart, Jupiter was associated with the 6th house and served to amplify the drugs he took, supposedly for his own benefit (Jupiter in Leo, the sign of ego). In Cash's chart Jupiter does not have an effective opposition to Saturn, which is clearly in the 11th. Just as there are whole sign aspects, there are "whole house" aspects as well. In Cash's chart, Jupiter is in the house of work and service, while his Saturn is in the house of friends and ideals.

With both Cash and Taylor, there was a Sun-Jupiter mutual reception, Sun in Pisces, Jupiter in Leo. In Taylor's case, this tied her 3rd and 8th houses together, that she profited financially from her husbands, or would have done, if she had stayed married to any of them.

With Cash, the Sun-Jupiter mutual reception tied his 6th and 12th houses together. Which had the unfortunate result of further hiding his drug use.

It is said that Johnny Cash had many friends. I look to the 11th (friends) but find Capricorn with Saturn nearby, stiff and formal at best, reserved and aloof when not. Instead I look at the precise Sun-Moon trine. This is a man who expresses himself, his mind and emotions, easily and directly. He is open in ways that those who do not have this trine are not. People respond with friendship, even if the man himself — Sun in 12, Moon in 8 — is in fact distant. Unlike Taylor, whose friends were close and intense, Cash was friends with every US President from Nixon onwards. He found them all very likable people, remarking that friendliness was a factor in elective office.

Which takes me to his Venus-Uranus conjunction in Aries. In the 7:30 am chart, Aries/Libra are intercepted. This means the planets trapped in those signs are not readily apparent to others. Like Elizabeth Taylor, debilitated Venus in Aries is in mutual reception to Mars in Pisces. Which fuses them, and their houses, into a sort of conjunction. Venus-Mars interchanges such as this give great sex appeal, but in Taylor's case I could not otherwise see them, from 3rd to 4th houses, as a significant part of her life. This is not the case with Cash.

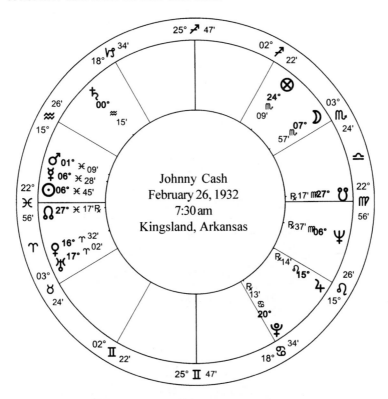

In Cash's chart, Venus-Uranus, which is already hidden in an intercepted sign, is scooped up by Mars, struggling to assert himself in Pisces, hiding in the 12th. With Sun-Mercury also in 12 and the Moon in the 8th, Cash had all his personal planets hidden away.

Truthfully it is easy to delineate the charts of the famous. We know what to look for, or at least we think we do. If I did not know who he was, I would have put Cash's drug use down to the Pisces stellium, rather than the oppositions in the 6th. I might have puzzled out that Taylor would have multiple marriages, but I would not have thought them to be anything of interest, since her 7th house is empty. I would have guessed Cash to have been a very private man, and perhaps he was. Cash's wife, ruled by Jupiter in the wife's 12th house, should have been his guardian angel, protecting him from harm.

Would I have guessed that Cash would be a singer? No. Others may have the ability to see that in his chart, but I do not. I would have put him in an institution. In prison, or in the army? Twelfth house Mars, one who plots in secret. This can make for a general, but with Mercury in Pisces the intelligence to carry out plans is lacking. Sun in Pisces lacks drive, the Moon in Scorpio in 8 is hypersensitive to the feelings of those around him. While I hear that U.S. Grant wept after losing men in battle, Cash lacks Grant's mental strength. Under stress Cash retreats into drugs. Which makes him a prisoner, rather than a private. Or, in fact, one of the great singers of the 20th century, a man who sang a great deal of raw feeling. — *April 12, 2011*

❖ Herbert von Karajan, 1908-1989

Herbert von Karajan was born in Salzburg, Austria, on April 5, 1908. After a slow start, he became the most celebrated conductor of the second half of the 20th century. At the Berlin Philharmonic, he was the successor to Wilhelm Furtwangler, who might well have been the greatest conductor of all time.

In music I have affinities to a few select individuals. Von Karajan is one of them. You will forgive if I call him Herbie.

Of Karajan's birth time, there is no doubt. He was born at 10:30 pm, more or less. Astro.com gives the source as "*CM. Feurback, B.R. PC,*" whom I was unable to trace. The resulting chart has 28 Scorpio rising, with a 5th house Sun and a 7th house Moon, intercepted in Gemini. I regret I could not read this chart.

I am not offering weekly charts to write potted biographies, as such are not worthy of your time. I settled on Herbie several weeks ago and presumed I could write a simple delineation. Then I looked at his chart.

As astrologers we often use shorthand to identify ourselves: Sun sign, Moon sign, Ascendant sign. We can get a sense of the individual with just these three.

But only a sense. Signs give personality traits. The active Aries, the talkative Gemini, the pompous Leo, the sexy Scorpion, etc. It's more revealing to replace signs with houses, because houses are more immediate, they tell us specific things. Second house is money. Fourth is home and daddy. Fifth is party time, Sixth is work, Seventh is marriage and partners, etc. Where are your Sun and Moon?

The house that has your Sun identifies the affairs which the Sun "lights up." You "have eyes," you "see clearly," you "know all." The Sun brings light and life to the house he occupies. It's where you shine, it's what is plainly obvious. It's eyes because the eyes are what transmit the Sun's light to your brain. It's where you bring sunshine to the world. The house with the Sun is the source of your curiosity, it is what you discov-

47

ered as a young person, it is what you have compulsively explored as an adult.

The house with the Moon, on the other hand, is what you know by instinct. What you've always known. Your gut. Your feelings. The things you knew even when you were very, very small. Like the back of your hand. The affairs of the house with the Moon in it come without any effort on your part. You can do it with your eyes closed. If your Moon is in a good place, those things make you happy. If your Moon is on the receiving end of stressful aspects, then the house in which it sits are very seat of your fears. Just as the Sun develops his house through curiosity, the Moon develops hers by experience. Over time she learns the world (her house) is not quite what she thought it was.

Get simple keywords for each of the houses, and see if this is not true in your own life. Your life, my life, everyone's life, revolves around the houses with the Sun and Moon in them. (And if they don't, then your birth time is *wrong:* try the nearby houses.) The houses of the Sun and Moon tell us *what* you are doing. The signs tell us *how* you are doing them. Houses are far more revealing than mere signs. When you have the signs and the houses, you have the person. As if he had posed for nudie pics: He can hide nothing.

So what should I think of the chart of a great conductor who has the Sun in the 5th, and his Moon in the 7th? What does this man conduct? His wife, as featured soloist at parties? That might account for Fellini and his wife, Giulietta Masina, but not Herbie.

So I wanted to delineate Herbert von Karajan, but now I'm stuck. The time is wrong and I really don't have a clue. I consider the numbers, 10:30, are offered with confidence, as if there was no doubt. And then I think of old tricks. What if they got the am/pm backwards? I've known that to happen more than once. It's worth a shot.

So I set Herbie's chart for 10:30 am, and to my surprise, something resembling a great conductor, perhaps Herbert von Karajan himself, emerged.

Sun at 15 Aries, 11th house cusp at 24 Aries. That's someone who wants to lead others, but will have to find his way because the Sun is on the wrong side of the tracks (cusp). He will come with authority because Saturn stands behind the Sun. He will be known for music and beauty because the midheaven is Pisces, and only a degree away is Mercury in Pisces. Mercury in Pisces is inept with language, but for music and musical expression there is no finer position, not by sign, and not by house.

He is aloof and reserved because his Moon, although in Gemini, is in the 12th. Few know what he thinks or feels, because his feelings are hidden (which, from what I've read, was actually true). He talks to himself.

Compounding this we find Neptune on the ascendant which makes him mysterious and misleading. One of the few personal things known about Herbert von Karajan is that he joined the Nazi party in 1933, three days after his 25th birthday. Austria banned the party only two months later. Did that make Karajan a Nazi? If so, he wasn't a very good one: His second wife, whom he married in 1942 (when these things mattered), was classed as Jewish. A better explanation is that an impulsive 11th house Sun in Aries, needing a group to join, jumped into the wrong one, a typical headstrong Aries mistake.

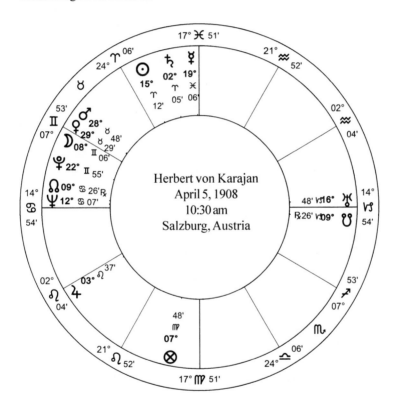

Herbert von Karajan
April 5, 1908
10:30 am
Salzburg, Austria

Another explanation, which has been widely discussed, is that he joined the Young Republicans of his day in order to somehow advance a conducting career that seemed stalled. I remember the utter panic I felt at that age when I had no job. In Herbie's case, Sun in Aries, Moon in Gemini, Cancer rising, can produce a great deal of nervousness, even if the 12th house Moon shows little on the surface. Which the MC in shapeless, formless, directionless Pisces does nothing to dispel.

Study the 10:30 pm and am charts closely and you will find something astonishing: At some time during that day, Venus shifted from Taurus to Gemini. Venus in Gemini is someone who speaks and writes with eloquence. Which von Karajan did not. Whereas, in Taurus, Venus easily sublimates Mars in Taurus, which it closely conjoins, to create harmonious, beautiful activity, i.e., direction. Details like this matter.

Herbert von Karajan had three wives, shown by Uranus on the 7th house cusp. At the age of 50 he married his third wife, the French Eliette Mouret, and at last had two daughters (1960, 1964). So far as children are concerned, this is not a very fertile chart. Sun and Moon are in infertile signs, the 5th house cusp is Libra, which is a guarantee of pretty children, but does not make them happen by itself. Venus and Mars are in fertile Taurus, but they are at the very end of the sign, which indicates children very late.

In this field I sometimes have personal ideas, which have no source other than myself. You can accept or reject, as you wish. Herbert von Karajan was the reincarnation of a 17th century French court conductor. Which is what it means to be a prodigy, that one is picking up where he earlier left off. I regret it is probably impossible to know exactly who. The court was in Paris, because Paris, specifically the Ile de France, was the center of art and culture and refinement in general. From this von Karajan drew his lifelong quest for polish and artistic perfection, because standards in Paris have always been very high. I imagine he thrilled to the much larger forces the 20th century gave him.

Finally there is the matter of his name. I have some experimental evidence that if one is self-aware, he will, by the end of his life, have selected his name for his next life, in some general fashion. If he was a French court conductor, then Herbert was a commoner who longed to be of royalty. In his next life, he got his "von."

In the 1960's his only rival was the American, Leonard Bernstein (1918-1990). I grew up in small Kansas towns, I did not really come to von Karajan and his recordings until the 1980's, by which time he was old and ill. I greatly regret I did not see him conduct. — *April 19, 2011.*

I was subsequently asked to justify the *pm* to *am* time change. I became curious when, in a formal, legal sense, the date changed. Was it at midnight, as is the current custom, or was it at *noon*? Consider that William Lilly, on pg. 152 of *Christian Astrology*, gives a time of 23:45 pm, with a chart to confirm it, which, to us, is 11:45 am on the next day. Von Karajan was born before there was radio, perhaps before Salzburg had electricity. In such a situation, from the viewpoint of the government, mechanical clocks might be unreliable, which would make sundials the legal standard. Which means the date would change at noon. But this is not the whole story, as it means someone has changed "22:30" for 10:30 pm, and then gotten the date wrong as well (Venus's sign change). Examination of official records will settle matters.

✤Bette Davis, 1908-1989

Ruth Elizabeth "Bette" Davis was born April 5, 1908, in Lowell, Massachusetts. Her mother, Ruthie, struggled with the birth, much as Liz Taylor's mother would, some years later. Bette was born at 7:00 am, 8:44 am, 9:00 pm, and 11:50 pm (*Source*: Astro.com). A hot-shot rectifier at the Church of Light has claimed 5:33 pm, but I presume he did not talk to mother Ruthie. Astrologers have never been big on actual research, a failing I share. We cling to our theorems and slide rules.

You will remember the date from last week's chart, as Bette was born the same day, month and year as Herbert von Karajan. To my great surprise, having been born the same day, they died a mere 82 days apart, at the advanced age of 81, in their 82nd year. (Herbie: July 16, Bette: October 6, 1989.) Very, very few people live this long.

From what I understand of astrological life-expectancy, the dates of death are, all by themselves, a powerful argument they had the same ascendants and planetary house placements. But this is unlikely, as Karajan had a 12th house Moon, whereas Davis was known for being temperamental. But there is something mysterious about the two charts. For every year that Karajan lived, Davis lived a year and a day. Precisely.

This reminds us immediately of secondary progressions, where each day after birth equals one year of life. The events of your 30th year are shown by the aspects made the 30th day after your birth, etc. The rationalist crowd wonders how such symbolic directions could be real, how days could translate into years, and are unhappy (as am I) with Biblical explanations.

I am working with an astrological theory that postulates the Earth itself as our primary astrological influence, the Sun and Moon as secondary influences, and the other planets playing comparatively minor roles. In my Earth-resonance theory, all the "symbolic" factors, such as those used in Vedic Astrology, Solar Arcs, and Primary Directions, as well as all those mentioned by Charles Carter, are all expressions of the Earth's own

51

resonance, so of course the Earth and its resonance will have more impact than, say, the transits and aspects of planets that are, in fact, far, far away. Which, when we look at the techniques of all the many astrologies on the planet, actually seems to be the case. The outlines of my theory are in my book, *Skeet Shooting For Astrologers,* and it's not that I'm plugging it, but that I seem to have stumbled onto something that has worth and to which I will be compulsively returning.

In my opinion, theories are never, ever, to be based on observation. Theories based on observations are, to me, upside down, since "facts" — very fragile things at best — are easily cherry-picked and unwittingly warped to fit. We have so many of these mediocre theories because most theorists are incapable of anything better.

A proper theory (those of Einstein and Newton come to mind) is an "Immaculate Conception" which is then put to the test, proven or disproven, by its ability to relate previously unrelated facts, to sweep them together and, collectively, reveal new and unimagined insights. I myself am strict about this. If a single relevant fact can be found that contradicts the theory, then the whole is thrown out and we seek some other Immaculate Conception to replace it. Which is the proper use of facts. Certainly two individuals, born the same day, who live to their 82nd year and die 82 days apart, are worthy of our study, come what may.

I flipped *pm* for *am* in Karajan's accepted time of birth, which, crude as that technique is, gave him 15° Cancer rising. Presuming that's more or less right, what if we were to add 82 degrees and give that to Davis? Each degree conferring one extra day of life? That gives Davis an ascendant of 7 Libra and a time of 5:26 pm. Not all that far from our wild-eyed rectifier at 5:33 pm and 8 Libra rising. If he's right then we could presumably reverse the process, subtract 83 degrees from Davis's 5:33 pm ascendant, and get von Karajan's ascendant. Karajan's chart was based on his recorded time of birth, the am/pm was presumably a transcription error. (If you're curious, I have, from time to time, used one chart to rectify another.)

Why would this work for these two individuals when, by 1989, at least 95% of all people born on April 5, 1908 were already dead? I do not know. I would look for an answer in primary directions, a forecasting method in which I am not skilled.

Having by roundabout means been led to the 5:33 pm chart for Bette Davis, let's read it and see if it proves out.

Libra rising, ruled by Venus. Note this critical difference from Karajan's chart: Venus in Davis's chart has slipped into Gemini. Now, instead of sublimating Mars in Taurus, only one degree back, (Venus rules Taurus), the two fight for dominance. Venus wants to go one way, Mars wants another. 29 degrees of one sign, 0 degrees of another, is a critical boundary.

Instead of being complete and self-contained, as in Karajan's chart, where it was in Taurus, Venus in Gemini is now ruled by Mercury. Mercury is still in Pisces, but here, in the 6th house, instead of conferring musical talent (as with Karajan), Davis's Mercury looks to the other side of the chart, to the 12th, of the actor (per Carter) and the sign Virgo. It's the same Mercury, it's the same degree. The difference is how the individual soul chooses to use it. This is why there can never be formal rules for chart interpretation.

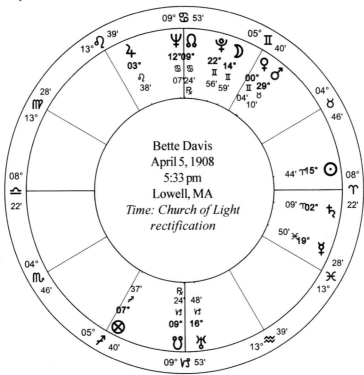

In Karajan's chart, the Moon was applying to a conjunction with Pluto, 14 degrees away. In Herbie's 12th house, no one saw this except Karajan himself.

Born six time zones away and hours and hours later, in Davis's chart the Moon is now only 8 degrees from Pluto, and both are in the 9th house. This is an aspect of intellectual intensity. Combine them with the friction of Venus and Mars, add an aggressive Sun in Aries, and Davis was known for playing fiercely independent women. And was one herself. It seems she was the antithesis of sexy.

In the early days of her career Davis was encouraged by her mother. In the chart we see Cancer on the MC (the house of the mother), with the Moon, its ruler, twelve houses from it, in the 9th. Whenever the ruler of a house is in the preceding sign and in the house immediately behind it (one house back), it stands behind it, supports it, in the nature of the planet and the manner of sign it is in. In this case, Davis's mother, the Moon, worked behind the scenes (12th house from MC), speaking (Gemini) on behalf of her daughter. Whether Davis was aware of it or not, the Moon's applying conjunction to Pluto indicates mommy's efforts on her behalf were rather intense.

Daddy: At the age of 7 Davis's parents were separated, with the mother taking her two daughters and moving to New York. Looking for daddy in the 5:33 pm chart, we find Capricorn on the 4th house cusp, exactly conjunct the south node. This reminds us of Jon Stewart's 4th house cusp and his unhappy relationship with his father. Capricorn on 4 is not good for the father. In Davis's chart, daddy is ruled by Saturn in Aries in the 6th, which, when you turn the chart, becomes daddy's 3rd. Saturn debilitated in Aries in 3 indicates he was off doing his own thing — and not very well.

Bette Davis's career took off fully 20 years before Karajan's, in the 1930's, as opposed to the 1950's. By the time Karajan comes into prominence, Davis was fading.

It is said that while married to her first husband, Harmon "Ham" Nelson, Davis had several abortions. We look immediately at the 5th house, to find it empty with Aquarius on the cusp. Davis's chart is even less fertile than Karajan's, since her Venus is in infertile Gemini. Presumably she had abortions for reasons of her career, but tracing the signs and their dispositors tells an interesting story.

Aquarius on the cusp of 5 is not fertile and, as it is opposite Leo, the sign associated with the 5th, shows a largely indifferent attitude towards children in general. Ruler Saturn is debilitated in Aries in the 6th, showing, on the one hand, that pregnancy may have made her ill, and, on the other, that children would be a financial drain (the 6th being the second from the 5th). Saturn, for its part, is ruled by Mars, in Taurus of the frontal attack, Taurus being the opposite of sneaky Scorpio. Mars and Saturn hate each other. Mars, the surgeon, compulsively terminates Saturn's difficult pregnancies. Astrology is often not nice, but it is always true.

Mars, for its part, is ruled by Venus in cold and calculating Gemini, which is ruled by Mercury in Pisces, which hardly knows what is going on from one moment to the next. Which is ruled by Jupiter in Leo.

Which would dearly LOVE to have children and lots of them, but can only look on, forlorn, from the wrong side of the distant 11th house cusp, the opposite house to where we find children. While we can continue with the dispositors (Jupiter ruled by the Sun, Sun ruled by Mars, which gives us a giant loop), having found a factor that relates to children (Jupiter in Leo opposite the 5th house cusp), we have found a *de facto* end of the matter. As a result of this difficult and convoluted scheme, Davis found children painful to contemplate, easy to ignore.

As with Karajan, Davis came late to parenthood, giving birth at age 39. A few years later she adopted two more (seemingly on a whim), and while I don't, off the top of my head, know where adoption may be in the natal chart, I am drawn towards Jupiter in Leo, finally having gotten itself into the 11th by means of a progression of some sort or another. Many years later, Davis's daughter, B.D. Hyman, accused her mother of being greedy. Davis shot back that if it were not for her money, B.D. would never have amounted to anything much. You will note that both of these opinions are neatly encapsulated in Saturn in Aries in the second house of children (Davis's 6th), as it withholds the financial support the child believes should be hers. — On balance I would judge the 5:33 pm time to be confirmed.

As with Elizabeth Taylor and Johnny Cash, and now with Karajan and Davis, we again see how the same planets, in the same signs (well, all but one) and making the same aspects, create radically different people when placed in different houses. Houses and their rulers are your keys to reading charts. Aspects are a sideshow.

While I don't much bother with forecasting, realize that accurate forecasts are impossible until you have a firm grasp of the individual himself. The factors that propelled Davis to an early start in life were missing from Karajan's chart, just as the factors that made him internationally renown late in life were largely missing from Davis's chart. I have not made that analysis, but I am confident it will concern houses and ascendants, not the planets themselves. — *April 26, 2011*

☩That Big Royal Wedding: Bill and Kate Wed

IT WAS final at about 11:30 am BST, April 29, 2011, Westminster. *The good news:* The wedding will produce a male heir. The 5th house cusp, of children, was fertile Scorpio. Ruler Mars was strongly placed in Aries, conjunct Jupiter in the 10th. *These are unmistakable marks of royalty,* note them well. This yet-to-be-conceived king will be headstrong, heartless and prone to acts of cruelty, but I will not live to see his reign. Well, it's been a couple of days. Maybe he's on his way!

The bad news: Just about everything else. I was asked if this was an elected chart, but that was before I had seen it. The merest glance? No court astrologer who valued his life would have anything to do with this awful disaster. This is another in a series of Windsor mistakes. The chart is essentially a staggering stellium, beginning with the void Moon at 26 Pisces, with Uranus, Venus, Mars, Jupiter all in Aries, and the Sun ending it at 8 Taurus. All opposed by retrograde Saturn in Libra.

Saturn immediately makes us think there is some powerful person who opposes this marriage, as this is inherent in such an opposition. The list of candidates is quite short, and the guilty party will have a clear astrological signature, thus removing any doubt.

Could it be the elderly Queen? No. She has no placements in Libra. Could it be the late Lady Diana Spencer, Princess of Wales? No. Kate Middleton's parents? They have no serious standing in matters of state.

How about William and Kate, themselves? *Okay.* In wedding charts the bride is forever the Moon. This Moon is void in Pisces, stranded in a cadent house. A very pretty lass, but lacking power, lacking position, lacking direction, lacking stamina.

Prince Bill? He is represented by the Sun in Taurus, which falls outside the powerful Aries stellium, having no association with the MC. Does the Sun not have rights in Aries? Yes he surely does, but he is forever upstaged when Mars, the actual ruler, is itself in that sign. We

56

then see the Sun is square to the Ascendant, meaning the groom was decidedly uneasy about the ceremony. We will learn why in a moment.

I really don't see the point of looking at William and Kate's natal charts, the wedding chart is so awful it could hardly be redeemed by the natals. I hear they both have Venus at 26-ish Pisces, such that the wedding Moon at the same degree would link the charts in nuptial bliss. With a void Moon in a cadent house, this is a false hope, for such a Moon is too weak for the job. Yes, Lilly says the Moon void in Pisces performs, but she will not perform well.

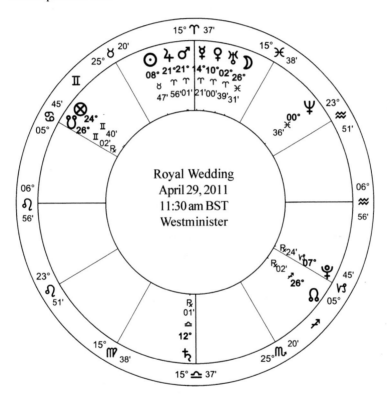

Then we turn to Charles, the Crown Prince. And we are astonished to find he has 5 Leo rising, while the wedding chart of his eldest son has 7 Leo rising. The houses of these two charts are virtually identical. Which, when combined with the relative weakness of the lights in the wedding chart, makes his son's wedding entirely Chuck's affair.

In Charles's natal chart we find Neptune and Venus both in Libra, conjunct the Saturn in the marriage chart, thus confirming Charles as

Saturn in the wedding chart. In his chart we also find a Mars/Jupiter conjunction, which is, again, a sign of royalty, but in Chuck's case we find it intercepted in the 5th, one of a number of indicators that Charles might reign briefly, but most likely, not at all. (The further analysis: Charles will become king when Mars (the Knight/Prince) conjuncts, i.e., becomes Jupiter (the King), but, alas, the king escapes into Capricorn before the prince can capture him. Note that Capricorn is the Queen's rising sign. When Charles' Jupiter escaped to Capricorn, thus denying Chuck his prize, it instead reaffirmed his mother's rule. Fate. An astute astrologer could have foreseen this 20 minutes after Chuck's birth. Perhaps a brave one did.)

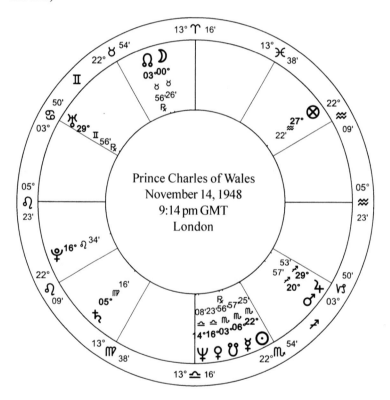

Prince Charles of Wales
November 14, 1948
9:14 pm GMT
London

Of the many factors that doom the wedded bliss of William and Kate, I may point out three critical oppositions:

First, Saturn opposite Jupiter. This is an aspect of failure. The two planets are naturally inverted, one to the other. Jupiter in Aries in 10 is the exuberance of public life. Which is important in a royal marriage, that the Prince and Princess are seen together in public. Saturn in 3 is the daily drudgery of satisfying common expectations, of, essentially, never being good enough. As hard as Jupiter will try to shine, Saturn, retrograde in 3 (the house of the media), will refuse to give the couple credit for their efforts.

Second, Saturn is opposite Mars. Saturn and Mars are not opposite by temperament. They merely hate each other. Note that both of these planets are strong by sign. As Mars is slightly stronger than Saturn, he will be able to plunge ahead before Saturn, tardy both because of its nature, as well as being retrograde, can put a stop to things. Since Mars represents the male half of the marriage and Saturn, as we have discovered, represents his father, it will be as if Chuck has William on a very public leash. The conflict is, again, between daily obligations (3rd house) and William's public persona (10).

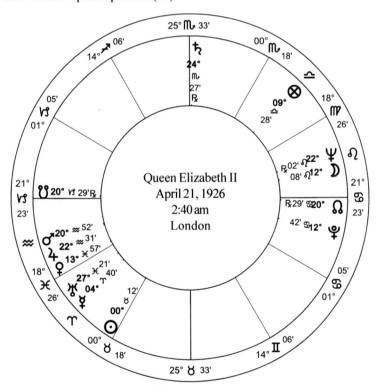

The marriage Sun in Taurus is ruled by Venus in Aries, which is ruled by Mars in Aries, which ends the matter, so far as rulerships are concerned. All the more telling that this Sun is not only square to the wedding ascendant, it is also square to his father's ascendant, thus reaffirming

Daddy's role and William's resulting disquiet.

Saturn at 12 Libra, Jupiter and Mars at 21 Aries, are these wide orbs? Yes, but remember that aspects are formed by signs. Degrees merely indicate intensity. Flabby astrology that takes no note of signs and houses has limited orbs as a result. When houses are included the effects of whole-sign aspects can be clearly seen.

But perhaps worst of all is the insidious Saturn-Venus opposition, only two degrees from exact. Were this chart the product of a court astrologer, this aspect alone would cost the fool his very life.

In the wedding chart Venus is debilitated in Aries. Which proves this marriage was not about love, regardless of what William and Kate feel about each other. Royal weddings are never about love, which is another indication this is a royal chart, not a normal one. Mars, the ruler of Aries, placed in Aries, has conquered Venus. Note that Venus, which has a strong affinity both for Pisces and the Moon, is in this chart the *de facto* ruler of the Moon, as Venus upstages Jupiter, distracted by Mars. Which makes Venus the de facto representative of Kate, the bride.

All debilitated planets long to be in the house opposite, perhaps never more so as when the planet that rules it is crowding it in the same sign. So to where does Kate (Venus) flee? Battered in Aries, she runs directly to the security of Saturn in Libra (Chuck), her father-in-law. A stressed Venus will always do this, will always run to the dull safety of Saturn if it happens to be in Libra. Kate has become a pawn in an ongoing father-son quarrel that, if the squares from marriage Sun to marriage/daddy ascendants are any guide, simmers, but never quite comes to a boil. In other words, William will tend to link the fate of his marriage to his father.

But still there is more. What are father and son fighting for? For what purpose has the innocent Kate been enlisted, and to what end will she be sacrificed? Well, as it happens the wedding chart is not merely a titanic set of oppositions. It is also a T-square. Charles and William are fighting over the apex, the focal point of the T-square: Pluto in Capricorn.

Which turns out to be the monarchy, represented by the Queen herself. Elizabeth has Capricorn rising. Its ruler, Saturn, can be found in Scorpio, at the very top of her chart. (Which is yet another royal indicator.) She is now elderly, though remember her mother lived to be 101. This utter perfection of astrological symbolism must be seen to be believed. In the wedding chart, the Queen turns up in the 6th house of health, represented by Pluto, the planet of profound, intense transformation. It is the Queen's health that is being fought over, and when the Queen is no more, the T-square between Mars (William), Saturn (Charles) and Pluto will bring a naked struggle for succession. When the Queen is finally gone, will the father charge ahead and claim the kingdom as his own? Charles' Mars in Sagittarius is ever hopeful of attaining its aim. Or will the massed forces of Aries in the wedding chart foil his attempt? Are the Prince and Princess who were linked on that fated day stronger than the one who opposes them?

Can this marriage last? I really don't know. In the wedding chart, Venus in Aries links both the Moon (Kate) and the Sun (William), to the consternation of Saturn (Chuck). Threesomes, whether happy or not, can be highly stable. Overall the male party — William — is stronger than the female, Kate, though both suffer. I would expect that Kate, being both a void Moon in a mutable sign in a cadent house, as well as a debilitated Venus, to become emotionally unstable. Which man will she choose? Mars, who owns her, or Saturn, who offers old and familiar comforts if she will but "cross the line"? For she cannot have both, and it will come to that. Which is why the court astrologer who proposed this date should flee now. Why are the Windsors so cruel?

This is not about sex. Sex is for the young. Saturn is old. This is about Kate's loyalty, duty and obedience. What she owes William as a consequence of her marriage vows, which the marriage chart represents. This is not part of the synastry between their natal charts and so cannot be found in them. William, in the guise of Mars in Aries, is too headstrong and careless to notice, and, in the guise of the Sun in Taurus, is too lazy to bother with. *Thus the opening to Saturn, in the misleading guise of duty to Charles as representative of the monarchy.*

Di was of noble birth. She would have seen this coming. Kate is a commoner.

I was living in London at the last big royal wedding, of Chuck and Di. Staged in the much larger St. Paul's Cathedral, it was a grand affair. The entire nation had the day off. I slept in. Hazel, my neighbor, had a TV and we glanced at it from time to time.

But I did see a brief YouTube of William and Kate exchanging vows. People who care about these things, people who care about spectacle, will rehearse the two, will stage the event so they squarely face each other, peering far into each others' eyes, into their very souls, such that when the moment arrives, they will speak their lines with a power and conviction worthy of royal succession. Which is what the world expected.

Instead I saw two insecure people rush the vows. I saw William grind the ring onto Kate's finger. He was dressed all in red like a toy soldier, as if we needed reminding that Mars, the planet of red, was in Aries, the red sign at the very top of the wedding chart. I could almost smell the mothballs. The two seemed so much smaller than his father and his bride, at that other royal wedding, long ago. Can William and Kate grow into the awesome roles they must quickly assume? Can they succeed where Chuck and Di failed?

But to remember that fated day in 1981, I am old. Two weeks after that wedding I left my home in London, never to return.

Can your astrology perform these feats of analysis? No? Why the heck not? As Goethe said, *Be bold! Boldness is its own reward.* As Robson said,

As a word of advice to the beginner I would say — Do not be afraid to let yourself go in this way. You will make many mistakes to start with, but it is the only way to make your Astrology of practical use. There is too great a tendency nowadays to float about in a comfortable haze of so-called esotericism. The first need of Astrology is accuracy and definition, not pseudo-religious speculation, and it is only by concentrating on the practical and scientific side that we can really make Astrology of service, and obtain for it the recognition it deserves.

I wish to be completely wrong. I wish to be proved a fool. A bloody fool. I wish William and Kate a long and happy life together. Pray for them.
— *May 3, 2011*

✤More (ghoulish) Royal Fun: Kate and Diana

THERE was a lot of reaction to my notes on the recent wedding of Prince William and Kate Middleton. Many said it was unlike anything they had read elsewhere.

I am not a royal watcher, I don't pay them much attention, but one of the people I chat with does. I will call her the *Ophelia of the West,* as she lives out in that direction.

Ophelia told me that on the wedding day Kate was wearing the same makeup as Lady Di wore the week before she died. That William gave Kate the same engagement ring that Charles had given Di. (A huge sapphire surrounded by diamonds, and, yes, I know how charged stones work.) Ophelia said that William was a mama's boy. He was when his mother was alive, and, according to Ophelia, he still is.

This makes Kate an enterprising schemer who took advantage of a weakened man by playing mommy to him. Which sounds true to my ears, and would be understandable under the circumstances. William had an unhappy childhood and needs time and help in order to heal. It's a private affair and not for outsiders to judge one way or the other.

But when Ophelia told me this, I heard something else. Something that finally put this strange wedding into context.

It was Lee who came to my office in Ventura the afternoon of August 31, 1997, with the shocking news that Di had been killed. The clairvoyant I worked with at the time said that although her body was dead, Di had merely been knocked unconscious. She "awoke" midway through her funeral, which I thought would be an overwhelmingly unhappy experience, but I was informed she took it in stride. Thereafter I gave Di no further thought. I presumed she would drift off, as the dead usually do.

And I should have known better. Back in 1996 was the famous Dally murder, which happened in Ventura, straight in front of all of us. A mother of two, Sherri Dally was murdered by her husband and his girlfriend, the body dumped in a ravine, where it was eventually discovered by detectives acting under the direction of Pam Coronado, a personal friend of mine who has since gone into the trade professionally, hence the reason I can name her. Pam did not get credit for it at the time, though she should have.

In an unrelated meditation group, we contacted Sherri, who made it very clear that she was going to protect her two children, on the one hand, and on the other, go after her no-good husband and his evil girlfriend, come what may. As to what eventually became of that, you will have to ask Coronado how, exactly, she led the police to Sherri's body.

So when Lady Diana Spencer died under somewhat mysterious circumstances, it should have been obvious, to me at any rate, that Di was

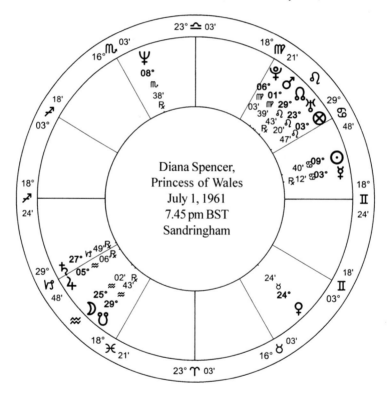

Diana Spencer,
Princess of Wales
July 1, 1961
7.45 pm BST
Sandringham

going to remain with her two boys, and that she was going to go after Charles, whom she blamed for her untimely death. This is *not* to say that Charles had anything to do with Di's death. It *is* to say that Di *thinks* he did, and in this case, her opinion is absolute, so far as Diana Spencer is concerned.

Those of you who lost your mother at an early age may have sensed her presence for some time thereafter, as I do not think this is unusual in these circumstances.

So when William started dating, it would seem that Di sorted through the females until she found one she could work with. If William was carrying a torch for his mother, then the only females he would have considered would have been those who reminded him of Di.

By this roundabout means, we come to the synastry between the very dead Lady Diana Spencer, and the very living Kate Middleton. Di was born July 1, 1961, at Sandringham. For many years her time of birth was murky (see Geoffrey Cornelius, *The Moment of Astrology*), but 7:45 pm was eventually settled upon, which looks good to me. I will highlight

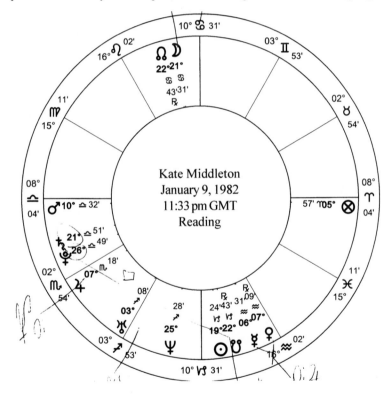

one aspect of her chart.

Di had Saturn at 27 Capricorn, retrograde, and Jupiter at 5 Aquarius, retrograde, on either side of her second house cusp, which was 29 Capricorn. This is an example of a "conjunction" spread over two signs. It sums up Di's life.

Saturn retrograde, she was at first thought an ugly duckling, but then, to the surprise of many, a somewhat plain older man from the government (Saturn in Capricorn, now direct) transformed her by marrying her as he changed signs (entering Aquarius, entering a new phase of his life). But immediately Di found her freedom (Jupiter) restricted. It was freedom she never knew she had, since Jupiter at birth was retrograde. But Saturn rules Jupiter in Aquarius, so as time went on he bore down harder and harder until he finally crushed (conjuncted) her, as Saturn is wont to do. And in fact, Di was crushed in an automobile. This was played out on the

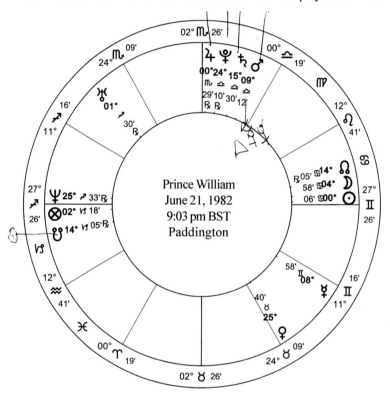

Prince William
June 21, 1982
9:03 pm BST
Paddington

second house cusp. You will note that Jupiter is exalted in Cancer, which is the 8th house cusp, which is the house of death. Which, by polarity, makes the second house that of life. Jupiter is also the ruler of Sagittarius, Di's ascendant. Saturn's actions at the house opposite death indicates demise by external means. This is 20/20 hindsight. I have no idea if these observations have any other use.

KATE MIDDLETON was born January 9, 1982 at 11:33 pm in Reading. The first thing to note about her chart is that she was born *during a lunar eclipse* that was *visible from her place of birth.* At the moment of her birth the Moon was in the very deepest part of the Earth's shadow (1° from the north node) and was presumably completely invisible. A lunar eclipse relates to females. For his part, we note her husband, Prince William, was born nine hours after a solar eclipse. A solar eclipse relates to males. *This is an extremely rare couple.*

Here is some of Kate's and Di's synastry:

Di's Sun is conjunct Kate's MC.

Di's MC is conjunct Kate's Saturn.

Di's Ascendant falls in Kate's 3rd house.

Di's Saturn is conjunct Kate's Sun and south node, and square Kate's Saturn and Pluto..

Di's Jupiter is conjunct Kate's Mercury/Venus conjunction.

Di's Neptune is conjunct Kate's Jupiter.

Di's Moon in Aquarius is trine Kate's Saturn, inconjunct Kate's Moon and semi-sextile Kate's Sun.

Di makes contact with Kate by the physical objects that Di once owned that Kate now possesses. Most principally, the ring. You will note the Tibetans use a similar concept to confirm their newly reborn Top Lama.

We might sum this up as Di having a heavy-handed Saturnine influence on Kate. Remember that Di's Saturn was in Capricorn, which is very heavy.

Given the evidence at the wedding, it would appear that Kate Middleton has become obsessed by the discarnate Diana Spencer. In such cases we commonly find the person obsessed (Kate) to have a quite weak chart. Which we have: Her Sun is conjunct the south node, which drains her of energy (this will become more apparent with age), while the Moon is entirely destroyed by the lunar eclipse. It is literally not "there". It is missing, she has no idea of her emotions, nor, I imagine, instinct (what is commonly called, "women's intuition"), nor her role before the public, which is the Moon in 10.

In her favor she has brash Mars in Libra on her ascendant. Mars ruling the 7th from the first means she manipulates her partner to get what she wants, which she then displays as hers (transference from 7th to 2nd (Scorpio) via the agent (Mars) in the 1st).

Mars otherwise has little in the way of aspects to back it up: The squares to Sun and Moon are separating and wide, and both the Lights are seriously debilitated. Mars has nice trines to Mercury and Venus, which, regrettably, merely give him a touch of color, as that's about as much as you can expect of trines.

Ophelia alerted me to Kate's retrograde Venus. It's hard for me to

get a reading on that, other than to note that she probably favors project-
ing herself as an "even-tempered" (Libran) intelligent (Mercury) person,
in other words, that Mercury, which is conjunct Venus, is much the stronger of the two.

Unlike Kate and Di, between Kate and William I found no significant
synastry at all. As they are born 5½ months apart we may discard Jupiter
through Saturn, as their positions will be approximately identical in both
charts, in other words, there is nothing in the outer planets that make Kate
and William of interest to each other, any more than anyone else of their
year of birth (1982).

They have Mars conjunct, which makes for a rough sort of sex, but
that won't make for a relationship *per se*. Between their two births, Mars
went retrograde, which means Mars held essentially the same position for
months on end. William has his Sun and Moon conjunct in early Cancer,
which means he is trying to find Kate's Moon in Cancer, which, despite his
efforts, is sunk entirely out of sight (eclipsed) and very nearly out of his
grasp, as it is 20 degrees away from his Sun. William's Mercury is trine
Kate's Mercury and its appendage, retrograde Venus. William's Venus in
Taurus is stranded. Kate's debilitated Sun and Moon give it weak aspects. This is a poor basis for a monarchy!

The most important thing these two have in common are severe,
complimentary, hurts. You will see this from time to time. Those who
struggled through unhappy childhoods, where they kept their heads above
water while barely staying sane while praying for a rescue they never
thought would arrive. When they finally do find a kindred soul, they latch
on to it with the ferocious desperation of a drowning man and then, claw-
ing themselves to safety on an island, they stand back to back (*not* face to
face), and battle for survival against a cruel world. This is the meaning of
the solar eclipse in William's chart, and the lunar eclipse in Kate's: The
hurts they were born with, and have endured every merciless day since.
These two have eclipses for synastry, they need nothing else.

I HAVE observed a similar relationship in members of my own family
and I am ashamed to say that I was the cause of it. Judging by a marriage
now in its 40th year, this sort of dysfunctional relationship can be highly
stable, and the reason is most curious. Because they share little (aside
from rescuing each other), they give each other wide latitude in all other
matters. Which makes the relationship invulnerable (despite appearances)
and gives the temptation to act out, either singly or together. To do
anything, to try anything that comes to mind. A life of desperation, if you
will, which can eventually become destructive to those around them. Kate
and William are essentially incompatible, yes, but they trust each other

absolutely and fear the outside world utterly. Their marriage is one of mutual fear, not love.

Which brings us back to their wedding, where all of this is now on display, plain to see. The massive conjunction in Aries, sucking in both William's eclipsed Sun, now in Taurus, and Kate's eclipsed Moon, now in Pisces, all focused upon Saturn in Libra, representing The Other, The Stranger, who must be defeated at all cost.

Which brings me back to Lady Diana Spencer, the undead Queen of Hearts. She it is who wants the showdown with Charles, she it is who sends forth her son and his bride to do battle. You may think this is speculation on my part, but note the following carefully:

That William and Kate are damaged and therefore defensive is not the same as William and Kate who want to fight the whole world. (My brother and his wife, born ten days apart, merely want to be left in peace.) Neither William nor Kate are fighters, neither of them have "fighting charts", aside from Kate's Mars in the 1st (bullying). They have been in the public eye long enough that we know their personalities. It is their wedding that has brought combat to them.

Will battle be joined, and if so, who, William, Kate or Charles, will prevail?

I greatly regret to say the answer can already be known.

We have previously observed that Mars, in an applying conjunction to Jupiter, elevated Princess Elizabeth to Queen, as Elizabeth, the King's niece, was not born to reign. We have seen the same applying Mars to Jupiter conjunction in Prince Charles's chart. Earlier I had said that as Jupiter escapes Mars, that Charles would never reign. I was agreeing with clairvoyant predictions and finding astrology to suit, but that was before I looked at what came after.

Look now at William's chart. He has, not Mars applying to Jupiter, but Mars applying to *Saturn*. If Mars/Jupiter elevates absolutely, Mars/Saturn *hurls down*. Please note that I am choosing my words with great care when I say that William will not be king. I do not know why he will not reign, I do not know how nor under what circumstances he will be "hurled down."

Look again at Diana's chart. Instead of Mars applying to Jupiter, Saturn applies to Jupiter. In her case, instead of Diana becoming queen, Saturn crushed Jupiter.

Look at Kate Middleton's chart. There is Mars in Libra, and Jupiter in Scorpio. Between them, Saturn and Pluto. Judging simply from astrology, she fares no better that William.

Above and beyond it all, Charles. He has largely usurped his aging mother, the Queen, in all but title, which, briefly, will some day be his. Represented by Saturn in Libra in his son's wedding chart, there is no reason for him to rise to the bait (Kate). Saturn in Libra is secure and has no interest in venturing forth. Venus in Aries (Kate) is restless and Mars in Aries (William) is foolhardy. Thus the newly married couple will compulsively goad Saturn. Above it as well, Charles' grandson, yet to be born, who will rule from an early age. He already has the promise of Mars and Jupiter conjunct. Which puts his birth in July, 2013, the conjunction in Cancer. Conjunct his father and mother, in square to their wedding vows.

Many of you will be unhappy that I have dragged Diana Spencer into this. Many of you are quite certain that ghosts do not exist, that *"when you're dead, you're dead,"* or, at best, that St. Peter and the Devil himself will personally fight over your soul, whatever a soul turns out to be.

All of which is rubbish. You might as well declare the Earth to be flat and the Moon made of green (i.e., unripened) cheese. Ghosts can be found throughout human history, and in all cultures, regardless how isolated or obscure, and the only talent it takes is a willingness to look. Which is precisely what a dead-end, crassly materialistic society most fears to do.

There is no reason whatever for William to draw his father into combat. It defies logic, it defies reason, it defies expectation. If, over the next year or two, he does, we may take it as *prima facie* evidence that Diana, mother of one, wife of the other, is behind it.

I am not a forecaster. I have not the talent, I have not the training, I have not the interest. I frankly consider it gauche. The immediate future for the Windsors, as it appears before me, is tragic. The events I see cry out for someone to stop them. Throwing a diseased engagement ring into the Thames would be a good start. — *May 10, 2011*

May 2012: I initially presumed Kate Middleton would quickly discharge her royal duties and produce an heir, but a year has now passed and she has not. It would indeed be eerie if she were to give birth in July, 2013.

UPDATE to Kate Middleton's chart. The Australians are using 11:15 AM, not PM, as I said last week. From 11:33 pm to 11:15 am, flips the chart almost precisely. From Libra rising, to Aries rising. Much to my embarrassment, Anrias agrees with mid-Aries rising, i.e., the 11:15 AM chart. — *May 24, 2011*

✤Sathya Sai Baba is Dead

BELIEVED by millions of adherents to herald the arrival of the new age, and by the Benjamin Creme crowd as a precursor to the Second Coming, Sai Baba died on Easter Sunday, April 24, 2011. He was 84.

I have many friends who are, or were, devotees, who must now feel bereft. Baba's radiance never quite reached me. A glance at his chart tells me why: Sun, Moon, Saturn and Pluto all in water signs, made for an emotionally acerbic man. I am air and fire, I found kinship with the intellectual Rajneesh, or would have, had I figured out his clever sex disguise before he disappeared from the scene.

Like Rajneesh, like Maharishi Mahesh Yogi (the Beatles' guru), Baba was one of a number of modern celebrity holy men. His ashram, at Puttaparthi, was large. According to Wiki, he had some 1200 international ashrams and unknown millions of adherents. I was surprised to read his body was buried, not cremated, but then learned the bodies of holy men are traditionally venerated. Just not chopped to pieces, the way Catholics treat their saints.

I was going to write some remarks on his chart, but when I looked at it, I found it did not speak to me. I was going to set it aside, but this morning I saw Baba in a railway carriage and me there with him, so I think I will describe that.

HE is an old man, old and tired. He sits, languidly. I should explain for American readers who have never seen a proper train, that a railway carriage is typically divided into more than a dozen small compartments that span about ¾ths of the width of the car. Each compartment has a door leading to a narrow passageway, and this particular compartment also has a door opening directly onto the station platform, as if it were a London commuter train.

Baba is still wearing his long, thin ashram robe. It seems he would rather be in a business suit, but is too tired to summon the energy to

71

change, as this sort of thing used to be one of his favorite siddhis. He has
a small valise, but the only things in it seem to be toiletries (Baba shaves!)
and a pair of shoes. We do not talk. There are only the feelings that come
from him. Overall, he is tired. He has worked his whole life. In his chart we
can see Sun-Saturn tightly conjunct. The Sun is ahead of Saturn, as if the
Sun wants to run away from his duties, but cannot, as it is at the very end
of its sign, Scorpio. That it is Scorpio tells us the majority of his work, like
the bulk of an iceberg, was hidden and will always remain so. The love he
wanted, represented by Venus, was forever just beyond his grasp, a mere
22 minutes of a degree away, but in Sagittarius, an alien sign. Baba, like
virtually all Indian holy men, did not have normal relations. In Baba's
case, this was not by choice, but through inability. His efforts to understand this, in practical terms, came to nothing much: Mercury was debilitated in Sagittarius, retrograde, and on the far side of Venus.

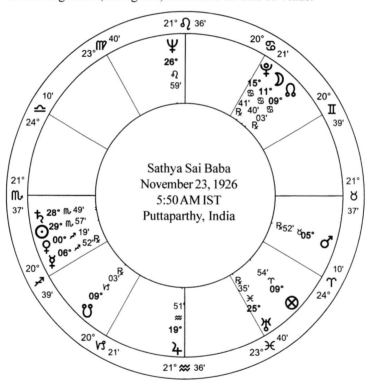

Perhaps in compensation, there are stories he took up with young
boys, the children of his adult followers. For this, we see Uranus, retrograde in Pisces, tight on the cusp of the 5th. Uranus represents, 1. What

is erratic, 2. Youth, and, retrograde, 3. What would not be approved, nor understood. Pisces tells me that though there would be great love, it would not be personal to any individual. Pisces is ruled by Jupiter in Aquarius, which tells me there would be many boys. Jupiter is under the tutelage of and in square to Saturn, which is the dirty old man himself (Baba). That Jupiter is in opposition to Neptune in the 10th says that his followers would close their eyes and wish it all away.

I mention this because, first, gurus, priests and holy men, in general, often have this problem, and, second, because those who are preyed upon in this fashion (they are never volunteers) are most often seriously hurt. When they seek help they are invariably told they should sacrifice for the sake of the guru, which only compounds the damage. Back a quarter-century ago, Caroline Myss, at UCLA, made the connection between the sacrament of Communion and the sex chakra, which, if you expand your concept of "communion" sufficiently, explains, though does not excuse, this problem.

Baba, in fact, had a well-known "Praetorian Guard" of older single females whose job it was to keep young willing females away from him. Which is one of the things I learned from friends who visited the ashram. How this particular "guru quirk" works out astrologically will change from guru to guru. You must learn to read a chart dynamically.

It also helps to remember that holy men, as we have seen with Baba's Sun-Saturn configuration, are not seen as flesh and blood, but as inhuman stick figures. Such a life can be lonely and unbearable, and I wonder why anyone would want it. Were those guards self-appointed, I wonder? There is only so much management a guru can enforce over his staff, as Jiddu Krishnamurti learned to his dismay.

In Baba's chart (November 23, 1926, 5:50 am, Puttaparthy, India) we can clearly see why this man became a solitary figure, rather than, say, someone's employee. Sun-Saturn conjunct, he appears severe. Moon-Pluto conjunct, he can be powerfully intense. Mars in Taurus, retrograde in the 6th, he does not play well with others. There is a story, perhaps true, that as a child he was beat up by bullies, who carved letters into his scalp.

It was said he had the ability to materialize objects at whim. The rational crowd wants this to be trickery of one sort or another. Myself, I don't have a big problem with whole-cloth materialization. Materialization is the concretization of projected energy. Sun-Saturn, Moon-Pluto, in trine to each other, can easily generate the necessary forces, which are known under a variety of names, one of them being prana. The only mysterious part is the stabilization of those energies, which is what precipitates a solid form into the material world. In Christian terms, this stabilizing force is known as the Holy Ghost. In chemistry, it's known as a catalyst. You are more familiar with the term vitamin. I wish I knew the exact secret.

So what makes this man a religious guru, as opposed to say, your average prana-stuffed street pandit (aka David Blaine)?

It would appear to be Baba's north node, Moon and Pluto, all in Cancer. Technically they're in the 8th, but the sign on the cusp of 8 is Gemini, which means these three want to identify with the 9th, even though they're not in it. It has taken me some years to work out exactly how house cusps work. For a long time I used a simple "whole sign" concept, where all the planets in a sign were residents of the house that had that sign for a cusp, but now I think that planets that fall outside (i.e. before) the cusp are *"on the wrong side of the tracks"* and are running (i.e., eager) to get into it.

Which makes them ne'er-do-wells. Poor relations, if you wish, or even nouveau riche. Always a bit gauche around the edges, always eager to claim what isn't quite theirs. Baba shows this quite clearly, in his intense (Moon-Pluto) desire to be a great religious figure, to the extent he claimed to be the reincarnation of Krishna himself. Or, if you're not quite comfortable with that, permitting the claim to be made in his name. This is an absurd claim on its face, not because the Gods cannot take incarnation like any of the rest of us (of course they can), but because no god, no god whatever, will ever make that claim. Such a claim merely gets in the way of their work. It hampers them. In supporting the claim, Baba used his mastery of various siddhis to transform himself into various guises. Reports I have heard is these were always done privately and often while in a car, for his personal amusement. I am sitting opposite Baba now, in the railway carriage. He clearly wants to do this, for my pleasure, it seems, but is too tired. He can only smile wanly.

SAI BABA claimed to be the reincarnation of Shirdi Sai Baba (died October 15, 1918, birth unknown). Which was widely discounted by Shirdi devotees, who pointed out how very different the two men were. Shirdi died destitute and had a mean and hungry look about him. Looking at Sai Baba's chart, can we know if the claim is true?

No, we really cannot, but there are clues. One, the very tightness of the Sun-Saturn conjunction makes us think of a previous life that was hard and tiring. That they are crammed into the very last one degree, eleven minutes of Scorpio makes us think rebirth as Sai Baba was rushed (which, only eight years out of body, it would have to have been) and that many compromises were made — which, again, would seem to be the case. That it was in the very last of Scorpio, and that Scorpio is known to be largely hidden, reminds me, again, that there was a great deal about Baba which will never be known.

But I can take some potshots. One, birth so soon after death means the normal post-death process was aborted. Presumably Shirdi Sai had devotees who were eager to have him as their son and who would willingly generate his next body. If this were true, then Shirdi chose among the various candidates. The resulting parents would have little, if any, karmic affiliation, and as a result there would be little physical resemblance between Shirdi and Sai. (Karmic affiliation, not direct lineage, makes for similarity from one birth to another.)

It is common in these cases for the person-to-be-born to impress a vivid dream on some immediate family member, usually the mother-to-be. In it, he will introduce himself and give a vision of the life he wants to lead, the goals he wants to accomplish. This sort of dream, by the way, is not unusual. Many mothers have them.

The concentration necessary to reincarnate in this way guarantees that memory will be maintained, from one life to the next. Which is not unusual, either. Those who die young, especially in war, often reappear quickly and retain much of their memory. See Stephen Crane.

So as they say on Mythbusters, Baba's claim of prior birth is plausible. To me, at any rate. So if you are young and a devotee of Baba and your sex life is under your control, you next could have the honor. — Does this sound like what you read in the Bible? *No*?

Outside the railway carriage the countryside speeds past. There is a loud clickety-clack to the rails, so we are not in any advanced country. Here and there the sun is breaking through the low, gloomy clouds. Baba is suddenly looking refreshed and alert, as if rest has already done him

good. Or maybe it's the promise of sunshine. The train is slowing. Baba has his valise in his hand and seems to be preparing to depart. While he was alive he said that after he died he would quickly reappear for a third and "final" incarnation. It looks as if he spoke the truth.

Baba clasps my hand and gives me a cheery goodbye, the only words he spoke, and leaves. The train starts up again with a lurch. I wish him much success at his new destination. Perhaps I will meet him for real, some day. *Reassignment.* — *May 17, 2011*

✤ Newton : Goethe : Polarities

THIS week I want to talk about genius. Not just any kind of genius, but that genius that is so powerful, so straightforward, that it cannot help itself, that it cannot be anything but.

This is the sort that Johann Wolfgang von Goethe (August 28, 1749, Frankfurt) had, who said of himself that he was born at noon on a full moon. And I thought, Moon here, Sun over there, I know what this is, I have it myself. So he invented *Sturm und Drang ("storm and stress")* — ? Well, of course. Sun and Moon pulling each other to pieces across the sky, that's what a full moon is all about.

And then I thought about Isaac Newton (1643-1727), who said he had merely walked along the seashore, discovering the occasional pretty shell in the sand. I know that one, too. Sun over here. Moon over there, the competing lights illuminate every detail. Brings everything into sharp focus, into great contrast. I'll bet Newton's a full moon, too. So I got his data: January 4, 1643, 1:28 am, Woolethorpe (Grantham), England, and set up the chart. Sun at 14 Capricorn, was that right? That's where the Sun is nowadays but that's not where it was back then because England was on the Julian calendar until 1752. So I checked carefully. Newton was born on Christmas day, 1642, Julian. Which means a modern chart, set for January 4, will be correct.

And what did I find in that chart? Sun in Capricorn, Moon in Cancer. Full moon.

Whenever you see this kind of polarity in a chart, Sun in one sign, the Moon in the opposite sign, making a full moon, the native is polarized. He bounces back and forth from one side of the chart to the other. Not so much because of the signs, but because of the houses they occupy. From one house to its opposite. He innately sees both sides, but not of any issue. He sees both sides, all sides, of the two *opposing houses*. Which makes finding *which* pair of the houses critical in understanding full moon natives.

76

If you're looking for people "like you", people who sort of do the same things that you do, look for those with Sun and Moon in the same houses. Same signs, too? You can try for it, but you won't find it very necessary. Matching houses are enough. This is what I'm up to this week. I have Sun in 9 and Moon in 3. I know these two men.

To be official, with Goethe we must first tweak his chart. Rodden and others have taken his direct statement, birth at noon, and given us charts with the Sun precisely on the MC. This is "justified" because it's what he said, and "justified" because he was really, really famous, which is a MC/tenth house delineation if you're not especially fussy about it. (Few "famous" people have 10th house Suns.) But what is "noon"? To Goethe it can mean the noon-hour, it can mean the midday meal. In a factory, lunch can be as little as 15 minutes. In Paris of the old days, "noon" was two hours. To resolve this we must consider houses.

Goethe's sun can be in the 9th, or in the 10th. In the 10th it will drive him outwards, into public life. As his Moon is past the exact opposition, if Goethe's Sun is in 10, his Moon will be in the 4th. The 4-10 polarity is political. It is patriotic. Moon in 4 is love of land, love of ancestry. Goethe lived through the French Revolution and the Napoleonic Wars. For anyone who wanted to make a name for himself in this way, there was abundant scope to do so. Goethe did not. He favored benevolent despots.

Goethe is known to us as a poet, a writer, and a savant. His Sun is therefore in 9, his Moon in 3, birth is 12:30 pm or later. Checking Anrias, his face appears to be "wet" (Scorpionic), rather than fiery, which makes late Scorpio rising rather than early Sagittarius. Pluto is in the vicinity of the ascendant, which should be notable. Donna Cunningham observed Pluto rising made for interesting grandparents. I regret I don't know about Goethe's grandparents, but Pluto rising also makes one touchy, and a bit isolated socially. Which was true of Goethe.

Late Scorpio rising puts his Venus-Jupiter opposition in 10 and 4. The signs are still Virgo to Pisces, just like his Sun and Moon.

Goethe and Newton and myself all have full moons that fall across the 3rd and 9th houses. The houses of intelligence, the houses of lower and higher mind, of the mundane and the spiritual, of instinct (3) and intuition (9), of nature spirits (3) and formal religion (9). The Sun-Moon polarity across 3 and 9, if it finds support in the rest of the chart, can literally know anything, and everything. On Earth, under the Sun, even the secrets of the gods themselves. This I know, first hand.

Many people are intelligent, and there are a variety of astrological signatures for it. Einstein, for example, was a genius mathematician with an interest in music. Music is very mathematical, which surprises many. But with Sun in Pisces and Moon in Sagittarius, Einstein lacked Newton's and Goethe's (and my) awesome ability to create pure knowledge, seemingly from nothing at all. Full moons across 3 and 9 are polymaths. While Einstein may well have had many interests, his actual talents were narrow. Newton and Goethe dazzled in every subject they touched.

The signs tell us how this is done. The Taurus-Scorpio polarity, for example, slung across 3 and 9, should produce an intense, earthy, pragmatic knowledge. One might become a great magician, for example, manipulating heaven and earth.

I learned this from Vettius Valens. He says "God" is in the 9th, while "Goddess" is in the third. Easy to extrapolate that by "God" he means a

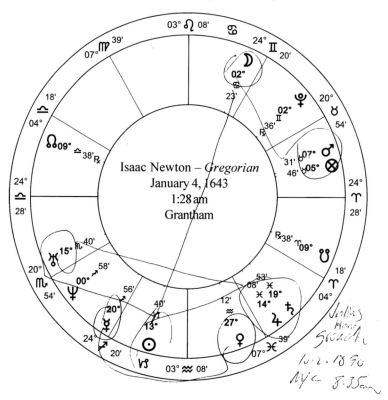

solar sun god, as this is essentially what all monotheistic religions (except Judaism: Jehovah = Saturn) amount to. Ninth house by definition. "Goddess" in the third took me a minute. That's Mother Earth. Valens has unwittingly shown us the difference between Christianity and Wicca, for example, but he has also given us more.

I associate Mother Earth with instinct. Which means that intuition, its opposite, is 9th. Which reaffirms the underlying nature of these two houses and shows Vedic astrologers are not wrong in giving an ideal placement of the Moon in the 3rd, and an ideal placement of the Sun in the 9th. Perfect instinct, combined with ultimate intuition. These placements both Goethe and myself have. Newton, if his time is accurate, was the reverse.

So if the 3 and 9 polarity does not produce a great savant, it might well produce a great magician or spiritual leader. The qualities are inherent in the houses. The expression is simply a matter of signs.

Consider Aries-Libra on 9/3. Enormous reckless drive coupled with an urge to swipe anything that's not nailed down (Libra, the sign of the

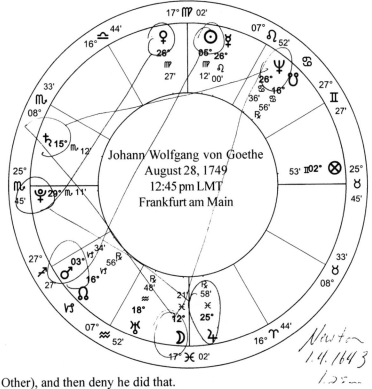

Other), and then deny he did that.

In Newton's case, Sun in Capricorn is study and hard work. Moon in Cancer is psychic sensitivity. The last thing Newton wants is to be a psychic and give expression to his feelings (Sun in the Moon's sign of debility), but, like an elephant in the room, he cannot get away from his emotions. At length he tackles the Moon's ideas, if only to prove them wrong (the opposition never stops being an opposition), but in the process, brilliantly transforms them. Which is the very essence of the polarity.

But once he has, he is somewhat embarrassed with the results. Feels they will not be accepted, as they are so radical. So he tends to sit on them, often for many years. Which in fact he did with calculus.

He publishes the least of his findings. These are not the things he is most certain of (he is certain of all his findings, for whatever can withstand the pounding of the Sun-Moon polarity is certain to be true), but rather, publishes only those things that might be of use (Capricorn) to others. This is in part because he fears exposing himself. It is useful to examine his method:

Isaac's Moon "feels something" — a bop on the head, perhaps. Isaac's sun blinks once or twice, picks up the apple and works out a formula. The Moon takes that as its new starting point and feels something else.

As this game goes on, the subject under study goes through profound changes: now red, now squat, now outside, now falling, now multiple, until, by what looks very like subtractive sculpture (think a block of marble and a chisel), a final, stable form is reached. One which amazes Newton himself, who, from the time the apple landed, until the final theory emerged, had never imagined any such thing.

This is the essence of the full moon: The world is different every time you look at it. As soon as you see something and say to yourself, Aha! I know what that is, some stupid voice in the back of your head says, well, what about THIS? And immediately you say, well, you're right, but what do you think about THAT? This is the Sun and Moon, literally tearing things apart, forcing you to hammer out what is REAL. Which is never what you thought, and never, ever, what is commonly accepted. Except, from time to time, by sheer accident.

All too often, and for too many things, every subsequent time you look at them, you find they've changed. So your understanding of them changes, too. People never know what to expect of you. The net effect is like a factory that takes casual observations as raw materials and extrudes manufactured knowledge. It is an awesome ability. Thus, wandering on the beach, looking at sea shells. The Sun-Moon polarity gave Newton eyes. He could see what others could not. That's how Newton's mind worked, and this is why.

Precisely the same process happens with Goethe. His Sun is in Virgo. His Moon is in Pisces. (With both of these men, note the Moons in water signs, an ideal placement, where they can easily sense the world around them.) Goethe repudiates the formless, shapeless world around him (Pisces), seeking instead to find the specific details that will satisfy his restless mind. (Sun-Mercury in mutual reception.)

Am I doing the same thing now, straight in front of you? Yes, and in my own fashion. Moon in Leo in 3, I am the dominant force in my personal environment, and always have been. I am proud of my position, I am proud of what I survey, which I know instinctively to be right. I eagerly take this to the Sun, in Aquarius, who, as with Goethe and Newton, is unwilling, but for different reasons.

In my case, distrust. Sun in Aquarius represents the group. The group is suspicious (in opposition) to the Moon (Leo/leader). The Sun says, We followed you the last time, where did that get us? The Moon retorts, I only do this because you yourself refuse to lead (Sun in Aquarius), and then in frustration the Moon adds, Okay, I give up, I don't care, I will go pout. Which is so like a Leo.

Whereupon the Sun thinks that maybe something can be done with the Moon's instinct after all. Leo/Aquarius across these two houses creates distrust and indifference. It paralyzes. Ultimately the Sun masters the Moon and dithers about doing his own thing, without regard for anyone or anything else. Because the abilities are enormous, if or when the Sun's work comes to light, it attracts a great deal of attention.

Such as with this newsletter. Now it seems the newsletter is gaining notice. And the Leo Moon perks right up. Is it my turn at last, it asks? As if it were a silly puppy. And the Sun replies, No, it isn't. The opposition does not go away simply because the hair is now gray. The rational Sun, not the emotional Moon, knows this well. The Moon's turn will never come. Dave is not Goethe. Many of you will say, Of course Dave is not Goethe. Dave is putting on airs. Which is precisely an Aquarian Sun's point. Such is life.

Men such as Newton and Goethe are among the most precious beings on the planet, presuming that ultimate knowledge is what the world seeks. But does it? As each learned, each in his own way, the world regrettably does not.

The world is as it is. It has a need for X tons of refined gasoline a day, a need for X gallons of whole blood, a need for X units of heat, X sacred blessings, and so on. Men such as these, men with oppositions that can touch the infinite, can easily overwhelm the world, giving it far more than it needs, more than it can imagine, more than it can stand, which is why, I think, that these men are so poorly used.

The majority of Newton's surviving writings are on alchemy, for example. Why this subject? Because, on the one hand, he had early on exhausted most every other subject, and, on the other, alchemy had pretty much the same reputation astrology does today, among those in "proper society." It was spurned, the work was believed to be impossible, and those who attempted it were fools, or frauds, or cheats. But after he had toyed with it, put it through his Sun-Moon processor, Newton could see the essence of it, its ultimate truth, and found it a worthy subject for his study. Minds such as his seek out challenges, seek out the impossible. It would not surprise me if he eventually succeeded in creating the Stone, in fact it would surprise me more if he did not.

Goethe writes prose, he writes poetry, he writes plays, he paints, he conducts research. Goethe in fact picked up Newton's work on color and stood it on its head. Goethe said his work on color was the finest thing he ever did. Both men remain enigmas to this day, we have still to fully understand them.

WE get a fuller picture of these two by considering the rest of their charts in context with their full moons.

With Goethe, we note his Sun in Virgo, ruled by Mercury, debilitated in Leo. This is a mutual reception, which usually binds together the houses in which the planets are placed. With Goethe, both planets being in the same house, Sun and Mercury take on each others' characteristics. The Sun gets nobility and power from Mercury's Leo, while Mercury gets the Sun's knack for managing details and fluency with words.

Note that in Goethe's chart, the Moon has passed by the exact opposition. So instead of being squarely opposed, or spoiling for a fight (applying to an opposition), the maximum tension is already over. The two are content to live and let live, or perhaps lick their wounds, if you will. So you will note that in Goethe's chart, both the Sun and Moon each have a "helper".

The Sun's helper is Mars in Capricorn, in a tight trine. This gives Goethe's Sun a friendly set of hands, as it were, to help him get his work done. Mars in Capricorn is eager to work, the Sun is eager to have him.

The Moon's helper is Saturn, in a trine from Scorpio. Saturn steadies the Moon and gives it patience and shrewdness. Off a bit to one side, both are trine to Neptune, forming a grand trine. Medieval astrologers held grand trines to be evil, but in a full moon chart, the more aspects the better.

You will then note three disassociate planets in Goethe's chart: Venus opposite Jupiter, the two of them trine and sextile to Pluto. If we use whole-sign aspects, which I often do, these are in aspect with the Sun and Moon, but in Goethe's chart I see them as independent actors. With a total of eight houses occupied (I am using a 12:45 pm chart), these various groupings give Goethe a great range of ability, a great range of color, if you wish.

We can trace the same thing in Newton's chart. Here the Moon is moving into its opposition with the Sun, it will be exact in about 20 hours. This is like preparation before battle. So what do each of them bring to the arena?

Newton's Moon has a sextile to Mars, which makes it magnetic (Mars rules iron, the Moon is in water, which shocks). The Sun, for its part, is well-aspected, with sextiles to Uranus, Jupiter and Saturn. Jupiter-Saturn are conjunct in Pisces (winner: Jupiter) and trine to Uranus. As these are trans-generational and outer planets, this grounds Newton to the society in which he lived. Off to one side, Mercury and Venus, in sextile. They belong to neither luminary.

We are all on a quest to understand ourselves, astrology being the tool that enables us to satisfy this craving. I have a chart which is broadly similar to these two men, and I am, I suppose, their peer. The primary difference, in my chart, is my planets are not scattered from 1 to 30 degrees. They mostly fall in a single 10 degree range. While I am no more "single-minded" than they were, of the ten planets in my chart, I can take eight of them, plus the ascendant, and draw them into a single multi-phase grand aspect.

This isn't Astrology 101 anymore. We have turned the corner and now ask where these men came from, *why* they were *who* they were. We all incarnate for a reason. Newton, Goethe and myself each incarnated in order to learn, to know. We each got charts that enabled us to achieve this goal, but each of our goals are different.

So, seek out those who have Sun and Moon in the same houses as yourself. These are your true "time twins." You will learn much. — *May 24, 2011*

✤Rapture!

WAS May 21, 2011. And this isn't 20-20 hindsight. Any fool could have predicted the outcome. I, chief among fools, in fact did so, before the Bel Air post office clerks at some point back in March, I think.

Harold Camping had done the hard work of finding the date, and then even harder work to bring it to the world's attention. But even he could not do everything. He had no idea how events of that day would actually play out. Since I have my Sun and Moon in the opposite houses to his, I had the necessary contrast to complete his work. On Saturday, May 21, 2011, the Rapture actually happened. Here's how:

God might be supreme, but ever since the Burning Bush episode he hasn't wasted time with pyrotechnics. If he wants to send us a delegate, he has him take ordinary birth, just like the rest of us. So if he wants to rapture people, knock their clothes off and lift them bodily into heaven, he already has the means to do that.

It's called tornados.

And though I've heard Harold, some 89 years old, has backed away from his May 21 prediction and now favors October 21, this only shows the old man has gone senile. There are few tornadoes in October.

So if you've had enough and wanted rescue (and don't we all!!), then on the ordained day, you must seek out a tornado. As it happens, the midwest is full of tornados at this time of year, and as it happens, the Weather Channel will tell you exactly where you may find them. — Such was my prediction. Any reasonably intelligent elder of Mr. Camping's church should have had bus loads of eager Rapturees standing by, waiting on the forecast.

An on May 21, the day itself, the Weather Channel, in fact, broadcast live from Tornado Ground Zero, in NE Kansas / NW Missouri. Top weather broadcaster Mike Bettis, along with Dr. Greg Forbes, the nation's leading tornado expert, were **live, in the field, physically chasing the Rapture Tornado,** broadcasting to the entire world as it happened. Yet only

84

one person was raptured. How could Camping's people have missed this? It was so obvious!

God put a lot of work into this. He was not happy with the result. The very next day, he forcibly raptured more than 100 innocents of Joplin, Missouri. He picked Joplin to send a message to nearby Tulsa, the source of much related nonsense. — *The loss of life was a great tragedy. Not a joke. My apologies.*

HAROLD CAMPING

MY remarks about Mr. Camping, like my remarks about his Rapture, will be sarcastic and tongue-in-cheek, but before I start I wish to say how loathsome I find preening idiots like him. He has ruined the lives of thousands, and very likely caused actual deaths, due to his absurd ideas and his egoistic certainty that he was right.

Harold Camping, according to Wiki, was born on July 19, 1921, in Colorado. Someone on-line has Boulder as his birth place, which is as good as anywhere. His birthtime is unknown.

To my surprise, Harold Camping is a full moon birth. I would not have guessed. So as I cannot read a chart without a time and as I think placing a full moon to be relatively easy, I will proceed with my usual guesswork.

Full moon in houses 1 and 7 is me against the world. Or at any rate, Me against You.

Full moon in 2 and 8 is My money vs: Your money. On a bad day it's *how much do I have to pay not to die?*

Full moon in 3 and 9 I explored last week. Does Harold look smart to you? No, I don't think so either, but he is a religious nut (9th), so let's set this aside for later.

Four and Ten is a patriot or a leader or a very public/private person of some sort.

Five and Eleven is compulsively creative, or sexual, or very into sports and teamwork. That's not Harold.

Six and Twelve is a sickly recluse, or a doctor in a large institution, or a cook in the military, or a cog in a wheel, etc.

And that's all the possibilities. The only one that sounds remotely possible is 3 and 9. So how do we make a full moon across those houses into a complete idiot, as Mr. Camping has proven himself to be?

Well, the Sun in Camping's chart is not alone in Cancer. Along with him are Pluto, Mercury and Mars. That's a stellium of four planets. Religion is the ninth house and Harold has always been a very religious man. He was a member of the Christian Reformed Church from birth up to 1988, when he was 67 years old. Harold's acceptance of his parents' religion makes me doubt he has four planets in Cancer on his 9th house cusp. Planets want to Do Things, and the more planets, the More They Want To Do. Four planets in Cancer on the 9th, Pluto and Mars among them, at some point in his life Harold is going to have a very deep, personal crisis that must be resolved by some 9th house means. Which are, deep study and reflection, or extensive travel, or religious re-examination. In his life, Harold has done none of these things. As sketchy as his Wiki entry is, this much is still clear.

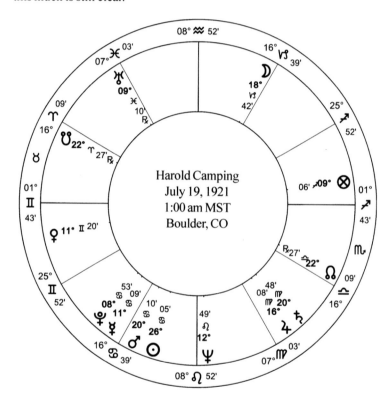

We put his Moon in 9, a very different picture emerges. Harold's Moon is in Capricorn, where it is debilitated. You may think I'm a genius and simply know things, but in fact I *have books* and *know to use them.* I went straight to Oken, where, of Moon in Capricorn, I read,... *as a feeling of security through the structure and control of the immediate environment, as well as a tendency to use an instinctual understanding of people for self-aggrandizement.*

Sakoian and Acker, another favorite reference, says, *The Moon in the sign of Capricorn indicates a reserved and cautious nature inclined to be cold and austere. Natives with this position take life seriously and identify emotionally with material rather than spiritual values.*

Reserved and cautious? Would that explain why Camping "emerged" only in old age? When Camping first predicted the End of the World in 1988 he wasn't exactly young. But what about this "materialistic" side? Doesn't religion transcend the materialistic? Let's go a few pages further into Sakoian and Acker:

Moon in the 9th house: *This position of the Moon indicates a deep emotional attachment to religious, social, and ethical values instilled in early childhood.... The Moon in this house can limit the scope or depth of spiritual understanding, through emotional bias and identification with parental attitudes and experiences.... If the Moon is afflicted, a narrow, dogmatic social and religious outlook can result.*

So Camping's Moon is cold, austere, materialistic and traditional, with limited understanding. There might be other rectifications for Harold's chart, but this looks good to me. That gives Harold a birth time of about 1:00 am. Get yourself good books and never be afraid to use them. That's what they're for.

So, how does a weak, defensive Moon, all alone in the 9th, turn into a major spiritual leader? Because it's not enough to place one planet. We must place all of them.

I should explain to all that when I rectify and read charts, I always use the Placidus system. The exact origins of the Placidian system are somewhat murky, it may go much further back than the 16th century monk for whom they are named. The system is based on the time it takes a sign to rise in the east, and functions as a shortcut for primary directions. A rudimentary system was used by Valens (2nd century), but it took Arabic numbers to actually calculate cusps with accuracy. Placidus is phenomenal for rectification and natal chart interpretation, which is what I use it for. *Other house systems have other uses.* You must pick the house system that is appropriate for your work. If I am asked I might deliver a very boring article on the subject. (See pg. 92.)

BUT back to Mr. Camping and his third house cusp, which we have determined to be Cancer. I am not interested at the moment if all four Cancer planets are in the 3rd, or if some are hanging around late in the 2nd, as all clearly want to be in the 3rd, one way or another. The question is, can they be shown to work in the 3rd in a way that is similar to how Mr. Camping has led his life?

At this point I would probably peek in another book, but this is a useful test of how good Sakoian and Acker really were. They describe the third house as *thinking.* The next page, they add *periodicals, papers, books, writing, telephone, television, radio, and speech.* A little further on they include, *short distance travels and comings and goings which bring us into contact with people.* Elsewhere I have heard that the third house rules ordinary schooling.

When I put all of this together, the third house, to me, represents daily life. When I see a stellium in the 3rd, or when I find the Sun or Moon in the sign of Leo in the 3rd, I judge that we have someone who is busy about town, or who wants to be a big shot in his community. Not a big shot to his family, not a big cheese in his state of residence, not someone who craves political power. A powerful third house makes for a town gadfly. Not a leader, as the third grants no leadership qualities. Third house dominant people who end up as mayors (for example) get there by acclamation, rather than any craving for power *per se.* Third-tenth house blends are another matter, of course.

Which pretty much describes Harold. Remembering that his Moon is weak and in a cautious sign and opposed by a good many planets, it is understandable that wasn't until 1958, at the age of 37, that he first got into radio. Which, right from the start, was the means by which he could preach the Old Time Religion he was born into. Radio quickly came to dominate his life. Harold had found his calling. Ever since then he has gradually, slowly, cautiously, taken the wraps off his 9th house Moon. I often say that debilitated planets want to be in the house opposite. Camping's Moon, in Capricorn, is debilitated. Camping's Moon wants to be a star on the radio, which in fact he has been since at least 1961. What does he do on-air? According to Wiki, he gives Biblical interpretations. At various points he has taken calls live on-air, so he presumably gives answers straight off the top of his head. This is the sort of thing full moons across 3 and 9 are good at.

So how does someone who, after a slow start, end up truly believing himself to be uniquely brilliant? How can a Sun/Moon paring across 3 and 9 be wasted with advanced Biblical Numerology? How can Harold Camping be so incredibly wrapped in his own ego as to prophesy events which are not only flatly impossible but which have no historical parallels whatever? (Not anywhere in the known universe!) How could he be so dense as to never once chance across the myriad number of others who have previously failed? Utterly, miserably, humiliatingly, devastatingly failed? Not a single success in sight, not now, not ever?

This, too, Mr. Camping's chart will tell us. Moon in Capricorn in 9 is rigid and dogmatic in terms of religion. Sun in Cancer in 3 is personable, direct and likeable. Mars gives energy and enthusiasm. Mercury in Cancer picks up the Ascendant and Venus (both in Gemini), making radio an outlet for Camping's verbal expression, which, Venus in Gemini, is always composed of the most beautiful words. Pluto would give them all a kick start, but he is far, far away at the very beginning of the sign. Early in Camping's life, transiting Pluto conjuncted Camping's Mercury (age 3), his Mars (age 9), and his Sun (age 14). If a time of 1:00 am is more or less accurate, Pluto opposed his Moon around the age of 9. These transits presumably left lasting scars and may well have reaffirmed a deep belief in God as his personal savior, being that the 3rd house is opposite the 9th, of religion, and that religion may well have functioned as his personal "life raft" as it were. The Pluto-Moon opposition was presumably his unique spiritual test. Combine with a formidable intellect and the result is a militant certainty as to his very personal calculations.

So here's how Harold Camping stacks up. Newton has Sun and Moon in the same houses, but opposite signs. (Isaac Newton: January 4, 1643 NS, 1:28 am, Grantham, UK.) In Newton's chart, the Moon in Cancer is strong, but the Sun, in the Moon's sign of debility, repudiates it, forcing a "rational" rather than "emotional" nature. But, paradoxically, the strong Moon feeds the Sun all his best ideas anyway. Note that both Camping, and Newton, feature debility. Camping's Moon in Capricorn is debilitated, whereas Newton's Sun, in the sign of the Moon's debility, simply wants his Moon to go away.

In my case I have Sun debilitated in Aquarius in 9. Again, debility. Sun in Aquarius is never sure of itself and is always ready to step aside for something else.

Look now at the results: Newton takes what the Moon feeds him and with it produces a "hyper rational" reality, one that the world as a whole has accepted for some 300 years.

In my case, my Sun's insecurity leads to a constant churning of ideas. The results are brilliant, but often invisible and just as often lost altogether.

With Camping, the Moon's babyish insecurity forces the Sun to pander to it, which is the nature of the opposition itself. Thus Camping early on got stuck in childish delusions. Look at the picture. It was taken in 2011, presumably before May 21. It shows an *eighty-nine year old man.*

Look at his beaming face! Look at his confidence! He has forecast the *End of the World*, a disaster of unparalleled magnitude, an event that will change not only his life, but the lives of every single person he knows, beyond comprehension. He is proud of himself and his ability. Like as not he himself can expect to lose personal friends, perhaps even family members, who didn't quite "measure up." But no matter! He holds his head high. The human equation, reality itself, is trivial by comparison. Camping has God in his pocket, Camping is God's Master, Camping is greater than God. Camping is drunk from 89 years of his own knowledge.

Such is the power of a full moon across the third and ninth houses, such is the importance of the signs the Sun and Moon are in. And such is the power of astrology. I am in awe.

LAST week I said the Sun and Moon in 3 and 9 could touch the infinite, could know the secrets of the Gods themselves. I am flabbergasted to learn that Camping has taken me at my very word. May 11, 2011, was not the first of his proposed dates. Camping had previously speculated on May 21, 1988, and September 7, 1994. I have read elaborate astrological analysis of May 21, 2011, the day itself, but in my opinion this is trivial. Camping's dates relate to Camping and to no one and nothing else. If Camping has a 1:00 am birth time, the Sun on May 21 of any given year is very near that ascendant, and the Sun on September 7 of any given year is very near Camping's Jupiter. The midpoint of Camping's Sun and Moon is, in fact, his nodal axis. The Sun on October 21 is only a few degrees beyond his south node, i.e. only a few degrees beyond his Sun/ Moon midpoint. Camping's elaborate calculations may be nothing more than rationalizations for his south node and two solar transits. Sun/Moon = Node is defined as a relationship. At first I was puzzled, as Camping seems to have had no significant relationships over his long life. But then I realized that, as with everything else, house positions define midpoints, just as **houses define everything in astrology.** In Camping's chart, his 9th house Moon is God, his 3rd house Sun is knowledge, the nodal midpoint becomes a *Knowing Relationship with God.* That Camping himself identifies October 21 as a significant date defines this as a south node relationship. The fool's relationship. Need I say that October 21, 2011, will come and go without event?

Harold Camping's chart is uniquely structured that he has spent his life in a quest to materialize, concretize, God Himself. Camping says the Bible is true, and while it might not necessarily be literal (Camping is not that dumb), his analysis, the sort that only a 3/9 dominant person can do, has given him concrete results. *The day the world ends.* Think about that! It is a staggering accomplishment. That he is wrong only shows the epic scale of his attempt, the sheer boldness of his claim. We may lay the blame for his failure to his debilitated Moon, with perhaps a nod to childhood Plutonian trauma.

Of Camping's revised date, October 21, 2011, my wife said, Well, they can be raptured, the world ended, with a hurricane!

No, I shot back. That would be Noah. God ain't gonna do that again, he already said as much. This is where I think the strain of Camping's failure to understand the events of May 21, 2011, has led to mental disability. Perhaps if we are lucky it will only be temporary. The world expects great things of Harold Camping, and while his remaining time may be short, our hopes have been raised.

As I had no space on pg. 1, **my wholehearted apologies for trivializing the massive weather disasters, human suffering and loss of life, of this past spring.** — *May 31, 2011*

❖How to Pick a House System

THERE are at least a dozen different house systems, none of which anyone understands. Ask an "expert" and you will get a description of how this or that system divides up the sky, but nothing at all on how to use it. This is more confusing because house systems are not fads. They emerged over time, according to mathematical ability and geographic location. So I will start at the beginning.

Houses are where everything in astrology comes to a single focus. Planets, signs, aspects, triplicities, midpoints and much more. It is therefore important that the house system fits precisely so that all those other details work as one.

So you're a jaded middle-aged male, entertaining a friend. The stripper has just appeared on the catwalk, wearing a gorgeous full-length evening dress, with elbow-length white gloves. That's her "house system." You're a pro, you know what her naked fundamentals will be, but (you're in the rag trade) you're curious how she's fitted herself together, her and all those garments (the package). You're like the astrologer who knows his stuff, but doesn't know how or why it works the way it does. You're not salivating over the act to come, so much as wishing you could personally peel off the layers and discover how she got them all to fit so perfectly. — Now that I've got your attention . . .

The necessity for houses, independent of signs, is a factor of latitude. At the Equator all house systems produce more or less equal houses, as you can see by the examples on the next page, where the same date and time is used to produce charts set at the Equator, 20°, 40°, and 60° north latitude. In Tropical regions you can use equal houses on all cusps. The midheaven won't be exactly there, but there's a lot of astrology you can do without an exact MC. And besides. All those fancy methods of rectifying a chart mostly work with the ascendant anyway. Rarely the MC. So long as the sign on the MC is right, you'll do fine, etc., etc.

Well, that's settled. Equal houses in the tropics (23° N/S of the

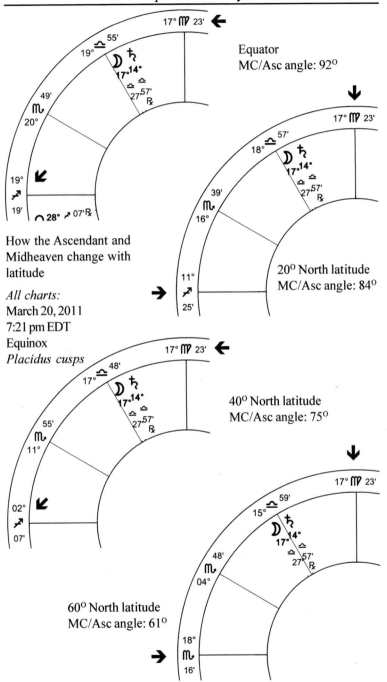

Equator
MC/Asc angle: 92°

How the Ascendant and
Midheaven change with
latitude

All charts:
March 20, 2011
7:21 pm EDT
Equinox
Placidus cusps

20° North latitude
MC/Asc angle: 84°

40° North latitude
MC/Asc angle: 75°

60° North latitude
MC/Asc angle: 61°

Equator), something else for the rest of the planet.

But not so fast. Turns out, the sky is a complex thing and early astrologers didn't have a number system that would let them describe it by means of houses. Early number systems, such as the Attic, the Ionian, the Roman, the Chinese, the Mayan, were all variations on hash marks. You could count, you could add, you could subtract and if you memorized tables, you could do simple multiplication and division. But that was it.

So far as houses were concerned, the gnomon on a sundial will determine noon. From that, simple tables were constructed, based on the day (or, more likely, the week) of the year, along with the latitude (more exactly, the klime) to give the angular separation, Ascendant to MC. The length of the gnomon's shadow at any given moment on any given day was the ascendant, as noted in the table. For night births, or when it was cloudy, there were water clocks (clepsydra).

Which in practice meant that for centuries astrology stalled at about 30 degrees north: Alexandria (31 N). Yes there were dabblers with Caesar in Rome (42 N), but the main school was further south.

Valens, for example. He was one of the most demanding of early Greek astrologers. He had the ascendant, he had the MC. He wanted houses. Real houses. Not equal ones. The best he could do was divide the zodiacal longitude, Asc to MC, by 3 and call that his cusps. Which are Porphyry houses. (They far predate Porphyry (3rd century), or Valens himself (2nd century), for that matter.)

Porphyry has lately been revived by Jeff Green and his Evolutionary Astrology, but they are not really houses, as they do not represent either the Earth's unique space, or time. Porphyry is just an alternative version of signs. My best guess is that Green's use of them is whimsical.

(What about Chinese and Tibetan and Celtic astrologies? Turns out, none of these were sky-based. Why? Because they were all too far north for the simple number systems (aka hash marks) they had. Astrology is more complex than has been realized. It is more complex than this overview.)

What changed? A culture that didn't really need numbers invented them anyway. By around 300 AD, India had invented what we know as "Arabic numbers." Which are numbers based on position, rather than symbolic hash marks. If they had invented them 600 years earlier, Alexander the Great would have brought them back to Europe. Instead, around 900 AD the expansionary Islamic Caliphate got them. In no time they (not the Hindus, it seems) had added decimal points, thereby creating the modern number system.

Islamic astrologers wasted no time in inventing the first proper house system: Alcabitius. In this system, the *time* it took for a degree to move from the ascendant, to the MC, was trisected. The degree on the ascendant at the first third was declared to be the 11th house cusp. The degree on the ascendant at the end of 2/3rds of the stated time was declared to be the 12th house cusp.

All the while Christian Europe was locked in a life or death struggle with Islam, which is to say, Europe refused to have anything to do with the "heathens" to the south. This changed when the first Crusaders returned with lots of fabulous loot. Which initially only spurred more Crusades. Plunder would pay for wars, Europe at the time was destitute.

By the twelfth century things had begun to settle down and the rudiments of actual trade was emerging. The Twelfth Century Translators (that's the name they go by) translated scores of Arabic and Persian books, many of them astrological. In 1202, Fibonacci introduced the Indian-Arabic number system to Europe. The importance of this one event to western civilization simply cannot be overemphasized.

Together, these became the astrology of Guido Bonatus (died c. 1300). In their texts, the translators found Alcabitius houses, which they passed along. Which were the houses that Bonatus used. If you are a student of Bonatus or the Arabs, use this system.

Campanus of Novara was a contemporary of Bonatus. He served a number of popes. Using the newly introduced Arabic numbers, he invented the Campanus house system, which uses *space*. Campanus erected a Prime Vertical and trisected the difference between that, and the horizon (ascendant). I regret that to my knowledge there are currently no books in print from the "Campanus era," though many notable 20th century astrologers found Campanus to be of interest, among them, Dane Rudhyar, C.E.O. Carter, and Cyril Fagan.

So we now have three distinct house systems:
No system: Equal, Porphyry.
Time systems: Alcabitius, Placidus, Topocentric, Koch, etc.
Space systems: Campanus, Regiomontanus, etc.
I am aware there are still other systems — midheaven based, for example, but they have few adherents.

THE hard-working girl on stage is slowly giving up her secrets. Our jaded host is examining a glove that came flying his way. Before the show reaches its climax, there is still more we can puzzle out.

I note that Alcabitius houses, based on time, was an effort to put a foundation under Vettius Valens, who used the time it took a sign to rise as a method of forecasting. This amounts to Primary Directions, which, then as now, are difficult to calculate. Placidus was an improved version of

Alcabitius, and Topocentric amounts to a confirmation of Placidus by means of actual observation.

What do all these systems have in common? They are all *time based systems* and they are generally used with *natal charts*.

On the other hand, astrology in Europe, right from the start, was largely centered on *horary*. What does horary use? It has traditionally used Regiomontanus. Which is a *space based system*.

So, what is the difference between natal and horary?

Natal charts are dynamic. Progressions, directions, rectification, transits, and much more, are applied to them. A given natal chart is in use from the moment of birth, until the eventual death. Natal charts *change*.

An horary chart, by contrast, is used once and then thrown away. Only the most simple directions are ever applied to it. An horary chart, as well as its near relations, electional, mundane and decumbiture, are *static*.

Based on the foregoing, here is a simple rule:

For Static Charts, (i.e. Horary) use a *Space Based System,* such as Regiomontanus or Campanus.

For Dynamic Charts, (i.e. Natal) use a *Time Based System,* such as Alcabitius, Placidus, Topocentric or Koch.

Generally speaking, the more recent the system, the more polished it will be. In other words, chose Regiomontanus over Campanus, chose Placidus over Alcabitius.

Must you follow this rule? Of course not! It is merely a term of reference, a starting point, for those who need one.

Mastery of materials makes for specialized uses. In other words, some house systems have comparatively narrow uses.

Koch houses are unique in that its intermediate cusps — 2nd, 3rd, 5th, 6th, 8th, 9th, 11th and 12th, are known to be sensitive to ordinary transits. Joyce Wehrman exploited this 30 years ago with her *Winning* gambling system — which really works. Hard aspects to the Koch 5th house cusp will make you a winner on the slots. It's been proven more than once. It is, however, not an easy system to learn, and a birthtime, precise to at least the minute, if not the nearest 15 seconds, is critical. How to get your time that precise? Joyce suggested dealing yourself Blackjack hands, until you deal yourself a perfect 21. Having previously set your clock exactly to true Universal Time, you erect a chart for that moment and from it, extract your actual Koch 5th house cusp. You then rectify your chart to put that precise degree, minute and second there. Here is a further hint: The conjunction, square and opposition aspects to your 5th house cusp repeat every five hours 59 minutes. If that's what you found, then you should be able to repeat the win every five hours 59 minutes. This is because the Day, the time it takes the same degree to return to the ascendant (or your 5th house cusp), is 23 hours, 56 minutes.

Wehrman's "winning moment" is only about two minutes long. There might be as much as 30 seconds on either side of it. Hit it square and you will win, win, win. Miss by even a second and you will lose, and go on losing, hour after hour. I proved this to myself many years ago playing Windows Solitaire, Vegas style.

Topocentric, which for most latitudes gives results very similar to Placidus, produces less distortion above 55° north. If you commonly work with natal charts in those latitudes, you might try it out.

In the middle of the 20th century, Cyril Fagan and Brigadier Firebrace invented a Sidereal Zodiac system of astrology. It was based on the Fagan-Bradley ayanamsa and exploited solar and lunar returns. By definition these were precessed, as the sidereal zodiac is self-precessing. Back in the 1980's we thought precession was the thing to do, so we precessed Tropical returns. Which produced charts for the same exact instant, so wasn't that the same?

Turns out, according to one of my contacts (Dave Y), they're not. Turns out, the Fagan-Bradley sidereal zodiac produces valid signs when used to make return charts.

This was a surprise to me. What house system did Fagan use for his returns?

He used Campanus. Back in the 1980's, I was running charts for Kanya. He was the brilliant man who ran the Tree of Life in Harlem. He had everything in Sidereal/Fagan-Bradley, Campanus houses. At the time I thought it was the African-American school of astrology, because at the time I was unaware the Sidereal school (Fagan, Bradley, Firebrace etc.) had completely faded away in only ten years.

So how do we learn to use houses? As with everything else, we learn from the masters.

FANS of equal houses will say that I have shortchanged them. I myself wonder if they know how to use houses. I recommend the *Morinus method* as he is most excellent. I might add that we have just watched a pro strip down to bare nothingness and while she did so, she had every eye in the house, male and female, riveted on her. By comparison, the usual astrological wet T-shirt contest (house guesswork) is a drippy amateur mess. Your choice.

And no, nudes are not out of place. They are used in metaphysical literature, partly to grab wayward male attention, but mostly as a metaphor for the naked truth. Astrology can give us that, the-truth-and-nothing-but, but only if we are brave enough to demand it, to be willing to see it. Unlike our dancer, it is not always pretty. — *June 7, 2011*

✤ How to write a Daily Horoscope

(AKA ASTROLOGY'S GREATEST SECRETS FINALLY REVEALED)

OVER the years I have been asked many times for books on how to write a daily horoscope. So far as I am aware, there has never been such a book, perhaps as no one thinks such a thing is worthy. Of the history of daily horoscopes, yes, we have that. It's Kim Farnell's *Flirting With the Zodiac.* But not one word, anywhere, on how it's done. Consequently, even many of the people who write them for a living are unsure. So here are some guidelines:

The amount of space you have determines the level, the degree of detail. Starting with the most brief:

Daily horoscopes are based on the Sun sign and the day's Moon. That's really all they are. You are simply writing Sun-Moon aspects. To wit:

Conjunction: In what sign is today's Moon? Write that sign's horoscope like this:

Today you start new projects, new adventures, new this, new that. Tailor each to the specific sign in question. Moon in Leo? Then Leos have a proud, regal day. Moon in Scorpio? That makes for intensity, etc.

Sextile: Two signs to the left or right of today's Moon are Sun signs that are in sextile to the Moon. Keyword: *Pleasant surprise.* Sextiles are kind of weak, we are surprised when things work out better than we expected. In the case of aspects, *the Moon brings the essence of its sign to the Sun sign in question.*

Example: Moon in Virgo, Sun signs of Cancer and Scorpio. Moon in Virgo is detail, Cancer is sensitivity, the result is *an appreciation of the details around you.* Moon in Virgo is detail, Scorpio is intensity, you could go out on a limb and say, *sex tonight will be a humdinger!*

Square: Three signs from today's Moon are Sun signs in square. *Squares are aspects of stress.* I've looked all over the many aspect books but it seems that when authors come to write about squares, they're too stressed to observe that stress is what they're talking about. Stress is not like an opposition. Oppositions are what you can see, and what you can see you can deal with. Stress is trying and trying but not quite understanding why you keep failing, etc.

98

In this case, what is stressful about the day? What is stressful about the day is what the Moon, by sign, has brought to the Sun sign in question. Suppose today's Moon is in Capricorn. That's a cardinal sign, it indicates toil without reward, even failure. Square to the Sun sign of Aries, it means that nothing you try will work. Square to the Sun sign of Libra, it means your friend or partner can't be pleased and neither of you know quite why.

Trine: The next sign over makes trines to your Sun sign. *Trines make for wonderful, marvellous days.* You wake up in the morning full of hope, and the day does not disappoint. As with the other signs, not everything you do on this day is wonderful, only those affairs ruled by the sign the Moon's trine brings to the Sun's sign. Suppose the Moon is in Gemini and you're an Aquarian. Gemini is communication, Aquarians are one of many. So on this day, you could be the center of attention: People come to you for news. And, finally,

Opposition: Oppositions are confrontational. They demand you take matters by the horns, that you let chips fall where they may, that you take responsibility for the outcome, that you are precise, clear and defined. Which is a lot for most people. The conflict is shown by the signs themselves. *Note carefully:* **Some oppositions are social.** Leo/ Aquarius takes special handling, as in, Moon in Leo, Sun sign Aquarius, *Try to humor the boss.* Moon in Aquarius, Sun in Leo, *don't make a fool of yourself.* Moon in Scorpio, Sun sign of Taurus, Scorpio being intensity, makes for *Don't get in over your head.*

What about the other signs, those that are not conjunct, sextile, square, trine or opposed? In a basic, brief horoscope column, you write as if you were writing on the next level of horoscope, where you have a bit more room to play with. Which is,

You equate signs with houses. On any other level of astrology I think this is a cop-out, but not here. Indeed, at this point it helps to think of your daily horoscope as not a collection of Sun signs, but rather, ascendant signs.

If today's Moon is in the same sign as the Sun sign you're working on, that's still a conjunction. Conjunction, first house, that's pretty much the same thing. Again, tailor your forecast to the sign in question. Suppose the Sun is in Scorpio. Moon in the same sign, that's a day when you reach your full level of intensity.

Keeping the Sun (or ascendant) in Scorpio, the next sign is Sagittarius. Which becomes the second house of money and resources. You might spend money on something exotic, or get money from far away.

Keeping the Sun still in Scorpio, the next sign, Capricorn, represents the third house. For the day, third house affairs will come to the fore:

Brothers, sisters, errands, minor things. Keeping in mind this is also a sextile, that Scorpio is intense and that Capricorn requires work, you could say, *Things go well today with a bit of work.* And you would not be far wrong.

Actually, at this point I'd be tempted to cheat. I'd get a copy of Sakoian and Acker's *Astrologer's Handbook* and turn to Part 1, Chapter 4, *Rising Sign Overlays,* and base my horoscopes on their sturdy foundations. Here they are with Scorpio and Sagittarius:

Generally, Scorpios have good luck in financial matters and know how to make money multiply. They expand their activities through money, and there are usually adequate financial resources to further their ends. . .

Maybe they had daily horoscopes in mind, I don't know, but this is the closest anyone's ever come to writing a book on the subject.

THE final detail for a daily horoscope is to include all the other planets. Up in the sky above, where are Mercury, Venus, Mars, etc., really at? How to incorporate them?

With the Moon, of course. The Moon activates the other planets, by transit, when it is in the same sign with them (conjunction). Planetary energies dominate the sign the planet is in, and are then brought to the Sun sign in question in the manner of the aspect the planet/Moon makes to the Sun sign.

So, for example, Mercury is soon to go into Cancer. Mercury is communications, Cancer is what is personal. Say you're writing for Sun in Libra, and suppose today's Moon is in Cancer. That's a square. So, *Today you get upsetting news from a friend.* The Moon's passage through Cancer makes it *today,* its transit over Mercury makes it *news,* Cancer makes it *personal,* the square makes it *stressful* and Libra means *you know* the person who wrote it. We don't tell you to memorize keywords for nothing. Suppose Mercury was retrograde? Then, *Upsetting news is not what it seems.*

On the same day, Moon in Cancer conjunct Mercury, the Sun sign is now Scorpio. He gets happy news, as the aspect is a trine. What if Mercury is retrograde? Then the news is not as good as it appears to be.

Same day, Moon in Cancer conjunct Mercury, Sun sign is Capricorn: *Your request is denied.* It's the opposition. Mercury retrograde, *Things are not as bad as they seem.*

You are cautioned not to go overboard. Saturn hangs around in a sign for 29 or 30 months. Such as with Libra, where it is now. That's upwards of 900 days. Divide by 28, and that's 32 conjunction delineations for Libra, 32 opposition delineations for Aries, and 32 squares for each of Cancer and Capricorn. You write all of those and people will think you're a real downer.

For Jupiter through Pluto, it's enough to hit the highlights. Which are:

Initial entry into the sign. Go through the Sun signs twice, then drop it. After that, we've pretty much got the message.

Stations. Saturn went direct on the 12th of June. Neptune went retrograde on the third. Hit just once. If for any reason you can't manage a clear conception of the aspect and what it's likely to mean, it's best to avoid writing about it. From what I've given here, you will have lots of ways to approach the subject. If you're pounding these out on a daily basis, you're going to learn fast.

Imagine what you can do with, say, Venus. It moves as fast, or faster, than the Sun, which means that in any given month (Venus sign), you can write an entire relationship, spread among all the Sun signs.

At the moment, Venus is in Gemini. That's sweet words, well-spoken. When the Moon is in Gemini, the Sun signs of Aries, Gemini, Leo, Libra and Aquarius will be hearing pleasing things from friends and lovers.

On the other hand, Virgo, Sagittarius and Pisces will not be as pleased, as, one way or another, the messages Venus sends from Gemini will disappoint. In which case, we remember that fast-talking Gemini can tailor its messages for ulterior motives.

Remember your position before the public is a privilege which few ever attain. *Whenever possible, be cheerful, give hope.*

WEEKLY horoscopes are essentially seven dailies, packaged together. We don't have to try as hard with weeklies, we can be content to just hit the high points. With aspects, houses and planets, we have a lot to work with.

MONTHLIES are a whole different thing. With monthlies, we can bring in the Sun itself.

Suppose you're writing a monthly and are working on Aries. Right now, the Sun is about to go into Cancer. Sign/house swap, the Aries Sun sign individual is about to have a month dealing with home and land and ancestry and his daddy, etc.: 4th house. Plus, you can throw in as much daily stuff as you need to round things out.

With monthly horoscopes we have arrived at our unique annual cycles. What we all know from experience, that spring brings us this and the winter brings us that. That's the Sun in its annual circuit through our charts. I am more inclined to give the transiting Sun the benefit of hard aspects, which I did not give to the Moon. Monthlies are where it really pays to read your ascendant sign, rather than your Sun sign.

So, the individual is Aries, the month of the year (transiting Sun) is Cancer. Pluto is opposite, in Capricorn. Pluto is going to be in Capricorn forever and ever and ever (up to 2024 or so), so you don't want to write doom and gloom, but you do want to keep it in the back of your mind and not go overboard with cheerfulness. Every now and then conjunctions and oppositions reach out and bite. Even with the sort of horoscopes I'm outlining, you won't be able to forecast the day week or month you get bitten. So don't try.

And it goes without saying that you never, ever, mention Moon or planets or aspects or other signs in your work. But now that you know the secrets, you can grab an ephemeris and easily decipher any horoscope. Or, for that matter, spot the phonies. There's a lot of them.

YOU are strongly cautioned that writing horoscopes is a treadmill. Once you get on, it can be very hard to get off. It can quickly become repetitive and thankless. I think you should keep a stock of phrases and slot them in as necessary. You may think you're being repetitive, and you will be, but to your readers, you are being consistent. This can be tricky to balance.

The internet has sparked a huge demand for horoscopes. In every case, horoscopes are a way of driving viewers to a site, which increases traffic and generates revenue for the site owner, or it should.

For this reason, *you must get paid.* No ifs ands or buts about it. You might give them a free month, but if there's no money at the end of it, **QUIT.** Don't compromise and don't apologize. Don't put up with sob stories or promises. You might be writing first class stuff, but they might be internet idiots who will fail no matter what. If they promise to share revenue, that's a contract. Have them draw it up and take it to an attorney for his inspection. (Look them up in the phone book. They won't cost more than $100 or so, which is peanuts. And I shouldn't have to tell you not to trust their attorney.)

There are a lot of guys who run websites who are cheap and expect you to work for free. Some think Astrology isn't "real" and so they don't need to worry about you and your needs, since, to them, you're just a scam artist anyway. (Just like them.) Avoid these creatures.

If you should happen to be hired to write a month's horoscopes only to find there's no pot of gold at the end of it, say goodbye, take your copies and go peddle them. If you're good and have a flair, then with a bit of persistence you might find yourself a paying gig. If you keep at it you might eventually work your way up to national magazines, as Debbi Kempton-Smith and Michael Lutin have. Or national syndication. Which pays rather well. It's a rarefied world, but someone has to do it.

How much money? I'd want enough that I didn't have to worry about my finances. People don't tell me what they make, so I can only guess. I wouldn't touch dailies or weeklies for less than $500/week, and as I already have a day job, it would take a lot more than that.

In this regard, *be very careful about signing contracts* where you supply material at a fixed price, forever. Horoscopes have, in the past, quickly blown the roof off, indeed, a good, well-written horoscope invariably generates a huge following. Which is what your sponsor is hoping for. Horoscopes are just about the only area of astrology that can be genuinely well-paid. I'd want 90 day reviews written into whatever I signed. You risk that after the first 90 days you will be out of a job, but that's the big cruel world for you.

Again: *your attorney is your friend.* Every famous rock group was once just a garage band. Most of them were badly burned by the first contract they signed.

Good luck! — *June 14, 2011*

---

footnote: **green astrology, a work in progress**

In my book, *Skeet Shooting*, I gave a couple of theories for astrology. One, that the Sun-Earth relationship, not the constellations, create signs of the Zodiac; and that astrological energies, in general, were a form of planet-to-planet "resonance."

I've had time to think since and I've come to the surprising conclusion that astrological energies are primarily of the Earth itself. Only a little bit from the sky. That we've had it precisely backwards. In a stroke I've created a vast playground where everything in western astrology, everything in Vedic astrology, everything in Chinese and Mayan and Tibetan astrology, all have a place.

I've shot this idea to three or four people I know and, so far, the result has been silence. Not sure if they don't understand, or if they don't like it and are too polite to call me a fool.

I'm going to write this up in my next book (next year, I hope), but are there any brave folks who would like to see it serialized in the newsletter? Astrology is how you live in harmony with the Earth itself, which makes astrology the ultimate ecosystem. — *August 2, 2011*

♦ Emperor Nero

NERO Claudius Caesar Augustus Germanicus was born on December 15, 37 AD, at Antium, near Rome. He was the only son of Gnaeus Domitius Ahenobarbus and his wife, Agrippina the Younger, sister of Emperor Caligula. When Emperor Claudius took Agrippina as his third wife, he took Nero as his adopted son and heir. Which somehow displaced Claudius's own son, Britannicus, from the throne.

The chart is from Vettius Valens, you will find it on pg. 242 of the upcoming Riley/Roell edition. On pg. 241, Valens tosses it off, thusly:

For example: Sun, Mars, Mercury, Ascendant in Sagittarius, Moon in Leo, Saturn in Virgo, Jupiter in Scorpio, Venus in Capricorn. The Moon controls the second interval since it is two signs from Saturn. The same is true of the Sun, Mars, Mercury, and the Ascendant with respect to Venus. . . .

As Valens does not name the chart as Nero's, this doesn't sound like much of anyone at all. As he does not give actual birth data, we use the following method to find it:

Sun in Sagittarius, we are looking for a day in November/December. The pairing of Saturn in Virgo, Jupiter in Scorpio, happens once every 59-61 years, which are quickly found. As Valens was writing in the second half of the 2nd century (101-200 AD), we are looking at 22 BC, 37 AD, 97 AD, 157 AD or maybe 217 AD. Any of these years should produce Saturn in Virgo, Jupiter in Scorpio, more or less.

We then look for Mars, which has a two year cycle. Saturn at 29 years, Jupiter with 12, Mars with 2, when all three are taken together, December, 37 AD is found to be the only possible month and year. The positions of Mercury, Venus and the Moon suggests the 15th/16th as the date, and Wiki, not Valens, confirms birth to have been on the 15th. The Moon is one day into Leo, while Mercury has turned direct only two days previously, having made a station at 0° Sag.

Rectification. I don't think we should go overboard. The chart is

104

very old and most surviving accounts were written by Nero's enemies and may be suspect.

According to Valens, there can be any degree of Sagittarius rising. Early degrees put Virgo on the MC. Middle and late degrees have a Libra midheaven. According to David Anrias, late degrees of Sagittarius rising have distinct "droopy eyelids," which remind me of grandmother Roell, who had them. Surviving busts of Nero lack this feature.

A ruler's midheaven is, essentially, his administration. A Virgo MC is sanitation and health, in other words, public works. With Pisces opposite, and Rome as the Emperor's place of residence, a Virgo MC will result in aqueducts and engineering. There were Roman Emperors who specialized in that sort of thing, but Nero was not among them.

According to Wiki, *During his reign, Nero focused much of his attention on diplomacy, trade, and increasing the cultural capital of the empire. He ordered the building of theaters and promoted athletic games. During his reign the redoubtable general Corbulo conducted a successful war and negotiated peace with the Parthian Empire.*

Diplomacy and trade, culture, theaters, war and peace, are all symbolic of a Libra MC and a birth time of about 7:00 am.

But, you will say, with Virgo on the MC, Saturn is there, and when Saturn is in the 10th, the native comes to a bad end. Nero came to a bad end, did he not?

Indeed, Nero came to a bad end, killing himself in anticipation of a stranger doing it for him, but it wasn't a Saturnine ending. Saturn in the 10th compulsively takes on responsibilities until it is finally overwhelmed and crushed by them. Nero seems to have taken on very little in the way of responsibilities. Saturn is time itself. Saturn in the 10th (I have a brother with this, I've had 50 years to observe it) builds slowly, painstakingly and only comes to a bad end after much toil and hardship. Which is rarely before middle age.

So this is our chart for Nero: December 15, 37 AD, Antium, Italy, 7:00 am. The chart is not the same as what will be in the eventual book. In the book, all charts are in Porphyry (the house system Valens himself used), and none have outer planets. Here, the chart is in Placidus. Of the outer planets, we find the Sun conjunct Pluto, Uranus in the 9th with Saturn, and the Moon opposite Neptune.

Nero's chart is dominated by the Pluto-Sun-Mars conjunction in Sagittarius in the first. This is overwhelming cruelty, a bully, as it turns out. This will be focused in the area shown by the house in which we find Jupiter, the ruler of Sagittarius.

Jupiter is in Scorpio in the 11th house of friends and ideals. Scorpio on the 11th, these are powerful and dynamic, intense people. Jupiter makes for a lot of them. On the receiving end of Pluto-Sun-Mars, they are literally eaten alive, chewed up en masse. This is not a nice way to treat your friends.

WHY would Nero do this? We must remember that he grew up in a family that was already guilty of fratricide. A mother, Agrippina, widely believed to have been a poisoner. This is a kill-or-be-killed environment. Nero murdered his stepbrother, Britannicus, as well as his mother. In murdering his own family he was no different from many other despotic rulers, before and after.

This intensifies when we study Nero's 7th house, of partners and wives. It has Gemini on the cusp, which, for starters, means the people he most closely associated with tended to be two-faced. Say one thing and do something else. None of the planets in Nero's first house have any rights in the 7th, which put his wives beyond his direct control.

The ruler of the 7th house, Mercury, is in Sagittarius, in the 12th. This is the 12th house of secret enemies, meaning that Nero was likely to find himself associated with those who did not like or trust him. As Mercury, like the planets in the first house, is disposed by Jupiter in the house of friends, the way Nero controlled his wife was to lump her in with his friends and treat her accordingly.

Mercury being the planet of communication, in the 6th house from the seventh, Nero's wives (?) talked to everyone except him, inconjuncts/ semi-sextiles (take your pick) by definition having no relationship to the rest of the chart. This also shows why Nero was reluctant to marry to begin with. It was so much easier to simply use brute force in personal affairs and let things fall where they may.

There is more. Robson says a debilitated Mercury in the 12th leads to hearing problems. Nero is not known to have been deaf, but on more subtle levels, his hearing was not good.

Mercury needs details in order to function, which is why it does well in Gemini and Virgo, third and sixth houses, and poorly in Sagittarius and Pisces, ninth and twelfth houses. Mercury in Sagittarius and the 12th is twice addled. In Sagittarius the concepts are too broad for it to handle, and in the 12th, Mercury is muzzled and so cannot speak. Nero has a third factor, that his Mercury had two days previously turned direct and was still, on the day of his birth, virtually immobile in the sky. Stranded.

In such a bleak situation, Mercury looks about for support, but finds little: A weak sextile with Neptune, which only makes things worse, a weak trine from the Moon, a weak sextile from Uranus.

Consequently we may conclude that Nero wasn't terribly bright. In his makeup we find the overwhelming, brute force of the first house, which terrified everyone around him.

Then, Venus in Capricorn in the second house, trine to Saturn in Virgo in the 9th. Venus, the ruler of the MC, is the image of Nero the Emperor, popular with the public, able to enrich them (MC and 2nd house), able to solve diplomatic problems (9th and 2nd) and largely avoid war.

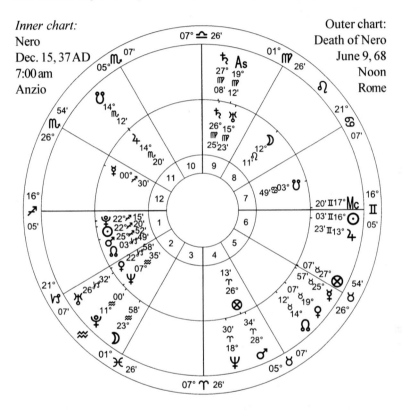

Inner chart:
Nero
Dec. 15, 37 AD
7:00 am
Anzio

Outer chart:
Death of Nero
June 9, 68
Noon
Rome

A year or two before he died he erected a 100 foot bronze statute of himself (roughly the same size as the Statue of Liberty), which ultimately came to be directly in front of the Coliseum, built a decade later, which was only slightly taller. This statue stood for three centuries, to the end of Rome itself. Efforts to replace Nero's head with the heads of others only resulted in Nero's head being put back. So far as the public was concerned, Nero was no ogre.

Finally, there is Nero's opinion of himself. A reckless bully who believed he had a good heart (Moon in Leo), a man who thought of himself as an artist (Libra MC), a musician, even an athlete (Sun-Mars conjunct). He was genuinely puzzled why his friends and associates did not understand him (Mercury debilitated), and why he was, in the end, abandoned to his fate.

Nero has the reputation as the first Emperor to persecute Christians, having them burned alive to illuminate evening parties. Analysis of Nero's chart suggests this had little to do with religion. Religion is 9th house, in Nero's chart we find Virgo on its cusp. Virgo is ruled by Mercury, which is hiding in the 12th and debilitated in Sagittarius. If these placements are accurate, Nero is, for the most part, unaware of other religions, since the ruler of a cadent house in a mutable sign and itself in a cadent house hardly rises to the level of waking consciousness.

COULD Christian persecution have been caused by Saturn's presence in the 9th? Saturn in the 9th tells us that Nero's religion was that of his ancestors, or, for that matter, of the society he lived in, Saturn being a generational planet. Saturn in the 9th is generally moral, the consequences being too dreadful.

Since Christians were, in fact, martyred during his reign, I note the 12th is the house of hidden enemies, in other words, those who secretly dislike us. Twelfth house ruling the ninth, it might be that religious fanatics made Nero their scapegoat. Nero's reputation has suffered at the hands of his enemies, who wrote most of the accounts that have come down to us. So far as Nero was concerned, Christians were probably just another group he could have deadly fun with.

What if Nero's birth time was a little earlier and Leo was on the cusp of the 9th? It's a good question and worth a look.

Leo on the cusp of 9 would be ruled by the Sun in Sagittarius in the first. Ruler of the 9th house in the first, when you're the Emperor, will make you project yourself as a god, or claim that god rules through you. Especially when the ruling planet is the Sun. It would have been aided by his Moon, also in Leo, which would have made religion a very personal matter. Nero was notably not guilty of anything like this.

So what about the burning of Rome? That's a different story. You will note the following inflammatory combinations:

Fire signs: Ascendant, IC, Sun, Moon, Mercury, Mars and Pluto.
Air: MC and Descendant. Air feeds fire.
Water: Jupiter in Scorpio. Scorpio has long been known as the sign of "firewater," i.e., alcohol.
Earth: Venus in Saturn's sign, showing what is old and decayed and presumably combustible, along with Saturn in another earth sign. And Uranus in Virgo, signifying that what is solid might turn out not to be.

This does not make Nero an arsonist, though it does not, of itself, absolve him. As the ruler's chart is the chart of his country during the period of his rule, it means Nero should be remembered for at least one good blaze, and, Libra at the MC, Mercury addled, that he might just have thrown up his hands and played while the city burned around him. Although Rome had an abundant supply of water, Nero's chart, with its shortage of water, shows there was little to battle a fire. Nor were there explosives to blow up buildings to create firebreaks — as was eventually done to put out the great Fire of London many centuries later.

It seems that in Rome, like in many ancient cities, once a fire got going, there might not have been any recourse, save waiting for it to burn itself out. During its history Rome was subject to many serious fires, which eventually forced sturdy brick and mortar construction. History says that after the fire Nero opened his palaces to the displaced, and gave his own money to the victims. This does not sound despotic to me.

WE come to Nero's death on June 9, 68 AD. Valens says this (and yes, you can skip to the end):

> *The horoscope is in its 31st year.*
> *The operative stars and the critical points are found as follows: when calculating the previously mentioned critical points, begin at the third row (=third interval), because the preceding two intervals, the first and the second, are inoperative. (The first is operative to year 12, the second to year 24, the third to year 36, and so on.) It is calculated thus: since the 31st year falls in the eleventh column of the third interval, and since Saturn, Jupiter, and Venus control the third interval at the nativity, investigate the stars in transit at the time in question to see if they transmit to another star or to themselves at a distance of 11 signs. Take the preceding nativity: the stars' positions at the time in question* [date of Nero's death—Dave] *were as follows: Sun, Jupiter, Mercury in Gemini, Saturn in Virgo, Mars, Venus in Taurus,* **Moon in Pisces** [emphasis: Dave]. *Now the stars controlling the interval of 11 were Saturn, Jupiter, and Venus, and we find at the time in question that Venus has returned to a position 11 signs from the Moon, but that no star has returned to a position 11 signs from Jupiter. Immediately I move to the fourth row. I find 32 in the eighth position. None of the ruling stars are critical in the fourth interval. I move to the fifth interval: the Moon and Saturn are operative in the fifth interval and are found to be returning to each other five signs apart. I move to the sixth interval: no stars are six signs apart. I move to the row of the seventh interval. [The*

chronocratorship is found to be passing through the fifth interval.] The seventh interval is found to be empty of any star (as mentioned above); Mars and Venus to Saturn <?>. I move to the row of the eighth interval: Venus rules the eighth interval because of the factor 4. It is returning to no star. Then to the critical point of the ninth interval: the Sun, Mars, Mercury, the Ascendant, and Venus rule the ninth interval; 36 is in this row. At a 4-year-interval the Sun, Jupiter, and Mercury are found to be returning to Saturn. Next I move to the tenth interval: the Sun, Mars, Mercury, Jupiter, and the Ascendant rule the tenth; in this row is the number 4; therefore the Sun, Mercury, and Jupiter are found to be transmitting to Saturn.

You are wondering what this is.

This is how Hellenistic astrologers made forecasts. Lacking ephemerides, with only a vague idea where the planets were at birth (or, for that matter, at death), they resorted to complicated counting schemes, which is what the preceding is. The overall framework is the 12 year cycle of profections. At age 31, Nero was in the seventh year of his third profection cycle, which is then used in many different and conflicting counts.

Valens is searching for an astrological explanation for an event which in his day was more than a century old. It seems he can make neither guesswork forecasts, nor find 20/20 hindsight.

Of this nonsense, William Lilly said,

I will only proceed to annual Profections, holding this opinion, That if one should follow the niceness of the Ancients *in every particular, it were impossible to judge one Nativity exactly in half a year's time.* (Christian Astrology, Book 3, pg. 716.)

Which Valens himself echoes elsewhere in his treatise, where he states that teams of astrologers needed months in order to make an accurate forecast. Valens gives mute testimony not only to the crudeness of Hellenistic astrology, but also the tremendous efforts the ancients made to comprehend and master it.

NERO died around noon on June 9, 68 AD, in Rome. Valens gives the placements (pg. 243), as he did with Nero's natal. Of note, Valens puts the Moon in Pisces, when it was actually in late Aquarius.

While the time of death is shown by the natal 8th house cusp, the natal 4th house shows the method of death, and the general circumstances surrounding it.

Nero died by his own hand, a dagger plunged into his throat. In his chart, we find Aries on the 4th, ruled by Mars in the first house. Death from the first house is a self-inflicted death, by definition. Moon in Leo intercepted in the 8th is evocative of someone who is cut off and isolated at the moment of his death, which Nero was.

So far as transits are concerned, Saturn had just passed over Nero's Saturn, which was presumably in its third and last pass of his first and only Saturn return. Saturn rarely brings such a calamity in its first return, but as it did in Nero's case, we may presume it was a particularly desperate scene.

South node was exactly conjunct Nero's Jupiter, indicating that his luck had run out.

Moon in Aquarius was opposite Nero's natal Moon and in the vicinity of his Neptune.

Transiting Mars was trine to itself, and inconjunct Nero's Saturn, thus showing the difficulty the government (Saturn) had in actually killing Nero themselves (Mars). In his final days on earth, Nero frankly shows a great deal of cowardice, which is the mark of a bully. According to historical accounts, the assassins were not at his doorstep, but merely in pursuit, some distance away. Nero's actions indicate panic, stemming, I think, from a debilitated Mercury that could not think things through clearly.

Nero's natal can be manipulated to put transiting Mars conjunct his Part of Fortune on that day. It would tweak his birth time to 7:10 am. Note that no one has ever used the Part of Fortune for this purpose.

Transiting Sun falls exactly on Nero's 7 am descendant. As it is in Gemini it would indicate the reasons for his murder were fabrications, as Gemini in this context (opposite the ascendant) is untrue by definition. Transiting Jupiter falls just short of the 7th, indicating, perhaps, that his savior would arrive too late. I use these many analogies as I have found, as other have found before me, that the sheer power and truth of astrology, even with

trivial details, cannot be denied. Every facet of the horoscope can be utilized, literally.

I HAD expected to write that Nero was an ugly, cruel ogre who got what he deserved. He was certainly despotic to those in his immediate social circle. What I found instead was a brash, impetuous hot-head who came of age far too young (Emperor at age 17) and paid the price for his inexperience. Astrology illuminates in ways that no other discipline can. — *June 21, 2011*

✠Newt Gingrich

NEWT Gingrich has been around since the 1980's. I never cared for the man, I do not even know his Sun sign. So before I started these notes, I tried to imagine what his chart would look like. Sometimes when I listen to a symphony I try to imagine what its score would look like. Turns out I'm better at imagining scores.

I had thought Newt would be coldly, calculatingly making primary use of his house placements, as that is what I usually see in a chart (Bachmann, Palin, Romney, etc.)

Instead I found that Gingrich's natal chart is based on a single dominant aspect. And it's one that's near and dear to my heart: A full moon. A very tight one at that.

The luminaries have the power, when in opposition, to overwhelm the rest of the chart. This was the case with Isaac Newton, it was the case with Johann Goethe, it was the case with Howard Camping (end of the world May 21, remember?), it was the case with Karl Rove (hi there, big boy!), and it is the case with Mr. Gingrich.

In checking various sources I find Newt's birth to have been a clear-cut affair, as all sources agree: June 17, 1943, 11:45 pm Eastern War Time (EWT, the same as daylight), Harrisburg, Pennsylvania. Aquarius rising, full Moon birth: Sun in Gemini, Moon in Sagittarius, less than one degree (two hours) from exactly full.

Sun in Gemini is witty, mercurial, two-faced, quick and fleet of foot. With Saturn nearby, it can be serious but would much rather not, as Newt's Sun is pulling rapidly away from the stodgy Saturn.

Moon in Sagittarius is carefree and happy-go-lucky. It wants no responsibilities, and, Sagittarius being mutable, is usually very good at escaping them. Team that up with a two-faced Sun and you have the perfect opportunist. There is no "conscience," the very idea is alien. Such a full moon will play both ends against the middle. Should this turn up in the chart of a political leader, he will invariably polarize everything

112

around him.

And, ever since arriving in Congress in 1979, this is precisely what Gingrich has done. He, more than any other person, single-handedly enabled the Republicans to wrest control of Congress from unsuspecting Democrats. He did so by shamelessly playing both ends against the middle.

I term aspects to the Sun-Moon opposition "helper planets." It is a rare full moon that does not have them.

Gingrich has two: A wide trine and sextile with Mars, giving the opposition even more dynamic energy (which full moons don't really need), and a tighter square with a mutable Neptune, which makes the opposition fuzzy, ill conceived, quixotic, illusory, deceptive. I have previously mentioned the danger of having Neptune prominent in a politician's chart. (See *Skeet Shooting.*) Newt is a prime example.

Moon in the 11th house, Newt wants to fire up all his friends and associates with his wonderful ideas. Moon in a fire sign, he has a great deal of raw energy. Moon in Sagittarius, there is a never-ending stream of wonderful ideas and proposals. Which, like the Moon itself, come and go with a rapidity that only Sagittarian arrows, flying through space, can match. The results are highly unstable, as we can see from Gingrich's own career.

Moon ruling the 6th house, these endlessly shifting ideas have to do with some sort of service. Jupiter in the 6th, those ideas will be larger than life. Note that Jupiter and the Moon are in mutual reception. Planets in mutual reception tend to fuse their houses together: Eleven and six, friends and service, ideals and service. On the face of it, being a representative is an ideal job.

DURING his career Newt has promoted many grandiose, emotionally appealing ideas. In that they are appealing, we can see the influence of the Moon. In that they are large, we can see the influence of Jupiter upon the Moon. In that they all collapsed upon arrival (i.e., contact with reality), we can see the deadly influence of Neptune. Few aspect patterns can be sorted as clearly as this.

I went to Newt's Moon first, putting his Sun aside for a reason. Newt's Sun is ugly. Vivian Robson, himself a Gemini Sun, writing at the end of his life, put it in these words, *"Gemini is essentially a cold-blooded sign, without affection and without morals. It is a kind of living question mark. . . Mental vivisection is a particularly Geminian habit, and is usually accompanied by extreme, but quite unintentional and unconscious, cruelty. It wants to "see the wheels go round" and is entirely unmindful of the effect of the process upon its victim."* (Astrology and

Sex, pg. 30) Which, in Gingrich's chart is enhanced by a Moon that willfully stands aside and cheers it on, which is the essence of a full moon.

So let's play what if. Many years ago, observing Newt's slash-and-burn style, I wondered if he was not the reincarnation of Maximilien Robespierre, the revolutionary French fanatic responsible for the Reign of Terror which ended with his own death on the guillotine in 1794. I liked that fancy. In its favor, the span of time from Robespierre's death in 1794, and

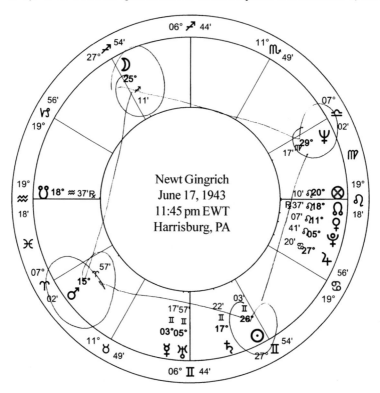

Newt's birth, in 1943, was about right. So was the time Newt spent in France as a teenager. But, alas, Astrology is an exact science and will not be denied. Robespierre's chart does not match up with that of Newt's.

That strange man, Donatien Alphonse Francois, popularly known as the Marquis de Sade, that's another matter: June 2, 1749, 5:00 pm, Paris. Sun and Moon in mutables in tight square, Mars in Aries (as with Newt), Moon is in the 11th in both. Sun shifts from 8 to 5, de Sade's Venus exactly conjunct Newt's Jupiter, de Sade's Part of Fortune becomes Newt's South Node/Ascendant, de Sade's MC becomes Newt's Part of Fortune.

De Sade had a very tight Sun-Moon square in mutables. During the course of a very dynamic life (Sun-Moon square is dynamic), he spent much of his life in prison, where he died. As a result he presumably became very careful of his environment, as many people in it clearly did not like him: This is one way in which a very tight Sun-Moon square in one life can become a very tight Sun-Moon opposition in the next. But I cannot say these two men are the same, as no one except Newt can know that. (For those of you who think lives have to follow in some precon-

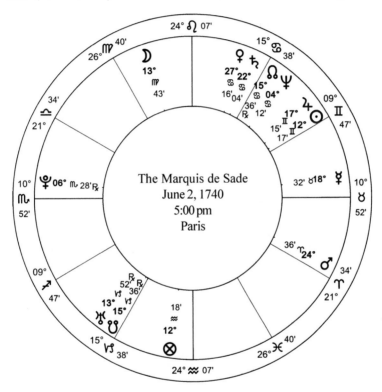

The Marquis de Sade
June 2, 1740
5:00 pm
Paris

ceived order, 12th house - 1st house - 2nd house, or Pisces to Aries to Taurus, or Taurus to Aries to Pisces, I tell you flatly there is no such simple formula. Every individual is different.)

IN reality there are billions and billions of souls all eagerly seeking (re)birth and it is absurd to insist these two men are one and the same. Great men—and de Sade was that — have friends, family, associates, fans and hangers-on. People for whom de Sade was the greatest and most interesting person they ever met, people who, if they got the chance, would eagerly ape him. With a clear connection to France, Newt might well have been one of them. But will I not apologize for citing Robson and then pairing Newt with de Sade (who was himself active in French revolutionary politics), because that's the level of intensity Newt Gingrich has.

Newt's Sun in Gemini on the 5th house cusp, is on the face of it a playboy who wants to know how women "tick." He will, and in fact, has, carried on with two women at once. Sun ruling the 7th, this is the basis of his marriages. Why do his marriages end when his wife becomes ill? Simple. The object of Newt's affection, Venus, is in Leo, ruled by the Sun, in the 6th house of illness. When that object become ill, and in the 6th house with Pluto nearby, Venus will always become ill, Newt no longer wants her. Newt then disposes of his unwanted bed-partner with utter disdain. Per Robson, Sun in Gemini does not comprehend its own cruelty. Moon opposing from the 11th house and Sagittarius never looks back.

In this, Newt's Moon is backed up by all his (11th house) friends, who always think his dalliances and escapades and romances and wives and girlfriends are trivial and in the way (Sun opposed by the Moon) and best got rid of anyway. You have here a portrait of an opportunistic monster. As well as his enablers, who in this case were members of the government of the United States, abusing their great power. Are you still surprised they, led by Newt himself, would attack Bill Clinton for precisely the same crime? What did they care?

Newt has, repeatedly, built himself up into a great position, only to shoot himself in the foot. His Sun and Moon, by signs, are the marks of a hypocrite. And because his Sun and Moon are tightly opposed, a transiting aspect to one becomes a transiting aspect to the other. When that transiting planet is powerful enough, Newt's games are exposed and his position collapses. I suspect there is no man alive who would be better served by a study of astrology. I am thankful Newt is not bright enough to figure that out.

Such as the reprimand given him on January 21, 1997, with transiting Jupiter and Neptune conjunct at 27° Capricorn, triggered in part by the Sun at 27° Cap, on January 12 and Venus conjunct Newt's Moon/opposed his Sun on January 7. All of which set off not only Newt's full moon axis at 25/26° Sag/ Gemini, but also his Jupiter at 27° Cancer.

On the day Newt resigned both his Speakership and his House seat, November 6, 1998, the Moon was in Gemini, Mercury was in Sagittarius opposing itself (i.e., resignation was not his idea), Mars was square his Saturn (stress), Uranus was at 8 Aquarius, which was opposed to the midpoint of his Venus/Pluto conjunction.

AND until this year, that was pretty much it for Newt Gingrich. He dropped out of sight. Earlier this year he returned, like a bad dream, to run for president. He seems to have put his third wife, Callista Bisek, in charge of his campaign. Remembering that Newt's romantic life is opposed to his professional career, you will not be surprised that it was his wife who torpedoed his presidential campaign, leading to the resignations of his entire senior staff. News reports said it was either them or her. No candidate can overcome an event such as this.

Callista Bisek Gingrich was born on March 4, 1966, in Whitehall, Wisconsin. Her birth time is not available (and I'm not in the mood to rectify it), but we hardly need it.

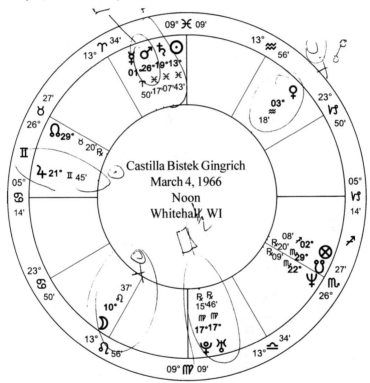

She has a tight Uranus/Pluto conjunction in Pisces opposite Saturn in Virgo. All of which is tightly square to, and a lead weight on, Newt's Saturn. Her Mars is square to Newt's Sun and Moon, which is not so much sexy as it is an endless irritant. Her Venus in Aquarius is opposed to Newt's Pluto in Leo; her Moon in Leo is somewhere in the vicinity of Newt's Venus. Her Moon/Venus opposed means Callista is essentially without love. Her Mars/Saturn conjunct opposed by Uranus/Neptune means her energies are highly repressed (Oken said it was like *"driving a car with the brakes on"*) and likely to snap at any time. Newt Gingrich, a fool at relationships, has found himself with more than he can handle. If he is "lucky" his sixth house will give her Moon some disease and he will escape. Mutable Newt, he's always looking to escape.

Newt Gingrich is an example of someone who should never have been allowed to have become as big and as important as he did. He is an example of what happens in "democracies" when opportunists run unchecked. He would be a persuasive argument in favor of universal astrological education and awareness, except that the ruling classes will never permit any such thing.

As such, Newt Gingrich, the manipulator of America, the polarizer of America, the ultimate destroyer of both America and its government, is a powerful argument in favor of hereditary rule. Because in any system built upon the casual change of leadership (the hallmark of democracies), men such as Gingrich will sooner or later emerge to destroy them, laughing as they do so. (Who are themselves eventually laid low by Mrs. Newt III types.) In the history of governments, there has never been an exception. In a monarchy, a bad king can be got rid of and a new king found. A bad ruling family can be disposed of wholesale. It's a messy, nasty process, but it's been done. The fact that it has been done and the threat that it might be done to them is one of the reasons kings toe the line. Like the Pope, kings cannot quit, they cannot resign. Unlike the Pope, a king's job starts at birth and is a life sentence. He does not aspire, as a child he knows the job will someday be his, he has no choice whatever. As the eldest child in a large family, I sense this quite clearly.

Elected leaders are different. Easy in, easy out, they have no cares and no responsibilities. They live for today. When that day is over, it's someone else's problem. Elected leaders are inherently opportunistic and invariably corrupt.

Monarchies beget new monarchies and are therefore more stable than democracies, which either grind themselves into partisan rancor (the French 3rd Republic, most Italian governments) or turn into wildly unstable dictatorships (the Roman Empire, the USA). I myself am tired of voting for the "lesser evil." We need honest leaders. Not evils. — *July 26, 2011*

✥Resonance, a work in progress

WHEN you get a theory right, one of the side benefits are ancillary details, things you were not looking for and had no reason to expect, that suddenly spring dramatically to life. For example, my revised theory of astrology. It says the Earth, beneath our feet, is the primary source of astrological energies. If a bell has a vibration, if an ordinary piece of metal has resonance when struck, then the Earth, with its vastly greater mass must have vastly more complex vibrations and resonances. And, as it is directly below our feet, those vibrations will permeate every person, place and thing on the planet. *Et voilà,* Astrology.

As an introduction this will have to do for the moment. I want to point out two things in connection with the never-ending debt wrangle:

First, the Earth's own vibrations account for the Earth's weather and its weather patterns. In other words, AstroMeteorology is nothing more than a synopsis of the Earth's astrological vibrations at any given moment.

Second, humans can, when organized, interact with the Earth's astrological vibrations on a wholesale level, provided they—the humans— are themselves making a coherent vibration of one sort or another.

Looking around, I would judge coherent human resonance to be rare, except in cases of widespread, extreme economic or political duress.

I am about to make a surprising conclusion, so I will again state the premises:

First, Astrology is a quality primarily of the Earth. Not of the sky.

Second, echoing Sepharial, these energies have their clearest impact on the weather.

Third, these energies are subtle enough that humans are not only influenced by them, but can interactively work with them. ("You create your own reality/The stars impel, they do not compel.") Note these last two hinge on astrological energies being local. Not cosmic.

Therefore, in times of widespread, extreme political and economic

119

duress, human discontent interacts with existing astrological energies to create bad weather.

You will immediately note widespread hardship in the 1930's as a trigger for the Dust Bowl. You will note that years of Vietnam protest and then Watergate culminated in a massive tornado outbreak in the spring of 1974. Widespread disgust with George Bush led to Katrina in 2005. Anger with the current government led to massive tornado outbreaks in the midwest earlier this year. Each of these events led to many innocent fatalities.

In every case, the weather did not happen exactly where the social unhappiness was the most severe. Instead, outbreaks of extreme weather were seen in locations that were prone to severe weather, at times of year when severe weather was common.

I therefore hypothesize the current budget battle in Washington will lead to a series of severe hurricanes, starting later this summer. For those of you who live in hurricane-prone areas of the country, take the time to check your home's hurricane/flood/wind/water/debris insurance. Remember insurance men are tricky. You need to check your coverage for specific storm components. And that your emergency kit is well-stocked and that you have an evacuation plan.

Be civil. Sometimes it really is a matter of life and death. Yours and mine. — *August 2, 2011*

May, 2012: Hurricane Irene struck the US northeast Atlantic coast, August 27-29, 2011. Its final landfall was at Brooklyn, NY. Wall Street, seat of American capital, is only a couple of miles to the west. Here in Maryland we had a very windy night, with widespread power outages that lasted most of a week.

✢ Planet Earth as Astrology

WHILE we are dazzled by the skies above, consider that planetary distances are vast, and that the known forces (light, gravity, electromagnetic radiation, etc.), by the time they reach us, are so weak as to be completely worthless. The signs of the zodiac are even more problematic, since they don't even seem to stay in the one place, and how is it, precisely, that empty sky has an impact? *Things* have impact. *Emptiness* does not, because that's the definition of empty.

Instead, consider the Earth. It is by far the largest thing of which we have any direct experience. (We can look at the Sun, but can't touch it.) The Earth has a diameter of 7,917.54 miles. It has a mass of 597,360,000,000, 000,000,000 metric tons. It is composed of at least 92 discreet elements and many, many thousands of compounds. Its temperatures range from -50°F on the surface, to several thousands of degrees at the center. The Earth has about 326 million cubic miles of water. It rotates on its axis in 23 hours, 56 minutes. It makes an orbit around the Sun in 365.256363004 days. It is inclined to the Sun, and has a large Moon inclined to both. It is subject to solar/lunar tidal forces, as well as eclipses.

The question I put to you is a simple one: Why do we think astrology comes entirely from "out there"? From a zodiac we cannot find? From planets that are impossibly far away? And yet we ignore the planet under our very feet?

It is staggeringly obvious that the Earth itself must be full of energies, vibrations, resonances, harmonics and much, much more. And that we who live on this planet, must be subject to every one of them.

Yes, I know that planets agree with their zodiacal positions, that transits happen with clockwork precision, that progressions and directions and primaries and much more, all can be traced directly to positions in the sky. But I would also have you note that progressions and directions do not relate to any actual sky positions, nor do the dashas and bhuktis of Vedic astrology, nor the stems and branches of Chinese astrology. If we're going to have a theory, if we're ever going to understand Astrology as a whole, we need a theory that explains all of it. Not just our favorite little pieces.

The "missing link" must be the Earth itself. It must be what the Earth itself supplies.

If we stand back for a moment and view the solar system as a whole, it is clearly absurd to imagine the planets have any direct effect on the puny individuals who live on the third rock from the Sun. It becomes blindingly obvious that planets, as wholes, affect other planets, as wholes, and that whatever these effects are, they are synthesized and combined with the Earth's own unique vibrations, which the Earth then radiates to us, and to everything in the vicinity of the surface of the Earth.

In other words, the "position of the planets" merely indicates how the Earth's net resonance (astrological energies) are changing from moment to moment. Since the Earth's own energies are presumably stable, net changes in the Earth's energies must be due to external events. Such as the ceaseless interplay of the Sun, Moon and planets.

It is as if the Earth was a prime number. Saturn comes along and adds a Saturnine " 1". What are we now? We are a prime number plus 1, we are still whatever we were before, but now with this Saturnine "1" as a net addition. If we were "41" before, Saturn's 1 makes us 42. Forty-two is different. Saturn goes away and now Venus comes and adds her "1". We have again gone from 41 to 42, but now, with a Venus vibration.

In this example, adding 1 to what we were before, mostly we're not changing at all. The Earth is vast, it has great inertia, it tamps down all but a tiny fragment of incoming influences, but because that one thing has changed, suddenly everything else has changed, too. It is like the Good Shepherd who ignores 99 sheep in favor of one which is novel.

Another example. The Earth as a plate of mashed potatoes. Add a trace of salt and they are transformed, but they are still potatoes. Add paprika and the potatoes change again. Add pepper, add thyme. 99.99% of what we are eating is still potato, but the taste has changed. Such is the subtlety of the interplay of Earth and planets.

Trapped on the Earth as we are, we typically respond as automatons. We are *not* responding to raw incoming planetary energies, because we have not the means to do so. We are responding to the *Earth's response*. As an instrument of incredible delicacy and precision, the Earth's resonances change minute by minute, second by second, according to the actual conditions of the planets in the solar system as a whole.

I suppose some idiot "scientist" will still say, well, there isn't enough gravity from Mars to make any difference on the Earth. Really? The position of Neptune was approximated by discrepancies in the orbit of

Uranus. Uranus is 1,784 million miles from the Sun. Neptune is 2,794.4 million miles. The difference is 1.01 billion miles. That's as close as Uranus and Neptune ever get to each other, which they only do once every 171 years. Most of the time Uranus and Neptune are upwards of three billion miles distant. *We* are closer to Uranus than it ever is to Neptune.

By contrast, the Earth is a mere 93 million miles from the Sun. The discrepancy in the orbit of Uranus was large enough that we could see it from crude telescopes more than one and a half billion miles away. The distances may be vast, but the effects—of mere gravity—are well documented.

SO, okay, what have we got, so far? We've got an Earth with a surface that looks a lot like the pad on an orbital sander. It's vibrating. It's always vibrated and always will vibrate. It's the loudest thing on the planet, but since we can't get away from it, we have tuned it out altogether.

Back when I was in college I had a part-time job with Pinkerton, guarding factories and warehouses against fire and mayhem. One of our clients was a fertilizer plant (now defunct) on the east side of Lawrence, KS. The manufacture of ammonium-nitrate fertilizer is surprisingly similar to the manufacture of ammonium-nitrate high explosives, the plant sat on more than a square mile of ground. This was because if the wrong thing got in the wrong pipe and went in the wrong direction, the result would be a very big hole in the ground. (The citizens of Lawrence had no idea.)

The plant was big to give blundering workers the time to call the next station, a quarter-mile downline, to tell them to shut the valves! It had its own railroad. In the overnight hours (the shift college kids worked) the company locomotive was parked on a siding on the far side of one of the buildings. In the winter it ran continually, as it would freeze if it did not. I first started in the winter, and one of my jobs was to walk across the building, open the door, and confirm the engine was, in fact, running. One of the plant's overnight supervisors laughed at my greenness. He said he could hear that damn engine everywhere in the building.

Why couldn't I? I wondered about that. In the spring I had my answer: In warm weather they shut the engine off at night and suddenly the entire building was quiet. I had mistaken the engine's rumble for some machine inside the building. The plant as a whole ran 24 hours a day, seven days a week, there were many buildings which were noisy. Because it was quiet outside the building, I had presumed the noise inside to have been produced inside. I had not imagined a locomotive, parked ten feet beyond the building, could possibly be rumbling inside the building itself.

Which is why we can't sense the Earth and its vibration. It is so pervasive as to be completely invisible.

So the Earth is like a giant vibrator. We are germs on the surface of the vibrator. We vibrate in sympathy. We have done so since our births. Which now starts to look very interesting.

Take the sandpaper off your orbital sander (a common workshop tool), turn it upside down (pad side up), and put a cookie on it. Now turn it on. The cookie will vibrate in sympathy with the sander. Leave the cookie there long enough, and if you can keep it from sliding off the machine, it will eventually fragment into smaller pieces. Each of those pieces will vibrate according to its position at the time it fragmented from the whole. In other words, their "birth moments." If we want to bother with the math, we can predict the future path of each fragment, based solely on 1) the time it separated, 2) its mass, and 3) any changes in the overall vibration of the sander itself.

No, we have not been crazy to insist on the importance of the birth moment. Once we get our eyes out of the heavens, our sander/cookie analogy proves the importance of the separation of the child from its mother. At the moment of birth, the mother loses an appreciable fraction of her overall mass, which amounts to a significant transit. The smaller mass—the newborn baby itself—loses its mother's vibration and immediately takes on the prevailing Earth vibration as of the moment of separation, e.g., its birth. The more precisely we know the time of separation, the more accurately we can forecast subsequent position. Which is precisely what astrology has always claimed.

But of itself mere separation from the mother does not make for a live birth. Some births are stillborn. That newborn must be claimed by an incoming soul, for if it is not, it will immediately die. Dead or alive it will still be subject to subsequent "vibrations" (astrological energies) but if dead will be unable to react to them. A live birth is therefore a binary, a dual process: The baby is produced of its mother, and then is animated by an outside force of some sort or another.

Or, to be precise, that newborn body, in a desperate attempt to preserve its own life, compulsively gasps for air, and with its very first inhalation, forcibly *sucks in* the soul for which it had been created. For the soul this is a traumatic event, it "gasps" in surprise. Many people in fact remember this moment, but not as "birth." They remember it, in dreams, as a "falling," for that is what it often is.

PREGNANCY and childbirth, to the waiting soul, are like a man watching his house being built. As soon as the house is finished, it quite unexpectedly sucks him inside. Where it will keep him for many years.

The time that elapses between separation from the mother and the first breath is rarely more than a few seconds. There are methods of rectification which will establish the time of birth to within a few seconds. Which of these two events are being timed, and what does that mean, in practice?

Rectification has to do with the moment the body takes on the surrounding vibration, as that is the benchmark for all subsequent astrological activities. Remember: Astrology is of the Earth and the baby's body is of the Earth. Therefore Astrology starts with the separation from the mother.

The soul is an interloper. An outsider. Arriving just a few seconds later, it is forever mismatched to its own body. It is forever just slightly unhappy as a result. Discontent. "Soul" is the forty-dollar word that no one really understands. In place of "soul," think of your general state of consciousness. It is human nature to be discontented with its condition. Now we have an idea why.

So we have an orbital sander for the earth, with cookie fragments bouncing around on it. It is plainly obvious that any change in the vibration of the sander will produce immediate changes in each cookie fragment: Which are transits.

It is also plainly obvious that, based on their original positions, some of those fragments are going to run into some other fragments and then bounce around together, for better or worse, like bumper cars: *Synastry*. Changes in the underlying vibrations will produce immediate changes in the relationship between those fragments (cars), whereupon the occupants of those cars (the souls, or individuals) decide if there will be friendly words spoken, or not. Again we see the contrast between the astrologically driven body, and the independent soul trapped in it.

ALL of which is of the primary vibration. But the Earth also has a number of distinct secondary vibrations, chief among them, the precession of the equinoxes. Precession is due to a wobble in the Earth's axis. You can see the same thing in a spinning toy top. There is the rapid spinning of the top itself, and, in addition, a much slower, secondary spinning, a wobble. The Earth's secondary vibrations are, for the most part, too slow to turn up as anything that humans can sense directly, but that's not the whole story.

Each one of us has our own slower, secondary vibrations. In astrology, we call these progressions and directions. They are the secondary vibrations of our primary ("transit-sensitive") vibrations. In other words, progressions, directions, converse and direct, are not of the Earth, nor of the sky. Not at all. They are unique to each one of us. When a personal secondary vibration aligns with the Earth's primary vibration, in other words, when a direction or progression is activated by a transit, events occur.

We are now establishing Astrology (it now deserves the capital A) to be a concrete, discrete science. One that can be studied objectively. Some will say that I am vulgarizing a spiritual science into something materialistic. To their surprise (I suppose), I agree. I am. Earth-based Astrology is so strong, so pervasive, so penetrating, that it must have concrete, material results. While there is also a spiritual side, we should be satisfied with nothing less than a material explanation. We have our feet on the ground, in direct contact with our Planetary Vibrator. Which is exactly where they belong. — *August 9, 2011*

May, 2012: This was the moment when the final theory emerged before me, one I had been groping towards for several years. I have developed it further since. I am dedicating a book to it and its ramifications, that the work not be lost in pages of these unrelated essays.

✤Hurricane Irene

I expected to lose power late Saturday night and not have power again until late in the week. I fell asleep watching the Weather Channel, woke up, saw the power was still on, watched some more, fell asleep again and in general had a long night. Dawn arrived, the rain ended, and **there was still power.** There was a phone call. Harford county reported 50,000 power outages. On TV I heard 4 million were without power. We were among the lucky.

You will say I predicted this. You will go back to the August 2nd newsletter, where I said, *the current budget battle in Washington will lead to a series of severe hurricanes, starting later this summer. For those of you who live in hurricane-prone areas of the country, take the time to check your home's hurricane/flood/wind/water/debris insurance.*

I did not predict this specific one. I did not predict the time, I did not predict the location. Hurricanes make landfall in the US every few years. If your theory says that upset people generate bad weather, it's pretty much the same thing as saying *grass grows green in the summertime.* It's not much of a prediction.

But Irene has arrived, and in time for America's 8th Saturn return. Saturn in 1776 was at 14♎46. As of Sunday, August 28, 2011, Saturn is at 14♎46. The 8th return has to do with things of the number 8, among them, transformation, money, resources, and death. (Which I extracted from the astrological 8th house, as it's as good a source for "eightness" as anything.)

Happy Saturn Return America! By the time it was done, Irene had powered up the Hudson Valley into Canada. Pictures on TV looked horrific.
— *Special Hurricane Edition, August 30, 2011 (modified)*

♣Claudius Ptolemy on Weather

THE sign of Aries has a general tendency, arising from the presence of the Equinox, to promote thunder and hail. Certain of its parts, however, operate in a greater or less degree, according to the nature of the stars which compose the sign: for instance, the front parts excite rain and wind; the middle parts are temperate; and those behind are heating and pestilential. The northern parts, also, are heating and pernicious, but the southern cooling and frosty.

The sign of Taurus, in its general character, partakes of both temperaments, but is nevertheless chiefly warm. Its front parts, and especially those near the Pleiades, produce earthquakes, clouds and winds: the middle parts are moistening and cooling; those behind, and near the Hyades, are fiery, and cause meteors and lightnings. The northern parts are temperate, the southern turbulent and variable.

Gemini, in its general tendency, is temperate; but its leading parts produce mischief by moisture; its middle parts are entirely temperate; its later parts mixed and turbulent. The northern parts promote earthquakes and wind; and the southern are dry and heating. Cancer is, in the whole, serene and warm, but its anterior parts near the Præsepe are oppressively hot and suffocating; the middle parts are temperate, and the later parts excite wind. And both its northern and southern parts are equally fiery and scorching.

Leo has a general tendency operative of stifling heat. The anterior parts are oppressively and pestilentially hot; yet the middle parts are temperate; and those behind are injurious by means of moisture. The northern parts produce variation and heat, and the southern moisture. — *From* **Book II** of the **Tetrabiblos**, *by* **Claudius Ptolemy**, *translated by J.M. Ashmand.* — *August 30, 2011*

✤ A Peek at Election Day, 2012

THE tireless gnomes at Planet Waves, in addition to finding Rick Perry's time of birth, also sent along the chart for next year's election, which will be on Tuesday, November 6, 2012. They set the chart for one minute past midnight in Dixville Notch, New Hampshire. This unincorporated village has a custom of voting at midnight, thus gaining supposedly useful media attention. Checking the town's Wiki page, I learn it is one of a number of towns in New Hampshire who pull this stunt. The results are not indicative, nor, so far as I am aware, of any consequence to the towns themselves.

But is it valid for astrologers? I thought of it this way. If we were to set a similar chart for a UK general election, would we set it for John O'Groats (famous for being the most northerly town in British Isles, though it isn't quite), or for the capital, London? If it were a French national election, would we set a chart for Mont St. Michel, in Normandy, or for the capital, Paris? I have visited the Mont. It is very pretty. If in Russia, for Vladivostok, or for Moscow? In Vladivostok, polls open hours and hours before they do in Moscow.

We should set our election chart for the polls in our capital city, Washington, because control of Washington, not Dixville Notch, is what is up for grabs. There is one other detail. 12:01 am is not when Dixville Notch *opens* its polls. It is when they *close*. Polls in Dixville Notch are open for exactly one minute. These various New Hampshire witching hour charts are studied in the hopes of determining the outcome of the election.

My aim here is different. I am not interested in who wins, but how the race will be played. It is the game, not the outcome. Which means setting the chart for when the polls open. By custom, if not local law, polls in Washington open at 7:00 am Eastern time. Thus it is.

The resulting chart has 17 Scorpio rising, the Sun a few degrees away at 14 Scorpio, with 26 Leo for a midheaven. The Moon is at 8 Leo.

Since American's national elections always take place on the first Tuesday in November, all such election charts will be broadly similar. Set for approximate sunrise, Scorpio will always rise, and, so far as Washington is concerned, Leo will usually be the midheaven. The Sun will be somewhere in the vicinity of the ascendant degree, marking the day as a whole of exceptional interest to the ruler (President), who is always symbolized by the Sun itself.

We attack the chart starting with the ruler of the Sun and ascendant: Mars. Election day next year, Mars will be in Sagittarius in the second house. Mars in Sagittarius is enthusiastic. It is tireless and restless. Alan Oken says it tends to shift blame to others, which is due to the Sagittarian enthusiasm for strangers, here being used as convenient foils. In a mundane chart, Mars in the second house means money for the military. You will note that America, since 1945, has continually shortchanged its military, not ever spending the money we need in order to be secure. So it seems the election next year will be all about spending even more on our brave men and women who serve overseas (Sagittarius, again). Better to defend ourselves over there than to have to do it over here. Besides, we can hire cheap foreigners to clean up the messes we make.

Remembering the foreign aspect as well as the recent Supreme Court decision (*Citizens United*), removing virtually all restraints on political spending, many already expect that next year record amounts of money to be spent, by among others, agents of foreign governments. Mars in Sagittarius in the second house is therefore double-edged. On the one hand, more money for the military, on the other, lots and lots of money from overseas.

Because with the recent Libyan escapade, where intense bombing cleared the way for a sham takeover by US/western-backed puppets (if you didn't hear the news, sorry to be brutal about it), it is plainly obvious to every foreign leader that they serve at the whim of the US President. This fact has hit particularly hard in Cuba, Venezuela, Syria, Iran, Pakistan and North Korea, if not Brazil, China, Russia and South Korea. They have not the means to stop a US military assault on their countries, which the first group knows to expect at any moment.

But, one way or another, they have money. Venezuela has a lot of it. The 2012 presidential election is an opportunity, perhaps the very last opportunity, for the leaders of these countries to buy their own personal safety. The examples of Saddam Hussein, Benazir Bhutto, Osama Bin Laden and now Muammar Gaddafi will not be lost on Bashar al-Assad, Hugo Chavez, Mahmoud Ahmadinejad, Kim Jong-il and the aging (and retired) Castro himself.

Foreigners have always spent money in Washington, but up to now they have done so discreetly, as the consequences for being caught were too enormous. (The exception has been the Israelis.) The Roberts Supreme Court, which is clearly on the take, (they always favor money over people), has opened the gates. Next year's election chart shows the results with great clarity. Mars in Sagittarius in the second house shows that next year's candidates for office (not just the presidential candidates) will eagerly solicit foreign donors. And, by the way, religious money. It is just that sleazy.

But it gets worse. Opposite Mars in Sagittarius in the second, is Jupiter in Gemini in the 8th. While the 8th house is Other People's Money, the shorthand for that is Wall Street.

Jupiter in the 8th house means there is going to be a lot of Wall Street money in the election next year, and while that might not be a surprise, a close examination of Jupiter shows just how bad it will be.

Gemini says the dealings will be two-faced, in other words, the money won't be for what you think it was for. It will be for something else. That Jupiter is retrograde means that the money itself is illegal, from illegal sources. Which, given Citizens United, we are powerless to stop in any effective way.

Finally, and most damningly, Jupiter, ruler of Sagittarius, disposes Mars. Which means that instead of buying politicians and thereby ensuring their own personal safety, international rulers will merely be scammed. Wall Street will steal their money just as they've stolen everyone else's. Will Mercury, ruler of Gemini, put a stop to it? No, for Mercury is itself in the sign of Jupiter, Sagittarius. Which is a mutual reception. When planets are in mutual reception, they tend to play together as if conjunct. When they are in mutual reception in their own debilities, they spin out of control and go straight down. In opposition they compete with each other to see who can be worse. In other words: Every.Single.Chart.Detail has meaning. And that's still not all.

In terms of profession, Lilly gives the 10th house to the job itself. In the election chart the midheaven is Leo, ruled by the Sun. The Sun, as we have seen, has been captured by Mars, which in this chart represents both the military, as well as rich deluded foreigners. The midheaven degree is late, and the 10th house as a whole is empty. The late degree means the election "comes late", which very likely means, "has already been decided." As in 2008, we vote merely to ratify an empty choice. That the tenth house is empty means we do not expect very much from the person who gets it, and it does not matter which candidate gets the job.

In this chart, the Sun rules the Moon, which in its turn rules the 9th. On the one hand, this gives the election a highly religious overtone, as in, "I am a better friend of Jesus than he is." Which is nauseating enough.

Cancer on the cusp of the 9th, we are viscerally afraid that evil foreigners will attack us in our beds. Terrified, we turn to Jesus to save us. Which is why the election will go to the man (man, woman, WHO CARES!) who panders best to Jesus Christ on the one hand, and the military on the other. All the while drowning in a sea of money. The Part of Fortune, in Leo, simply reinforces it all.

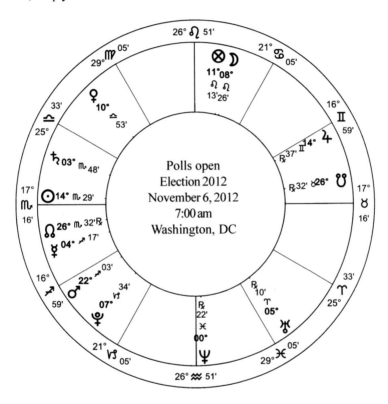

The Morning After

As upsetting as this is, what comes next makes a mockery of all of it. The evening of the election, at 7:05 pm EST, Mercury goes retrograde.

The roughly 75 days, from the election, to the Inaugural, is when the final deals are made. Typically the president-elect sells offices to the highest bidders, grants favors to his personal friends, and in all other ways corrupts his office before he even gets it. This is the American way, and it was instituted right at the very beginning, ostensibly because it takes a long time (initially four months) for the newly elected president to walk from the wilds of western Georgia to his new office on the Potomac.

No, really. Even in 1789, the Founding Fathers themselves (mostly from Virginia, not Georgia) were making every deal they could.

Mercury retrograde means those who expected a payoff from their candidate will be double-crossed. Mercury in Sagittarius will have made a lot of foolish promises, far more than it can make good on, even if the sign was a strong one, such as Virgo or Aquarius. Which Sagittarius, so far as Mercury is concerned, is not. When Mercury turns retrograde, it will make no effort. It will simply walk away (turn around) and leave the hopeful foreigners hanging.

While I can understand foreign desperation to stop this mad Washington military machine, I am frankly astonished at their gullibility. Starting with the Natives, Washington has never respected its treaty obligations. Well, but we treat real foreigners differently, don't you know?

Really? In recent years the State of Texas has repeatedly put foreign nationals to death who were denied their rights under treaties signed in Washington and ratified by the US Senate. When challenged in the Supreme Court on precisely this issue, the winning, certified, legal excuse was two fold: One, Congress had never passed enabling legislation, which means the treaty was void on the face of it, and that the US Government, in its role as member state on this planet, is in no way responsible for the actions of its constituent parts. Which means the treaties the US signs apply only to the District of Columbia itself, as it seems the US government is responsible for nothing else.

Mercury goes retrograde at 4 Sagittarius. It retrogrades back into (nasty) Scorpio on the 14th. It turns direct on the 26th at (surprise, surprise) 18 Scorpio, very nearly dead conjunct the election ascendant. Whatever you thought the election had brought, good or bad, it will have been undone by this time. Direct, Mercury reaches Sagittarius on the 12th of December and finally catches back up to where it was on election day on December 15th. Which will be the end of the fix. In earlier years I had presumed that when major changes such as this had finally cleared, that everyone would know. It turns out I was wrong. It can take the public a long time to catch on. Pity.

I am sick to my stomach about next year's election. While elections in the US have never been quite what was claimed, it seems that since Bush vs: Gore in 2000, the powers that be haven't even made a pretense.
— *August 30, 2011*

✤The Republican Party, part I

FROM Penelope, I have the chart for the Republican Party: February 28, 1854, Ripon, Wisconsin. Penelope gave the time as "noon." I decided to see if I could do better.

I first went to the Wiki site for Ripon, WI, where I learned the meeting was held at a schoolhouse, which still stands, though not at its original location. Since schoolhouses are usually in use during most days of the week, I needed to find out what day of the week February 28th was. I got that from Ancestor Search, though an ephemeris of the period would have done as well.

Turns out, the day was a Tuesday. A school day. I presumed the school day in small towns in Wisconsin was more or less the same as it was when I was in school in Kansas, from, say, 8:00 am to, say, 3:00 pm, give or take half an hour on either side. Thereafter kids came home to their waiting mothers, and if that sounds like the Cleavers, well, it's supposed to.

Ripon was a new town, only having been settled six years earlier. The school house was perhaps a year old. The community presumably served the surrounding farmers. In February most farmers are inactive, except the dairymen, who work year round, generally at sunrise and sunset. And there would have been dairy.

So our next question is what time the sun sets in Ripon on February 28 of any given year. Which a standard astrology chart will give us: Set the sun on the 7th house cusp, read off the time. More or less, that's sunset. Which was about 5:40 pm (CST, as I forgot to set things in LMT).

So the setting was a schoolhouse, the day was a school day as well as a work day. School ends late in the afternoon, children return home, the evening meal is prepared, the head of the house returns, food is eaten, the dairy men milk the cows and put them away for the night, and only then can evening activities begin. The first meeting of what was to be the Republican party thus begins no earlier than 7:00 pm.

I am unable to determine what, if anything, happened during this

133

epochal meeting. Some thirty people attended. Presumably there were speeches, comments from the floor, debates, motions that were defeated or approved, etc.

In other words, time passed. Presumably once a final resolution of some sort had been agreed upon, the meeting ended. For a meeting starting around 7:00 pm, an hour does not sound long enough. If the meeting was brief, it would most likely have been noted as such. On the other hand, meetings that last three hours or longer are generally remembered as tiresome and, oftentimes, contentious. Presuming the people who met were more or less like-minded (people in small towns are often like-minded), two hours, more or less, is often enough to get the job done.

By this method of deduction, it is reasonable to take Penelope's noon chart and set it for 9:00 pm, the approximate conclusion of the meeting, the time when a final result, whatever it may have been, was agreed upon.

Other details: *The dog that did not bark.* Snows in Wisconsin can be fierce. If there was snow, there would have been no school, which means the men could have met at any time of the day, except that if there was no school, there would not have been much of any activity in Ripon on the day. So we may presume the streets were clear and that classes had previously been held.

Second, these men were presumably godless heathens, as you will note the meeting was held in a schoolhouse, rather than a church. I am glad they did not meet in a church, as it would have been nearly impossible to establish the time of the meeting if they had. It was a new town and there may not have been a suitable church building, or it may be the promoters were not associated with any of the local clergy, or it may be they were serious about Church/State separation. It is said they took the name of their new party, Republican, from the Declaration of Independence. Which is as much a list of grievances as a statement of principles, but it might be they had the First Amendment in mind as well.

WITH these preliminaries out of the way, we can now examine the chart, the result of these men's work on that night.

Set for 9:00 pm — which is an approximation — the chart has cardinal signs on the angles, indicating great strength and dynamism. Libra rises, showing a desire for equality (these were antislavery men), but underneath a placid exterior, Libras will manipulate others to get what they want. This should be kept in mind.

Chart ruler Venus is exalted in Pisces. Which, by comparison to the signs it actually rules (Taurus and Libra), Venus in Pisces is over the top, overdone, overripe, excessively idealistic. With Venus in Pisces are

the Sun, Neptune and Mercury. Which is a pronounced religious fervor
and a willingness to sacrifice, even face martyrdom, even in defiance of
common sense, which a debilitated Mercury in Pisces notably lacks.

Now look where this falls in the chart: At 9 pm, as well as at 8 pm,
Pisces falls on the cusp of the 6th, and 8 pm and 9 pm, Venus and the Sun
fall outside of the 6th. I have said before that planets falling on the wrong
side of the cusp are ne'er-do-wells, that they will try all the harder to prove
their *bona fides*. Which is the case here.

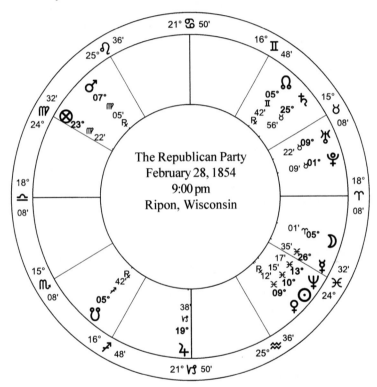

What is the sixth house? **SLAVERY**. The men who met that night
were ideologically driven to rid the world of that scourge, even at the cost
of their own lives, as shown by the Sun's own position. Cardinal signs on
the angles, they would do whatever was necessary. Chart ruler Venus, as
well as the Sun in Pisces, they would be indiscriminate as to the means, as
well as tend to excuse themselves with endless religious rationalizations.

Now look across the chart and find Mars opposing from Virgo.
They knew they would be confronted, they expected to pay the ultimate
price. They could rationalize and say that as Mars was in the sign of

Mercury, and as Mercury was on friendly terms with Venus, that they had a "spy in the enemy camp," which so far as the Civil War went, may well have been true. People do not consciously rationalize their actions with astrology (as I have done here), but, knowingly or not, they invariably make full use of their charts.

THIS chart may be analyzed for its role in the Civil War (the election of Abraham Lincoln as the party's first president may well rectify it precisely), but my immediate goal is the present day. Just as Venus wants to be in the 6th house, Mars wants to be in the 12th. Mars in the 12th is a strategist. The best military men, the best chess players, invariably have Mars in the 12th: It keeps their plans secret.

In Virgo, these plans are detailed and precise. Mars retrograde, they are wrong. Opposed to Mercury, they run counter to logic. Opposed to the Sun, they are hostile to life itself. Opposed to Pisces, they are ugly and contrary to religious principles.

But, using whole sign aspects (and why not?), Mars is supported by trines from Jupiter, Saturn, Uranus and Pluto. The trine from Saturn, while wide, is particularly telling: Even my enemy likes me. (Saturn and Mars hate each other.) The Pisces-Virgo opposition is the major source of dynamic energy in the Republican chart.

A chart with cardinal signs on the angles, ruled by Venus in transcendent Pisces, backed up by the vitality of Sun, deluded by Neptune, saddled with a debilitated Mercury, forever irked by Mars (off in his own corner laughing at them), is, in sum, a chart that believes in its divine right to rule, regardless of the opposition it engenders.

Once the issue of slavery had been dealt with (no, it was not really, it is still an open sore, but enough of this!), the chart of the Republican party takes on an interesting new life.

All the planets that want to be in the 6th house shift from the issue of slavery, to the unwashed workers, the serfs. As in, We know what's best for you. Which makes the Republican party a neo-Church, with all the rights and trappings of a proper religion. Party members become True Believers, party ideology is unquestioned, people find a "home" in their political church, etc.

Critically, as with the Church itself, moral welfare becomes more important than physical well-being. Having the right beliefs becomes more important than being well-off. The Republican party thus fundamentally confuses the role of the Church with the role of the State. You will note the intensely religious fervor Lincoln's Republican government generated during the Civil War.

This should be a minor thing, that even with a religious orientation (note debilitated Mercury in religious Pisces ruling the 9th house of religion) the overall aim of a political party is, in the end, political rule, and it would have come to pass, but for the critical position of Saturn.

In the Republican chart, Saturn is in Taurus in the 8th. Saturn in Taurus is insecure and greedy and grasping. If it were in the second house it would toil ceaselessly for a pittance, eventually rising to great wealth.

In the 8th, Saturn steals. Okay, you know this already, but look what happens when we set the chart in motion:

Saturn has rights in Libra, as chart co-ruler. As such, Saturn rationalizes his theft as the way things should be. He looks immediately to his proper ruler, Venus. In exaltation as well as sextile by sign, Venus gives her assent.

Which is to say that workers (6th house) should be happy (Pisces) with ideals, not money (Taurus/8th). Money belongs to Saturn, not to them. Why do Republicans hate trade unions? Because Pisces, as a sign, is disorganized. That's the way workers should be. Good little fish. A school of fish.

Saturn is then nudged by Jupiter. Jupiter is in Capricorn. Which is Saturn's own sign, as well as the sign of Jupiter's debility. Capricorn is the sign of the government. Whatever the government (Jupiter) has, is properly Saturn's, as, debilitated in Capricorn, Jupiter cannot claim it as its own. Thus we see the Republican tendency to grab the government's money. Which they were just as good at in the 1880's as they were in the first decade of the 21st century.

Where does this money come from? Two sources. First, the 4th house is land, including real estate and mines. Secondly, just as Saturn has rights in Libra, Venus has somewhat lesser rights (or perhaps, obligations) to Capricorn. Venus in Pisces in the 6th permits money to be taken from workers and given to the government, which Jupiter then eventually gives to Saturn. If Saturn and Venus were in true mutual reception, and if Venus was not lost in a weak cadent house, there would be "revenue sharing" between the two of them. There is, instead, only a vague "noblesse oblige." A "trickle down," if you will. This is the best that can be done, the best the Republicans can do.

I have not spoken of the Moon in the chart, which is in Aries in the 6th. Unless the degree on the ascendant should prove to be 5 Libra or less, the Moon has no rights in the 7th house. Nor, being in Aries, is it properly part of the 6th. Moon in Aries in the 6th is "mommy knows best," even though, lacking support from elsewhere in the chart (square to a weak Jupiter, that's it) she rarely does. Her ruler is Mars, who wants to take both her, and himself, and hide away in the 12th. Which makes the

Duels at Dawn:

Republicans devoid of warmth, of emotional support, of caring. The Republican religion is solar. It is the Savior, dying on the Cross so that you, young worthless serf, might be spared. Be happy with that. The Virgin (the Moon) is nowhere in sight, but the Magdalene's tears (Venus) might wash your feet (Pisces).

FOR a party that was founded with the Declaration of Independence in mind, there is a temptation to make the party's ascendant match the July 4, 1776 Saturn, at 14-something Libra. This is not necessary and would probably not be accurate. There is the question in my mind, could the Republican party evolve into something a little less heartless, a little more generous? At the age of 157, I am not hopeful. Having lasted this long and having remained largely unchanged for its entire history, it looks set to continue. Regardless of the fate of the country and people it rules, the party itself continues to go from strength to strength. I say this, not as a party member (I am not), but as a realist. — *September 6, 2011*

Photo: *A. Langdon Coburn.*

MR. VIVIAN E. ROBSON,

This is the 29 year old Vivian Robson (1890-1942), as he appeared in the June, 1919 issue of *Modern Astrology*. Robson was its newly installed editor. He was the successor to the late Alan Leo, who had died unexpectedly in 1917 (the two men never met). By training, Robson was a geologist. By profession, a draftsman. Unhappy with both, the previous year he had signed up for Alan Leo's astrology course, where he made outstanding progress.

The photo was taken by the noted Alvin Langdon Coburn, who had taken up a study of metaphysics (with ties to Theosophy, a favorite of Bessie Leo, Robson's employer) a few years before. Regrettably, in 1930 Coburn destroyed his entire life's work. Which means this blurry photo, from an old magazine, may be the only record of Vivian Robson that exists. He was, hands down, the finest astrologer of the 20th century. My thanks to Philip Graves for the picture, from his collection. — *September 13, 2011*

♣*Chewing the cud:* **More Republican Mayhem**

PETER emailed last week. "What about the retrograde Venus in the Republican chart?" I was gobsmacked. I was thunderstruck. I was slammed to the floor. I was blown to smithereens, and the smithereens blown to tiny bits and then stomped on.

I missed a retrograde Venus? No fair blaming lousy Solar Fire printouts, there is no excuse for not checking the obvious. A retrograde Venus changes the Republican chart in fundamental ways. So let's have another look at the Republicans, and the planets themselves:—

First, what are the chances of a chart with both Mars *and* Venus retrograde? I turned to Neil Michelsen's *Tables of Planetary Phenomena.* (I have books, I will use them.) On pg. 108, I learn that Venus is retrograde 7.2% of the time, and that Mars is retrograde 9.5%. Multiply those two and they are both retrograde .6850% of the time. That's 68 hundredths of one percent. In theory, that's some 250 days *per century.*

Then I got out the ephemerides and counted. As I don't have a 19th century ephemeris, I checked 1900-2100, a total of 201 years. Here is what I found. Mars and Venus were both retrograde:

> 42 days in 1905
> 26 days in 1918
> 23 days in 1937
> 8 days in 1950
> 4 days in 1969

For an actual count of **103 days for the 20th century.** Barely more than *one day a year.*

For the 21st century, as follows:

> 10 days in 2037 — a 68 year gap
> 12 days in 2057
> 30 days in 2069
> 2 days in 2076
> 14 days in 2082

140

28 days in 2089
1 day in 2095
For a total of **83 days in the 21st century.** *Less than one day a year.*

So far as 1854 is concerned, Venus went retrograde on February 6th. It went direct on March 21st, a total of 54 days. Mars was retrograde the entire time. For most of that period, the two planets were within a degree or two of exactly opposed. None of the mutual retrogrades of the 20th and 21st century were that severe. In all the other cases, the two planets' retrogrades merely overlapped. In 1854, the Martian retrograde ate the Venusian whole.

The normal delineation of Venus/Mars opposed says that if Venus is the stronger, then the native is hypersensitive and prone to abuse. It is the female who cannot stand to be "hit on", who is fearful of being stalked, who hides from the world.

When Mars is the stronger, we get the abusive male. Super macho, women are his for the taking, their feelings, their beings, of no interest to him. So long as he gets his way.

Critically in these traditional delineations, it is presumed that Mars is retrograde. Except for lunar oppositions, virtually all oppositions have one retrograde planet. It is as if there are two fighters in the ring. One—the direct planet—comes out of his corner swinging. The other—the retrograde one— emerges from the opposite corner, cowering. *Ma! He's picking on me!* Does victory then go to the direct planet? No. It's not so simple. When pushed the retrograde planet may well lash out: The cornered animal. I wish I could tell you there were simple mechanical rules for astrology, but there are not. You must look at each individual case.

When both opposing planets are retrograde—which is rare—it is as if the fighters have torn up the rule book. They are both in the ring, but they are there despite themselves. When both cower, victory goes to the better placed, better aspected planet. Since whatever planet that squares one, will square the other, and whatever planet that trines one, will sextile the other, tightness of orb is critical. As well as any planet that conjuncts one and opposes the other.

In the Republican chart, retrograde Venus, being well placed in Pisces, does not want icky Martian interference. Only one degree separate from the Sun, she is still within its warm rays. So far as retrograde Mars is concerned, he has his plans carefully laid. He will do what he wants. He is not responsible for Venus' serfs or slaves or whatever she is calling them this week. So far as he is concerned, the best defense is a good offense.

As I mentioned last week, the Virgo-Pisces opposition is the main source of power in the Republican chart, and it is a curious sort. Venus has its ideals. It is the chart ruler, it is backed up—quite powerfully—by the Sun. Neptune and Mercury, both of questionable motives, are in Pisces and along for the ride, but that's okay. All four planets in idealistic Pisces, in the house of slaves, serfs workers, doctors and even small animals, surely Team Venus can be trusted to take care of us!

But it is precisely because Venus is retrograde that the Republicans are, and have been, unable to deliver on their grand promises.

What, in fact, was the Republican plan to end slavery? Answer: There never was a realistic plan. Not at all.

The most likely plan, simple-headed, muddled, highly dangerous, a plan that was endorsed by Abraham Lincoln himself, was to simply **ship the slaves to some other country**. There to fend for themselves. By 1860, slave "repatriation" had been on-going for some 40 years. One result is known today as the nation of Liberia, which was formally founded in 1847.

Upon taking power, all the Republicans needed to do was send the army to the South to round up eager slaves. Up to 1863, Lincoln's actual plan (opposed by all freed slaves) was to strand them in Haiti or Central America. A slam-dunk. Nothing could be more simple. Why do you suppose that immediately upon Lincoln's election, the Confederate states seceded, even before he was sworn in? Fearful the Yankee army would invade, fearful the slaves would rise up to greet them, why do you suppose the South attacked Fort Sumter? Southern backs were against the wall. Were Southerners retrograde Martians or retrograde Venusians? Doesn't make any difference! Throw the Yankees out, everything else was negotiable.

In this respect, the Republicans are paternalists gone sideways. They come with impractical plans (retrograde Mars in Virgo) that cannot actually be put into action (opposition to the chart ruler, a retrograde Venus), but which can result in unintended consequences. Such as stumbling into a Civil War.

Or shutting down the government in 1994 to make some petty point. Or stopping the Florida recount in 2000. Or holding the nation hostage over a debt ceiling.

Such Republican plans "for the good of all" are imposed on the unwilling serfs/slaves/workers, to the profit of institutions (12th house: corporations are people, too) and their financial backers (Mars trine to Saturn in Taurus in the 8th).

Which Venus, in league with Saturn in Taurus, permits. Elsewhere, Mercury, not very bright in Pisces, is smart enough to know it wants to be on the other side of the chart, in Virgo, with Mars.

HARDLY anything in astrology is more rare than a political party with both Venus and Mars retrograde. Surely this cannot be human! At first I thought, the Republicans are really ALIENS FROM OUTER SPACE, sent to infest unsuspecting earth creatures!

But then I thought, God sent the Republicans to Smite America back into the stone age where it belonged. The Avenging Angels of Amerika, one and all. And, well, they're just taking their time at it. Nobody ever said that God was in a rush. I can make out a case that he enjoys slow torture.

But, heck, well, no, that weren't it, either. Lookie here: From a standing start, the Republicans were running the country seven years after they were founded, and went on running it, in a more or less unbroken streak, until the economic system as a whole collapsed in 1929.

Whereupon Franklin Roosevelt rescued us—and them—and after 40 years of licking their wounds, Ronald Reagan brought the Republicans back from the dead. There is no difference between what the Republicans are now, and what they ever were. The nice, kindly, sympathetic Republicans of the 50's and 60's, the Republicans I grew up with, were simply a party in disarray.

With this kind of success, we should be honest and admit the Republican Party to be the true face of America. Maybe the shock of self-recognition will encourage us to do better. Do you see another Franklin Roosevelt in sight?

In his email Peter also remarked that the purpose of the Republican Moon in Aries in the 6th, ruling the 10th of Cancer, was to use its public position (MC) to push workers (6th) around. Which is another excellent observation. Do the Republicans treat us any better than they treated the slaves? Don't just think of Lincoln's *Emancipation Proclamation,* as that was the work of one man. Think of the horror of Reconstruction and its aftermath. Or the fate of Liberia.

Mark emailed to ask where I get the keywords that I use. While there are two excellent sources for this sort of thing (J. Lee Lehman's *Book of Rulerships* and Rex Bills' *Rulership Book*), I never quite got on with either one. In part I am guided by 25 years of study, but when I'm stumped, or unsure or just want a second opinion, I turn to Sakoian and Acker's *Astrologer's Handbook, Alan Oken's Complete Astrology*, Charles Carter *Principles of Astrology* and Vivian Robson's *Student's Text-book*. All of which are basic introductions-to-astrology books. There are many others. You should have three, if not four, such books in your library, each carefully chosen.

The technique I use can be found in Morin's *Book 21*, or in Patti

Tobin Brittian's *Planetary Powers.* It was best expressed by Vivian Robson, in *A Beginner's Guide to Practical Astrology:*—

> Having found the significator of the matter concerned interpret all aspects to it as things and people affecting it. Suppose Jupiter were chief significator of money and afflicted by Saturn. We should judge that money matters would be hampered by poor conditions, depressing surroundings, ill-health, or whatever Saturn signified in that horoscope. In other words, we should give Jupiter the chief consideration as significator of the matter enquired into, and interpret the action of Saturn in its relation to Jupiter, and not vice-versa. On the other hand if Saturn were the significator we should judge that fits of generosity or extravagance would affect the finances, because Jupiter is expansive in its action, and its afflicting aspect would cause trouble and loss. This general judgment is then refined by taking into account the sign and house occupied by the aspecting planet, and the houses it rules. Thus, suppose with Saturn as significator that Jupiter threw an adverse aspect from the 5th house. Then we should judge that the extravagance would arise from too much indulgence in pleasure, or from gambling, or other matters ruled by the 5th house. This would be modified by the sign containing Jupiter. A water sign would incline more to self-indulgence, a fiery one to gambling, a sign ruled by Venus to expenditure on women, and so on, thus enabling us to enlarge on the judgement obtained from the house position alone. We should next look to see what houses Jupiter ruled. If it ruled the 3rd we should judge expense and extravagance over journeys, relatives and other third house matters, and by blending the influences, that gambling losses (5th) would come through the advice of relatives (3rd) or some other appropriate blending. . . .

> This, however, is not the only way the influences would work. . . .

> There is method to be used, and it is one which needs considerable practice, but it is well-worth the trouble involved, and the student will himself be amazed to find how accurately the most trifling details may be predicted.

> **As a word of advice to the beginner I would say — Do not be afraid to let yourself go in this way. You will make many mistakes to start with, but it is the only way to make your Astrology of practical use.** There is too great a tendency nowadays to float about in a comfortable haze of so-called esotericism. The first need of Astrology is accuracy and definition, not pseudo-reli-

gious speculation, and it is only by concentrating on the practical and scientific side that we can really make Astrology of service, and obtain for it the recognition it deserves. *(Dave's emphasis)*

I wrote a great deal more this week, chiefly on how slavery really worked, but it was too much of a rant. (You want the real story of slavery? Female slaves were forcibly bred/mass raped on an annual basis, the majority of male slaves castrated at birth. The slave-owner himself did the siring/stud work/raping (pick your term). Such is how field slaves came to be. Because, as is well-known, slaves will not breed. *"Let slavery end with me"* is their bedrock belief. What do you think of Jefferson, now? House slaves were the product of the owner's slovenly daughter and an unexpectedly fertile black male. Presumably for every house slave, there was one dead black male. The real story of slavery is still well-hidden.)

Consider also *Rosemary's Baby*, which, metaphorically speaking, is what can come about when both Venus and Mars are retrograde. Just plain creepy.

America is, in sum, an extraordinary country. It has an extraordinary chart, the chart of the founding of the Republican Party. Next year I expect it to sweep the elections and by its misrule further advance its mission of self-destruction through greed. The rest of the world is trying to distance itself from us, by whatever means as come to hand. It is just that bleak. — *September 13, 2011*

Mad as hatters and not going to take it anymore:
✤The Tea Party

YOU have gotten used to this high-octane stuff. Astrology smashing through the week's headlines. Some week I will ran out of the easy stuff and you will tune in and find *Stardate 2879.3:* Time Twins Mr. Spock and Capt. James T. Kirk.

My intention is not to pass judgement on the US political mess (who am I?), but to demonstrate how you can use astrology to know more about the world in which you live. Learn how to fully read a chart, how to organize planets, houses and signs to make your own conclusions, your own realizations. Will your results be the same as mine? Of course not! The goal is to use my techniques (Morin's techniques, frankly), not to agree with my personal beliefs.

Some updates. So far as the Little Red (actually white) Schoolhouse in Ripon, WI and the meeting of February 28,1854,1 have been corrected. That meeting took place in a local church. I think my analysis of the probable time (in the evening) will stand. During the day, people attend to business. In the evening there are meetings, rallies, revivals, concerts, casual romances between strangers, etc. The second meeting, of March 20, 1854, was held in the school, very likely about the same time of day, which advances all the house cusps by one sign. Mars should rule.

Numerous people have emailed dates of other meetings, each claiming to be the "origin" of the modern Republican Party. It seems clear that by the summer of 1854 that something was afoot. In particular, the March 20th meeting has been called out as the true founding date of the Republican Party. Of that day, March 20, 1854, *The Wisconsin Historical Society* has preserved an account, which includes,

It was a cold and windy night. On the desk where the teacher was accustomed to preside, was a single candle. And on the benches were the men who sold goods over the counter, the minister, the blacksmith and the farmer whose horses stamped in the chill outside the candle-lighted building.

146

This was not a meeting for debate. Every man present knew why he was there—*it was to dissolve the local organizations of the old parties, to organize and adopt such measures as the inauguration of a new party required.* — The Milwaukee Journal, June 2, 1929 (My emphasis. Note references to night.)

Read this carefully. If there was no debate as to the need for a new party, then March 20 was not the inception of the Republican party, but its first organizational meeting. Distinctions matter. Of the February 28th meeting, the same report says,

In the meantime came the "Nebraska question, "with every Whig and Democrat in the country lined up. Should Nebraska and Kansas be admitted as territories with power to do as they pleased about slavery, despite the Missouri Compromise and its guarantee that there was to be no slave north of 36-30?

"No, " said the community on the hill, and hastened, men and women, to attend a meeting in the Congregational Church, called by Bovay and held on the last evening in February, 1854. The burden of the speeches concerned the subserviency of the old parties to the slave holders and the necessity of a new party. A resolution was adopted that if the Nebraska bill should pass, they would "throw the old party organizations to the winds and organize a new party on the sole issue of the non-extension of slavery. " (Emphasis mine. Again note the nighttime setting.)

Which makes the Tuesday, February 28th meeting, not the one of Monday March 20th, the do-or-die meeting, the one at which the necessity of a new party, and its fundamental identity, was debated and finally decided upon. Is there overlap between these two meetings? Yes, a great deal. History is messy like that. But we cannot understand the actions of March 20th without reference to the previous meeting of February 28.

TEA parties have been a venerable tradition on both sides of the Atlantic. In America we go out of doors and rant. In England tea parties are picnics attended by oversize animals and demented local businessmen. As a form of political protest there have been various informal "tea parties" in recent years, none of which amounted to anything much.

This changed on February 19, 2009, when Rick Santelli, a CNBC business news reporter, gave a most amazing rant from the floor of the Chicago Mercantile Exchange. The video clip is available on-line and you will see that it is clearly time-stamped: 8:11 am Eastern, 7:11 Central. Chicago is Central, thus the time: Thursday, February 19, 2009, 7:11 am, Chicago.

The gist of Santelli's rant—and it is a rant—is that the government is wrong to help underwater home owners stay in their homes. That the government is wrong to "subsidize losers," that there are plenty of people who would be happy to buy these properties on the cheap. Rather than tax everybody else to pay for bad mortgages. He was interrupted by one of his hosts who pointed out the mob rule aspect of his rant. Santelli then continued by saying that before Castro everyone in Cuba lived in mansions and that since Castro they all have to drive around in very old American cars. Santelli concluded by claiming that the 5% of the trading floor that was there with him at the moment (7 am CST) was a representative cross-section of America.

Santelli was born in Chicago on January 12,1953, the grandson of Italian, not Cuban, immigrants. He graduated from the University of Illinois Urbana-Champaign and, age 26, began a career at the Chicago Mercantile. In 1999 he joined CNBC as a business reporter. He is an expert with the Chicago Mercantile, which is why he was hired. In stressful times one often hears such rants. One remembers the classic "love it or leave it" of the Vietnam war. Which in the past the media has noted, and then moved on to a discussion of possible solutions for the problems which gave rise to the rant. But that was when the Republicans were in their post-FDR slump, and the Democrats, always and forever feckless, were still basking in his glow. The Republicans are now back up to speed and the Democrats have slithered back into the shadows they love so well. It's 1928–or 1860–all over again.

While there had been various "tea party" events over the past decade, in the days after Santelli's outburst, many "tea party" events were quickly organized. Which makes his televised statement a founding moment.

The Tea Party Chart

IN mundane maps the signs of the zodiac are not much used. The Tea Party chart has Pisces rising, which is an aspect of religion. On the first house cusp, with the Sun nearby, Santelli's rant was one of religious belief. Watch and listen to the video clip: He certainly believes what he says.

Chart ruler is Jupiter, in Aquarius. Pisces-Jupiter-Aquarius combinations to me are indicative of preachers (Pisces) haranguing their congregations (Aquarius). Jupiter conjunct Mars gave him a great deal of energy, self-confidence and zealous, warlike expression.

I am coming to view the north node, when there are planets in close aspect, as granting a degree of self-righteousness. I note the universal belief that the north node is "where we should be going," so if there is a planet conjunct the node, then the north node must make that planet's actions to be right and true and proper, at least as far as the individual is concerned. (You as observer may want to disagree.) When the north node is on the ascendant, or conjunct the ruler of the ascendant, then whatever the chart signifies would have the connotation of being right.

Which was certainly the feeling that everyone had at the time. That Rick Santelli had spoken Truth, however unpleasant. There is no profit in my pointing out that "truth" that distorts history and victimizes people is not a very useful truth. As I know well, there is no such thing as absolute truth, or, indeed, any sort of "truth" at all. "Truth" and its opposite, falsehood, are relative terms. To a weary, long-suffering, mentally addled public, such as America, what Santelli said was true enough. Just as Howard Camping's fantastic dream of the end of the world last May 21st rang true for countless millions. By contrast, Jimmy Carter's warning of energy dependency, on April 17, 1977, while certainly "true" was also most unwelcome. Truth is relative, it might even be a relative of yours or mine, but this is not something easily judged with a chart alone.

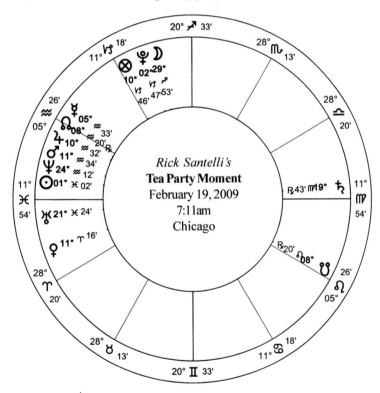

The house in which we find the ruler of the chart, along with Mars (for energy), the righteous node, as well as know-it-all Mercury, was 12. Here we have an enormous set of problems.

The twelfth house is perhaps the most slippery in the entire chart. It rules prisons and workhouses and insane asylums and institutions of all kinds. It also rules secret affairs and intrigue, which can include sex. A moment ago I went to the shelf and looked through Rex Bills and Lee Lehman's rulership books. I was looking to find the astrological rulership of corporations. I did not find corporations in Lehman's book, which did not surprise, as hers is a compilation of late medieval sources. Bills, a modern work, gives corporations as Jupiter, Neptune and Uranus. He does not give a sign, nor a house, but you will note that in the Tea Party chart, the chart ruler is one of Bills' rulers of corporations, another of his rulers, Neptune, is nearby, and the third, Uranus, is in the first house.

You will also note that both Jupiter and Neptune have natural 12th house and Piscean connotations, and that Uranus is associated with Aquarius and the 11th. I am of the opinion that corporations, which are, essentially, large organizations of (oftentimes) addled people, are 12th house creatures. Corporations are largely secretive as well as beyond individual control. This is important because, although Santelli's words were taken up eagerly by the public at large, it is very clear that he was, in fact speaking on behalf of the world in which he has lived, quite comfortably (or so I imagine) for more than 30 years. Which is the world of corporations. Not the general public.

Note the position of Mercury. If corporations are 12th house, then Mercury in the 12th may be said to speak on their behalf. Mercury in Gemini is glib. Mercury in Aquarius, another powerful placement, is a smart-aleck. The On-Line Dictionary defines smart aleck as *"an obnoxiously conceited and self-assertive person with pretensions to smartness or cleverness."* I myself have Mercury in Aquarius and recognize the tendency. Aquarius is, in fact, a sign of smartness and intelligence and, in its strange and aloof nature, also quite conceited. You will note the node is very nearly at the midpoint of Mercury, the obnoxious, and Jupiter, the chart ruler. You will also note the south node, symbol of "all that is wrong" is in the 6th.

Raphael VI, in his book, *Mundane Astrology*, defines the 6th mundane house as ruling, *"the public health and the general condition of the working classes and servants. It also governs national service, Army and Navy, the Soldiers and Sailors, Battleships, etc. The nature of the sickness affecting the country generally can be deduced from the planets in this house, or ruling over it according to the parts of the body ruled by such sign, etc."*

The nodal signs are, north, in Aquarius, in the 12th, indicating We the Corporations who are Right, vs: the south node, in Leo, representing you, the petty and mean and hopeless and drowning serfs (ruler Sun in Pisces, which is wet), who have no rights, no rights at all. On this point,

Santelli was explicit: Pay your bills and be happy, or shut up and take the consequences. (And for that, he was cheered?)

It is at this point that the analysis becomes grim. The past two weeks I have shown the Republican chart, with its strong, albeit warped 6th house paternalistic aspect. This week we have a hectoring, Aquarian/ Piscean corporate chart. In both cases it is working people who are being beaten up, first by a government (retrograde Venus leading to Jupiter in Capricorn) and now by corporations, direct from the trading floor.

You will note in the Tea Party chart that the chart ruler, Jupiter, not only rules the 12th of corporations, but also the 10th (Sagittarius) of the presidency itself. In the Tea Party chart we again see the government, now subservient to the corporation, making war against the workers, to the profit of the corporations.

Which is reinforced, yet again, by Saturn in Virgo in the 7th house. As Virgo is ruled by Mercury, it is therefore Saturn which was the aim of his rant. Saturn in the 7th normally signifies trouble in foreign affairs, but the target of Santelli's rant was not foreigners, but poor Americans. Sakoian and Acker, in their *Astrologer's Handbook*, tell me that Saturn in Virgo makes people who are practical, exacting and hard working. They are perfectionists, they tend to overwork, they do not get on well with others. They tend to be austere and gloomy and in poor health.

That Santelli had innocent poor people in mind would have been more clear, his rant would have had more focus, had there been an actual opposition between Mercury and Saturn. Virgo and Aquarius are inconjunct, which Valens describes as "turned away", in other words, not able to "see" each other. For those of you who are accustomed to working exclusively with aspects and are having a hard time with rulers, this kind of distinction is important. If the two planets had actually been opposed, Santelli's target would have been clear. But as they were not, the target of Santelli's rant was perceived to be more general, more diffuse.

And it's here where we find the power of astrology to reveal. Reviewing the analysis as a whole, I find that Santelli was speaking on behalf of corporations and against the working poor.

WHERE'S the money? Funny you should ask. In the Tea Party chart, both money houses are empty, though a debilitated Venus in Aries (remember the retrograde Venus in the Republican chart) is trying to get into the 2nd, but really wants to be in the 8th, which it rules. Ruler of the 2nd, Mars, is conjunct the chart ruler, Jupiter. Mars also rules Venus. Both Mars and Jupiter are located in the 12th house of corporations. One way or another, so far as the Tea Party is concerned, *all the money belongs to the corporation.*

The Moon in this chart is in the last minutes of Sagittarius, in the 10th. Tenth house Moons resonate well with the public. Moon in Sagittarius represents ideas we can all believe in. That it is void in the 29th degree means these ideas are old and burned up (Sagittarius is a fire sign) and no longer valid. You will note the Moon is less than three degrees from a conjunction with Pluto, and that the aspect is applying, in other words, the two planets are getting closer by the minute. This is another example how rulership astrology differs from aspect astrology.

Aspect astrology says the Moon and Pluto are in aspect, must be in aspect, because not only are they physically close, not only are they moving towards each other, but the Moon itself has an overly large orb of aspect. And while it is true that Santelli's rant galvanized the country (which Moon and Pluto will certainly do), it did not produce intense riots and civil disorder, which a true Moon/Pluto conjunction on the MC will do. Even when the planets are only three degrees apart, aspects are sign-based. Subordinate to that, intensity of aspect is degree-based. Out-of-sign aspects have the underlying value of the signs themselves, and adjacent signs, which are innately conflicting, have little if any relationship.

The Part of Fortune. In my work with Valens I am coming to value Fortune more and more. You will note Fortune in this chart is in Capricorn, the sign of government. It is ruled by Saturn, which is ruled by Mercury. Which again takes me back to Santelli's words, much of which were a rant against the government for mistakenly helping "losers." Valens says to look at the 10th house from Fortune, to see what and where that is. In this chart, the tenth from Fortune is the 8th, of, I hate to remind you, Wall Street (other people's money). Ruled by Venus, which is ruled by Mars, which is conjunct the chart ruler in the house of corporations.

It is a sad commentary on the country of my birth that such a moment as this became symbolic of hope, when there is no hope in sight. I am asked what I think may happen in the future, as if my opinion had merit, which it does not. Personally I would like to see a general strike, led by cunning operators. I am fearful of widespread riots, which will be suppressed with loss of life. I have no hope whatever for the elections of 2012. —
September 20, 2011

✤ Astrological Tools You Can Use

OVER at the blog, TMC points out that last week's Tea Party chart is a bucket, with the south node, or rather, Saturn as the handle. Which brings up **planetary patterns**. Planetary patterns were first developed by Marc Edmund Jones and expanded upon by Stephanie Clement. You look at the overall arrangement of the planets in a chart to find various patterns, among them, Splay, Splash, Teeter-totter, Bundle, Bowl, Locomotive, etc.

The See-Saw, for example, is all or most of the planets in a chart forming two groups which are more or less opposed to each other. If you have a cluster of planets in Aries and Taurus, for example, with another cluster in Libra and Scorpio, you have a Teeter-Totter, aka Seesaw chart. Clement describes a See-saw as,

> [T]he two groups of planets polarize the energy so that the individual tends to swing from one general point of view to the other instead of experiencing the flows of energy through the pattern. In psychology, extreme mood swings are sometimes described as bipolar mood disorders, and the Seesaw pattern reflects a tendency toward such a split in a person's energy.

(Aspect Patterns, pg. 93)

This is from the second paragraph in the chapter on Seesaw (the first paragraph was a physical description of the Seesaw chart itself) and already we see the author reaching for a specific conclusions that are far in advance of what her generalized astrology can support. One of her See-saw examples is the chart of Anwar Sadat, former Egyptian leader. As is often the case when working beyond one's means, Clement's delineation of Sadat's chart tells us nothing whatever about the man himself. She instead projects her concepts and then searches Sadat's life for an event to justify them.

WHEN reading a chart, you have an enormous range of tools at your disposal. Here are just a few of them:

153

There are: Specific planets. Specific houses. Specific signs. Specific relationships between all of them.

Signs can be:

Cardinal, which is to say, active

Fixed, or unchanging

Mutable, or changeable

Signs can be:

Fire, which is to say, active

Earth, practical, or slow

Air, impractical, or mental

Water, emotional, or sensitive.

Houses can be:

Angular, which is to say, prominent

Succeedent, which is to say accumulative

Cadent, which is to say, chaotic

Degree positions can be:

Early, 1-10, which is to say, young.

Middle, 10-20, representing maturity.

Late, 20-30, which is to say, old and worn out.

The very first and very last degrees of a sign (0-3; 27-30), which is to say, childish or senile, are especially critical in this regard.

Houses are not the same as signs. I don't care if Robson himself said otherwise. Angular is not the same as cardinal, succeedent is not the same as fixed, cadent is not the same as mutable. Signs are qualities. Houses are drivers. **A cardinal planet in a cadent house has a hard time punching its way out of a paper bag.** Punching, an activity, is the cardinal planet. The paper bag represents the limitations of the cadent house.

A mutable sign, such as Pisces, on an angular house magnifies the instability of the mutable sign. Exactly what kind of instability will be determined by the nature of the sign, in particular, its element. Sagittarius on the ascendant will magnify its *(mindless:* opposite Gemini, fall of Mercury) fiery energy and boundless *(Jupiter)* enthusiasm, in the direction of and to the aims of the house of its ruler, wherever Jupiter may be.

Signs have rulers. Libra is always dressed as Venus would have her. Leo always radiates the Sun. The planets in the houses they rule are of the nature of tenants in a rented house. The ruler always remains the landlord.

By contrast, houses DO NOT have de facto planetary rulers. Nor is any house associated with any particular sign. **Houses are like slaves.** They are like beasts of burden. No. 2 is a slave for money. No. 5 is a slave for romance and children. Houses must work with whatever planets and signs they are given. Which are their masters. Some masters are good, some are not, all are unique. Realize these subtleties and you will vastly enhance your delineations.

For example, take a chart with Sagittarius rising. The ruler of Sagittarius is Jupiter. If Jupiter turns up in, say, Cancer in the 8th, it will actively work (Cancer) to get lots (Jupiter) of money from others (8th house). As the chart ruler, this will be the reason for the individual's existence, whole cloth. Everything else is detail.

Could this also be about sex? Well, yes, but that will depend on the condition of the Moon (ruler of the 8th) as well as of Mars, ruler of Aries on the 5th. Sex a lot more personal than money-grubbing. Sex is like a hot-house plant. It won't grow just anywhere. And it could also be about death. Money, sex and death, all three are 8th house matters.

The house containing the ruler of the chart is the dominant house of the chart. In mundane matters, this particular chart, with Sagittarius rising, Jupiter in Cancer in the 8th, could turn up as the chart of an international (Sag rising) investment house, or as the opening gavel for a convention of undertakers. Or an international porn expo.

Mundane charts must be read according to the group which has claimed it. If there is an opportunity for close examination, you may find that undertakers can be quite sexy, that porn operators are well-known for luscious vampires, that very stuffy investors often consort with high class prostitutes *(the best money can buy, baby!)* and that in his short life Jack Kennedy, with a stellium in the 8th, had brushes with violent death (in WWII, and his ultimate demise) as well as with young starlets.

Further in your research, you will eventually come across ruling planets which are themselves in their debility. Which is to say, in one of the signs opposite to the ones in which they rule. One fine day you will be looking at such a chart, such as Bill Clinton's, with a debilitated Saturn in Leo ruling his (otherwise empty) 5th house of adventurous and fun Aquarius. And you will suddenly realize why he is always caught out in his petty extramarital affairs: Saturn literally jumps across his chart, from its debility in the 11th, to its rulership in the 5th, and exposes him. Catches him with his pants down around his, well, ankles. Aquarius rules the ankles. I miss Bill, we all do. I want a leader who's overtly lusty and fun. I want a guy with his head screwed on straight. Not moralistic and dour, or petty and evasive.

And having made this observation, of a debilitated planet jumping across the chart, you will then excitedly apply it to other charts. And to your amazement, find that it always works. Elsewhere I read that planets, in general, have effect in the houses that are opposite and square to their natal domicile (which is to say, where the planet is physically located, not the houses with the signs it rules), but I have never seen this to actually work. Debilitated planets work in the house opposite. It's in the nature of the debility itself. Whereas planets in rulership or exaltation are self-centered. They ignore the rest of the world.

On top of all of this you have triplicities (10° sections of signs, see Anrias, *Man and the Zodiac*), as well as Terms and their rulers, but I've never seen a need for that much detail.

In sum, you have So Many Tools! But so many astrologers limit themselves to aspects and orbs, aspects and orbs, aspects and orbs. Astrologers have learned aspects to the exclusion of almost everything else. It is self-evident that aspects can give only fragmentary results. Most people don't have a lot of aspects. Some people don't even have their Sun and Moon in aspect. Does that mean they are primitive and undeveloped, or warped and demented? Of course not! Judging merely on the basis of aspects is to severely shortchange the individual. Astrology is better than that!

Every chart, *every individual,* has 12 functioning signs, 12 functioning houses, and 10 planets and two nodes, which interact in many dynamic ways. Aspects do in fact highlight important details, but as these details are fragmentary at best, *aspects usually miss all the important parts of a chart.* As a result, too many astrologers are accustomed to a vague and incomplete astrology. They literally do not know any better. When real astrology is put in front of them, they can find it disorienting.

So let us return, again, to the Tea Party chart, of February 19, 2009 (pg. 149). As you can see, above, it is the bucket sort. Of buckets, Clements says,

> [T]he Bucket personality has a specific outlet—the handle planet. The nature of the handle planet and the house and sign it occupies will define the quality and direction of the individual's structured, directed activity. The Bucket personality is driven to dig deeply into the area of life defined by the handle planet. Much energy is put into figuring out how to get the best results from focussed activity. (Aspect Patterns, pg. 68)

Which is a logical development of theory. Clement's example chart is Albert Schweitzer (January 14, 1875, 11:50 pm, Kaysersberg, France). This is a chart with Libra rising, ruling planet Venus in Sagittarius in the 3rd. Which gives a love of adventure, frankly. It is in contrast to Sun, Mercury and IC all in dreadfully boring Capricorn, spurred on by an irritating Moon in Aries in exact square. Schweitzer started life as his father's religious tool (the family had a long history of religion and music) but gave that up for adventures abroad: Chart ruler Venus in expansive Sagittarius in a very mobile 3rd house. Acting against his father's express wishes, as shown by Sun in Capricorn in the 4th. That medicine was not his first career, that he had to struggle to become a doctor and go to Africa, is shown, quite clearly, by Jupiter's remote position in the first house. Schweitzer's Jupiter contradicts my usual delineation, of a planet outside the house with the same sign on the cusp.

In this case, Jupiter is in the first house, *not* trying to get into the second. The reason? Jupiter is barely 0° of Scorpio. And while it's as much a Scorpion as your newborn baby boy is a Smith (just like you), it is not nearly mature enough to know that it should want to be in the second. "Inertia," if you will, still has it in the first. This is what I learned from this chart: That a planet at 0° won't necessarily associate with its proper house cusp. This bears investigation.

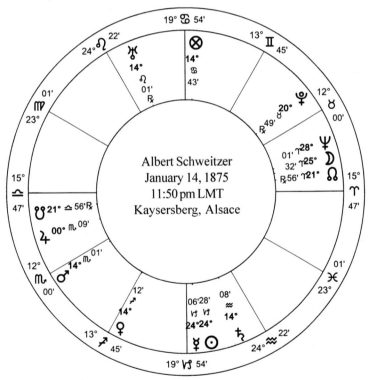

Once abroad in Africa, Schweitzer found his life's work. The chart is clear: Jupiter in Scorpio (the sign of intensity), somewhat stranded in the first, slowly but powerfully acts through the sixth house of medicine and healing, which happens to have Pisces, ruled by Jupiter, on its cusp. Jupiter also rules Venus, the chart ruler. Here, Jupiter has equal power to bring 3rd house Venusian dreams (Sagittarius, travel) to reality.

Lacking these essential tools, Clement can only say,

> *If Pluto in the 8th house is viewed as the high-focus planet, then the emphasis of the pattern is more on transformation and less on philosophy. Because Pluto disposits Jupiter in Scorpio, Jupiter has a strong inclination toward the transformative nature within his personality, so the difference is not as dramatic as it would be if the dispositor relationship did not exist.* (Aspect Patterns, pg. 73)

Which is a complete muddle. Pluto happens to be prominent, to Clement, because it is the trailing edge of the bucket. Clement bypasses a structural analysis presumably because her astrology is not strong enough to give her results she can actually use. Instead, she substitutes theory. Which results in *strong inclinations.* Which neither describes the man in front of us, nor gives us any useful means for our own work. To quote Robson, [*t*]*here is too great a tendency nowadays to float about in a comfortable haze of so-called esotericism. The first need of Astrology is accuracy and definition, not pseudo-religious speculation.* (Beginner's Guide, pg. 113)

DARE to use the tools in front of you, and you will achieve the promise of astrology. So what can we find out about the Tea Party's bucket chart? Let's start at the beginning and see where we go:—

In Rick Santelli's Tea Party chart, the ruler of the first is Jupiter, in Aquarius, in the 12th house. The 12th can represent horses, Aquarius can represent rebellious groups, we could say the Tea Party concerns an abundance (Jupiter) of wild mustangs. Metaphorically speaking, we would not be far wrong, though physically we'd be in outer space.

In this chart, Jupiter in Aquarius in 12 is itself ruled by Saturn in Virgo in the 7th. When we trace rulerships from one planet to another, we are following a natural and logical progression. In a mundane chart, the 7th is our enemy, as it very often is in a natal chart as well. (Sex as a lubricant helps us to overlook that, though never quite forget it entirely.) So when we see the chart ruler's ruler end up in the

7th, we know we have a dynamic chart, so to speak.

For its part, Saturn is ruled by Mercury, which is in the same sign as Jupiter. "Same sign" means "same party" or same group. Same sign also means same house. **Saturn and Mercury are in mutual reception,** which means the two planets are effectively conjunct and the two houses, 12th and 7th are effectively fused. As the two houses are in fact inconjunct, and as **inconjuncts are aspects of invisibility** (sorry to throw that at you), we can say the Tea Party is angry at things with which it cannot quite get to grips.

So, from a standing start (the Ascendant), rulerships have now led us both into the bucket, as well as directly to its handle. **The Tea Party chart is therefore a bucket chart,** with all rights, duties and privileges pertaining thereunto. Having gone about finding the bucket by backwards means, a guess is that it won't turn out exactly as Clement would imagine.

Clement would have Saturn in Virgo in the 7th as the primary planet in the chart. Since Saturn has led us to Mercury, can we use our tools to determine which planet, Mercury or Saturn, is stronger?

While Saturn and Mercury are in mutual reception, which should make them more-or-less equal in strength, Mercury is exalted in Aquarius, whereas Saturn is merely stuck in Virgo. (In one set of terms, Saturn at 19° Virgo is in its own terms. In another set of terms, it is not. To me, terms are one whole subset below rulers and exaltations. Which is to say, not on equal footing: Subtenants.)

With its exalted knowledge (of being superior, of course), Mercury in Aquarius can pounce on Saturn in Virgo, blaming it for the mess it's making.

It's useful to remember that Saturn is not always the stronger planet. Virgo is Mercury's bailiwick, Virgo is Mercury's responsibility. Mercury doesn't take kindly to Saturn making a mess in its sign. On crude levels—and mundane astrology is always crude—Saturn makes a mess wherever he goes.

Saturn in Virgo is all about not being neat. Not being tidy. Not getting the job done. Not being on time, etc., etc. Or, in Santelli's own words, not paying your bills, not keeping your house in order, and suffering the consequences. Astrological delineations must closely mirror the subject of the chart itself. As this does.

Backing up a bit, you could say that Pisces rising puts a spotlight on Jupiter in Aquarius in 12, who then passes the baton to Saturn in Virgo in 7, who throws it to Mercury in Aquarius in 12. All of which are straightforward rulerships. No hocus-pocus, no magic show, nothing up the sleeves. Mercury and Saturn then monopolize the game (i.e., the chart) by throwing the ball back and forth between themselves, shutting everyone else out. Mutual receptions tend to do this.

In this chart, as Mercury is the stronger of the two, it's Mercury railing against Saturn, and Saturn who finds he cannot get out of the way and that he has no good reply. Mercury, the planet of words, is giving Saturn a good scolding. Which, again, was precisely what Santelli was doing. So far as buckets are concerned, in the Tea Party chart, the primary planets are Jupiter, Saturn and Mercury.

I do not mean to speak ill of Stephanie Clement. She has worked and studied very hard, for very many years. I can trace her as far back as the days she worked at Michael Erlewine's Heart Center Library, in Big Rapids, MI. I feel like Thoreau, in Walden, who told a story of Indians and their baskets. Thoreau meant them no ill-will. He simply found it frustrating they had spent their time with baskets, when there were more interesting matters at hand.

LEARN to use all the tools at your disposal and your astrology will go from crude sketches, to technicolor movies. Astrology is a powerful thing. I am accused of bias, and while this is true and unavoidable, it is also true that astrology describes the world as it is. Not how we imagine it to be. There are charts I cannot present because their delineations will contradict commonly-held beliefs and ideas. But this is the sheer terror of astrology, that it sees all and knows all. No one, no thing, can hide.

Table of Rulerships:

The Sun rules Leo

The Moon rules Cancer

Mercury rules the signs on either side of these two: Gemini and Virgo.

Venus rules the signs on either side of Mercury: Taurus and Libra

Mars rules the signs on either side of her: Aries and Scorpio.

Jupiter rules the next set: Sagittarius and Pisces.

Saturn brings up the end. It rules the signs opposed to Sun and Moon: Capricorn and Aquarius.

Table of Detriments:

Detriments are opposite to rulers:

The Sun is in detriment in Aquarius

The Moon is in detriment in Capricorn

Mercury is in detriment with the signs on either side: Sagittarius and Pisces.

Venus is in detriment in Aries and Scorpio

Mars is in detriment in Taurus and Libra
Jupiter is in detriment in Gemini and Virgo.
Saturn is in detriment in Cancer and Leo.

Detriments have a puzzling relationship with rulers:

Sun and Moon are in mutual detriment to Saturn.
Mercury and Jupiter are in mutual detriment.
Venus and Mars are in mutual detriment.

In other words, when Mercury and Jupiter are in "mutual reception," Mercury in Jupiter's sign and Jupiter in Mercury's, they are also in mutual detriment: Gemini to Sagittarius, or Gemini to Pisces, or Virgo to Sagittarius, or Virgo to Pisces. (Uniquely, these two planets rule the four mutable signs. Which means both Jupiter and Mercury are mutable in nature.)

It is the same with Venus and Mars, and with Sun/Moon and Saturn.

Which brings us to enemies.

It may be said that when Saturn is in Leo it is the Sun's enemy (but not the Moon's), and when he is in Cancer he is the Moon's enemy, but not the Sun's.

By extension, Venus and Mars are enemies, as are Mercury and Jupiter.

By "enemy" it is meant that Venus and Mars, for example, are opposed in nature. Venus is conciliatory and agreeable, Mars is aggressive and penetrating. Mercury is detailed and vocal, Jupiter is expansive and, so far as Pisces is concerned, mute.

Exaltations:

Exaltations are a funny grouping. The planets do not rule, but are said to be well-placed, as follows:

The Sun is exalted in Aries
The Moon is exalted in Taurus
Mercury is exalted in Aquarius
Venus is exalted in Pisces
Mars is exalted in Capricorn
Jupiter is exalted in Cancer
Saturn is exalted in Libra

Fall

The fall of a planet is another funny grouping. Falls are the opposite of Exaltations. They are places where the planets feel uncomfortable:

The Sun falls in Libra

The Moon falls in Scorpio
Mercury falls in Leo
Venus falls in Virgo
Mars falls in Cancer
Jupiter falls in Capricorn
Saturn falls in Aries

Various relationships can be worked out.

Jupiter and Venus both have a positive relationship with Pisces. One rules, the other is exalted.

Continuing:—

Mars and the Sun have a positive relationship with Aries.
Venus and Saturn have a positive relationship with Libra.
Saturn and Mars have a positive relationship with Capricorn.
The Moon and Venus have a positive relationship with Taurus.
Mercury and Saturn have a positive relationship with Aquarius.

The opposites, of course, are also true. Saturn and Venus both have a negative relationship with Aries, etc. One is in fall, the other debilitated. (I often get fall and debility confused.) These relationships are the keys to delineating the various Astrological Ages, for example.

These are the ABC's of astrology. You should know these by rote, or, at the very worst, know where to find them in a book, and all introductory books should have these tables. Knowing these are like practicing scales and arpeggios on piano. Comes in handy.

Now do you understand how silly it is to give rulerships to Uranus, Neptune and Pluto? Or Chiron or Eris? One may say they have affinities to this sign or that, but in fact they can rule none. Rulerships are an organized system. — *September 27, 2011. With continued apologies to Stephanie Clement.*

✢ Ron Paul

LAST month the Republicans formed a circular firing squad in the form of debates. When the smoke cleared Rick Perry, Sarah Palin and Michele Bachmann were effectively out of the race and someone named Cain had snuck in. There's no point bothering with trivial candidates like Herman Cain. They will be out of the race before the end of the year.

The Republican race is coming down to Mitt Romney, who has the experience and the money to stay the course, and Ron Paul, who has acres of popular support. Neither man will give up, at least, not before some actual votes are counted. I delineated Romney's chart a few months ago. I haven't done Paul's as he has no birth time, and for the sort of astrology I do, I need that. Until recently I had no sense of the man. I looked at his Wiki pages, but as Wiki pages are written by hack sycophants there was no hope there, either.

But then it struck me that Ron Paul is your garden variety fanatic. True believer. Right is right and wrong is wrong. Black and white. All that sort of thing. And that made it easy: Ron Paul is a 9th house type. The 9th house is the house of, among other things, law and justice, truth and falsehood.

Which means that the chart ruler will be in the 9th, *or* the Sun will be in the 9th, *or* the Moon will be in the 9th, *or* a whole bunch of planets will be in the 9th, etc. And since Paul started out as a doctor, we should find a late degree on some house cusp or another (probably the 6th), with a ruler pointing to medicine, and some other planet actually in the house, in some other sign, that pushes him into politics. Where he has been for many years now.

So our theory says that Ron Paul has something about his 6th, because he was once a doctor but is not now, and some planets in the 9th, because he thinks Ayn Rand is hot stuff. (He named his awful son, Rand Paul after her, and don't confuse me with Randal. Paul did not name his son after an acerbic actor.) If you want to put a time under a chart that has

163

no time (like Ron Paul's), this is the sort of preparation you must do. If my previous experience is any guide, you will find you were completely wrong. And if so, that would be good, because it means the chart is telling you things. Giving you ideas. In trying a "wrong" idea, the chart itself might just lead you in the right direction. You won't know unless you try. Never be afraid to guess, never be afraid to be wrong. Not only is being wrong a great way to learn, it's really the only way.

According to Wiki, Ron Paul was born in Pittsburgh, PA, on August 20, 1935.

In looking at Paul's chart, I find his Sun late in Leo and his Moon late in Taurus, forming a square. Mercury, Neptune and Venus (retrograde) are in Virgo. Remembering the 6th and 9th houses are square, I set the Moon just inside the 6th house cusp, with the Sun just inside the 9th house cusp. Sag rises, the time is 3:20 pm EDT.

Sun/Moon in square is a darn good driver. It will make you itch, it will make you do things in life, give you challenges. In fixed signs a square from Sun to Moon means you have to endure it, there is no cure. If in cardinals you would be driven to action, in mutables life would be out of your control.

Though it's only my first guess, I'm struck by the 3:20 pm chart. Moon in the 6th, a late degree of Taurus on the cusp, the ruler is retrograde Venus in Virgo. Retrograde Venus in Virgo thinks itself dirty and can never get "clean enough" to overcome it. There are presumably sexual hang-ups as well. It applies this unease to the sixth and the Moon, the result is an OB/GYN with puritanical sexual views and an intense curiosity about "how girls work." You will note that Venus is ruled by Mercury, which is itself in detailed, analytical Virgo.

But without a lot of Taurus actually in the 6th house, the Moon and its medical career "runs out of room" almost as soon as it gets started. It might be that Paul took up premed in order to "get girls" ("play doctor" in other words), but by the time he actually got to med school he was married, which made his quest somewhat moot. This would leave him in a quandary, as his Sun, at 3:20-ish pm, "ran out of room" in the 9th even faster than his Moon did in the 6th, given that the Sun in Leo hasn't got a "sponsor" (i.e., ruler) elsewhere in the chart to help it out.

Eventually Paul realized that Mercury was the key to his quest. (He doesn't realize consciously, of course, as he has no knowledge of astrology, which is aside from the fact that this method of chart analysis is rare anyway.) Mercury, which had made him a doctor, could also give him the room his 9th house Sun needed but did not have.

Mercury in Virgo in the 9th, Paul could know right from wrong. Details matter. Does the 9th house give details? Yes, it does. It sells them wholesale, in big lots. Take them or leave them.

What kind of details did Mercury find? Look straight across the chart and you will find Saturn, dead opposite at 7° Pisces. At 3:20 pm, Saturn rules the third house. Saturn in the 3rd makes study a slog. Study, study, study.

Saturn also rules the second, which is Capricorn. You have to earn your keep, and what you earn is yours. Handouts are not permitted. In his medical practice, Paul notably refused to accept Medicare or Medicaid. In Congress, he refused to accept his government pension. He opposes welfare of all kinds.

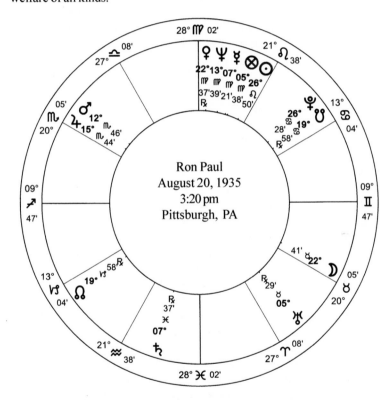

All of which Saturn throws back to Mercury. **Oppositions make for contrast**, which is the only way we can know the world. In the case of Paul's Saturn-Mercury opposition, Saturn tells Paul that hard work is required, and will be rewarded. Which bounces to Mercury in the 9th, which looks around, seeking an ideology that fits.

And finds it in the novels of Ayn Rand and the Libertarian Party in general. Note that Mercury isn't very happy with what Saturn has given it, since Saturn is in the sign of Mercury's debility, Pisces. It's like getting love letters from the one person you never wanted to hear from again.

I AM delineating a *guess* of Ron Paul's chart, but notice what I've just done. From the beginning: I've guessed his dominant traits, from what I can read in the newspapers.

I reduced these to astrological notation: The relevant houses that might express them. I then went to his chart and put those factors into those houses.

First degree of success: Ron Paul's chart would let me do that. I could not have done it with my chart and I probably could not have done it with yours. Then I started making stories. Mercury in Virgo in 9, that's, let me see ... details (Virgo) that come straight from God himself (9th house). Details handed to *St.* Paul on a platter. Sort of like the Burning Bush in the Bible. Details that Paul believes with his whole heart, his whole body, his whole soul.

But what's the context? Aha! Saturn sits dead opposite. Whatever God has given Mercury, in the guise of St. Paul, is going to be exactly the opposite of whatever Saturn has, and not just because of the opposition, but—*we know our basics!*—Mercury really doesn't like the sign that Saturn is in.

Since Mercury is stronger in Virgo than Saturn is in Pisces, Saturn is a sore point, an irritant, an *external factor.* So Mercury gives him a lot of attention. Mercury is *conscious mind* (the Moon is emotional and often unconscious), so Ron Paul is very much aware of this.

What is Saturn telling Mercury? In Pisces, that the world is a mess. Which Mercury knows already, since that's Mercury's own opinion of the sign, one of his least favorite. Saturn tells Mercury that daily life is a slog, that one must study hard, that help comes from siblings, but only if one has earned it (all 3rd house), that you start at the beginning and work your way up. (Capricorn on the second, ruled by Saturn.)

Which Mercury, by and large, refuses to hear (see Robson's *Student's Text-Book* on Mercury oppositions and deafness, which can be selective). Instead, Mercury runs to the safety of the house he is in and finds an ideology (9th house) with the details that satisfy his Virgo craving for such details. That rationalize his distaste for Saturn and everything it stands for. He finds Libertarianism and Ayn Rand.

Who or what was Ayn Rand? Here is part of her Wiki page:
In her philosophy of Objectivism, Rand advocated reason as the only means of acquiring knowledge and rejected all forms of faith and religion. She supported rational egoism and re-

jected ethical altruism. In politics, she condemned the initiation of force as immoral and opposed all forms of collectivism and statism, instead supporting laissez-faire capitalism, which she believed was the only social system that protected individual rights.

Let's use astrology to unpack this. Rejection of faith, isn't that sort of like a planet in a house it's not very comfortable in, like, I dunno, Mercury in the 9th? Reason in place of faith, wouldn't that be Mercury in Virgo in 9? Laissez-faire, isn't that kinda like Capricorn on the second, Saturn in 3? Work your way up by your bootstraps? Isn't there a fundamental conflict here, that one cannot both be rational and simply let things be? Isn't that like waiting for *laissez-faire* to turn up as the Hand of God—an entity you don't believe in? If rationality truly is the key, then won't rationality trump *laissez-faire*? Is not reason a light that peers into the darkness and brings illumination? Agreed, some subjects are harder for reason to penetrate than others, but I myself have pushed reason far beyond such a flimsy limit. *Laissez-faire* is simply a cop-out.

But aren't you using astrological make-believe to justify your rectification of Ron Paul's chart? Isn't that cheating?

No, it's not. I am *not* trying to impress an audience of astrological novices. I am not trying to pull rabbits out of hats. I am demonstrating to the astrological community the very close relationship between astrological symbolism and the personal preferences of the chart under study.

Ron Paul jumped onto the Ayn Rand bandwagon because her philosophy exactly matched his experience. Anyone who had lived as Paul had, and read what Rand wrote, would have done the same. Astrology merely confirms, it merely describes.

In support of the rectification, elsewhere I read that Ron Paul started life as a Lutheran, baptized his children as Episcopalians, before finally ending up a Baptist. Which is indicative of conflicts in the 9th house. One with no conflicts, including all those with an empty 9th house, keeps his father's religion. This is an absolute rule, as religion is not a casual thing to play with.

Lutheranism, to hear Garrison Keillor talk about it, is dour and severe. Episcopalians are a very close branch of the Holy Roman Catholic Church, in other words, the Real Deal, a branch acceptable to those who don't like Popes. In shifting from one to the other, we see Paul searching for absolute reality, a Mercury in Virgo in 9 quest. Baptists, on the other hand, believe that God has put us here to get rich and that we are doing God's Work by becoming rich. (Such has always been my understanding.) This fits tightly with Rand and Libertarianism.

I'd tell you about Libertarianism except it's never really been clearly defined, not even to this day. It's something to do with not liking government. Ideologies built on negatives *(don't like this, don't want that)* are often ill defined as a result.

Early on in his career, Paul was a doctor in the Air Force. Can the rectified chart tell us why?

Yes it can. Chart ruler Jupiter, in Scorpio, wants to be in the 12th house, of institutions. And he would have been, except that Mars, also in Scorpio, is racing to join the chart ruler and also jump into the 12th.

Either planet, by itself, would probably have given Paul a home in the military, but Mars and Jupiter together made him too big and too bold, not to mention too forceful and too sneaky. So he left, but not that many years later found himself hankering after another institution, the Congress of the United States. Where, not surprisingly, he has largely been a gadfly.

I am still struck by how easy this was. I conceptualized Paul as 6th/9th house, I set up his chart with the Moon in one and the Sun in the other, and I seem to have the man. Astrology is never this easy! This is hubris!

Another way of rectifying a chart, or at least confirming or refuting rising degrees, is to look for solar eclipses on that degree. (Nick DeVore's *Encyclopedia of Astrology* is a handy reference.) It is believed that an eclipse exactly on the ascendant leads to great changes in life. If, during your life there was a solar eclipse exactly on your ascendant, but your life continued on without interruption, your birth time might be wrong. At 9° Sagittarius, there were no solar eclipses in the 20th century, but there was in May, 2003.

So what about the Presidency?

As a president, Ron Paul would be scary. He knows right from wrong, he knows true from false, and he will act upon it. To the extent he can "unbury" his Sun, he will shake things up, because Mercury opposite Saturn lacks raw power, while Mars/Jupiter, with their boundless energy, are obscurely placed. Which makes his Sun in Leo the critical planet. So far as I can tell, in his life Ron Paul has never quite done this, his Sun has never quite "broken through."

Note that Ron Paul lacks the common touch. He is not a "peoples man." Sagittarius on the ascendant is an enthusiastic placement, but not a personable one. Virgo on the midheaven makes him critical. Venus retrograde makes him loveless, except that by this time in his life he has learned, courtesy of Mercury, its ruler, how to fake it. And faking it, when it comes to debilitated planets (Venus retrograde and in fall) is sometimes enough.

So often I find politicians with tight Mercury-Neptune squares or Mercury-Neptune oppositions, or the same with the Moon and Neptune. Which are, all of them, professional liars. **Paul is not.** Paul has Mercury in an applying conjunction to Neptune, six degrees and closing. Mercury in

Virgo is strong. It has the facts, it knows what the facts are. It would seem that in Ron Paul's chart, Mercury is reaching out to Neptune, reaching out for more than mere facts. It appears to me that Neptune's "beyond-facts" would be wrong, since Neptune in Virgo, by definition, has the wrong facts in the wrong way. Remember the 9th house actively suppresses facts, wholesale. Ron Paul's beliefs about how the world works, and why, are therefore most likely wrong.

So far as a choice between Ron Paul and Barack Obama, I'd take Paul over Obama. Easy. Paul, unlike Obama, will change things. Some for the better. Many others for the worse. I fear that Paul will rationalize his blunders, which will compound them.

So far as Paul vs: Romney, that's harder. Romney believes in money and vested interests. Romney isn't going to tell anyone to take a hike. Romney will plot, he will scheme, he will be complicated. Romney might just blunder through, but he will blunder.

Realize there is never going to be a perfect president. Such a man does not exist. We need to remember we are electing a human being. Not anointing a 4-year god. By use of astrology, we can know a great deal about who and what the next president will be. — *October 11, 2011*

✤Stephen Colbert, The Colbert Report

IT was Herman Cain's sudden rise in the polls that reminded me of the much neglected Stephen Colbert. Who has been running for President since 2008. If a B-movie star can be president, why can't an A-list comedian make a try?

I thought someone had asked Colbert his birth time, but it seems I was thinking of Jon Stewart. Colbert's birth time is unknown. Stephen Colbert was born on May 13, 1964, in Washington DC. He grew up in North Carolina. So let's find a birth time for this man.

On the day of Colbert's birth, the Sun, Mercury, Mars and Jupiter were all in Taurus. The Moon was in Gemini, Venus was in Cancer, Saturn was in Pisces. Four planets in Taurus usually means that one–only one– of the twelve houses will predominate and have a very grounded–Taurus –feel to it, but here we must be careful. Mercury at 1°, Mars at 4°, Jupiter at 7°, and then a big gap and the Sun at 22°, all Taurus. For the most part, a sign is the same as a house, which is to say that planets that are not actually in a house, but in front of it, will still act as if they are actually in that house. The exception is when the last planet in a sign is smeared across an angle and ends up in the quadrant next door. Where it stays.

You can think of angles in a wheel as being like four paddles turning slowly in a vat of liquid. The paddles/angular houses push angular planets in front of them. The sheer physicality of the paddles/angles forever separates what is in front of the paddles from what is immediately behind them. I am constantly trying to find concrete terms like these as there is so much fuzziness in astrology. Fuzziness which is based on well-meaning ideas that, well, *could* be like this, or *might* be like that or I dunno, what do you think, *etc., etc., etc.*

These "paddles" are of interest in Stephen Colbert's chart. Colbert has long been noted as a writer, and over time has shown himself to be quite very busy. Busyness is a Martian trait, which we can clearly see, as his Mars is tightly sandwiched between Mercury, the runner, and Jupiter,

170

the expansionary. Placing these by house is really too easy: The third.

The question arises, is Colbert's Sun also in the 3rd, or has it slipped into the 4th?

Sun in 4 in an earth sign is going to make for a man who is very much into home and ancestry and all the good things in life. Which would contrast with the other planets in Taurus. Three planets in Taurus in the third, on the one hand could be a highly energetic, down to earth comedian, while on the other, the Sun in Taurus, marooned in the 4th, would value home and family and ancestry and land. Stephen Colbert does not seem to have this added dimension.

From what I can read at his Wiki page, Stephen Colbert groped for many years to establish his identity. This points to an obscurely placed Sun (important to males), and/or an obscurely placed chart ruler. Sun in a cadent house is by definition obscure, which puts Stephen's Sun further along in the third. Not in the 4th. An angular Sun always knows who it is and what it wants.

I am moving towards placing Stephen's birth shortly after midnight on May 13, 1964. I've established Taurus as the likely third house, with the Sun late in the third. The next question is the signs on the midheaven and IC, the 10th and 4th house cusps. Of these two angles, the 10th house is easier for an outsider to place, as that's what we see of the individual. We have two choices:

If the third is Taurus, then the 9th is Scorpio, which makes the 10th Sagittarius–? If so, the ruler is Jupiter, which is conjunct Mars. Put them all together and Stephen would project as a super hero. And while Colbert has made parodies of himself as super heroes of various sorts, it's clear to him, as well as us, that these are, in fact, parodies. Parody is anathema to Sagittarius. It takes itself far too seriously to dare to laugh.

In Stephen's chart, and this is true regardless of his time of birth, there are 110° between the ascendant and 4th house, as well as between the 7th house and the MC. So we could have Scorpio on both the 9th and 10th house cusps. What would that look like?

Scorpio on the tenth would be a very different sort of thing. And it's not just the basic contrast between the two signs, where Sagittarius would want to project itself with simple, honest enthusiasm, while Scorpio would be a lot more intense, a lot darker. It also has to do, critically, with how the two rulers, Jupiter and Mars, drive (empower) the signs they rule, the midheaven itself.

Mars in Taurus is debilitated. If it's in the third, then it really wants to be in the 9th, in Scorpio, the sign it rules, and, oh, by the way, if Scorpio is also on the 10th and you're looking for somebody for that, count him in, too. This is an insecure Mars, a debilitated Mars, a Mars who, conjunct

Jupiter, wants to puff himself up, and, conjunct Mercury of language, wants to have **bold words** written (in Taurean stone) to describe him. All of it PROJECTED UPON THE UNIVERSE !!! (10th house) Can you smell Tek Jansen yet?

   Mercury in Taurus in the third makes it the most powerful planet of the four in Taurus, followed by the Sun and then Jupiter (not quite comfortable in the 3rd). Mars is the clear weakling, therefore when he projects himself, Mercury and Jupiter are standing nearby, ready and eager to mock.

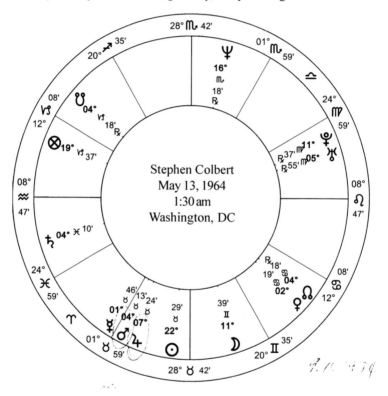

   Confirmation of a buffoonish Scorpio on the midheaven comes straight from the *Colbert Report* itself. The opening sequence features an eagle, wrapped in the American flag. The eagle is one of the symbols of Scorpio, which not only puts Scorpio on the MC, but also confirms the ruler, Mars, to be in debility in Taurus, as the opening sequence mocks it. Years ago when Martha Lang-Wescott (a dear friend, and a Scorpion herself) got into asteroids in a big way, she discovered, as she has often said, *that your chart is true, right down to the details.* Martha's writing is dense and difficult, but her conclusions are astounding. It is simply a matter of learning to read the details.

You may have thought you needed complicated mathematical formulas to rectify a chart, and while you can make rectifications using accidents (i.e., transiting events), you can also rectify by sheer observation. Indeed, the final test for all rectifications is that the resulting chart confirms the identity of the individual himself. That it can be read.

I have thus established Stephen Colbert's probable time of birth as around 1:30 am on May 13, 1964

THE critical factor in Colbert's chart is not the stellium in Taurus in the 3rd, but its opposition to Neptune in Scorpio in the 9th. The third house likes simple facts, but in Stephen's case, those facts are constantly being contradicted by a Higher Authority (Neptune).

This is one thing I learned in Vettius Valens, who puts the lunar goddess in the third, and the solar god in the 9th. The implications, to me, were profound. We already know the 9th to be the house of religion. Valens not only confirms the Sun god as 9th house (Christ, Buddha, Krishna, et al), but in a revelation, gives us the third house as Mother Earth (Mother Mary), the earth/fertility goddess. By extension—and not a very big one—the 3rd house is instinct, which we share with the animals, while the 9th is intuition. Instinct falls below our waking consciousness, whereas instinct is above it. Instinct is common and personal, whereas intuition is abstract and impersonal. Instinct is the feelings you have, what you know off the top of your head, without having to think about it.

Intuition comes in a flash, in an instant in time, fully worked out, but then has to be laboriously "unpacked" before it can be understood and used. Instinct is immediate and direct. Intuition is abstract and difficult. All of this, hiding in the polarity of the 3rd and 9th houses.

In astrology, the third house represents facts, but the ninth house represents truth. And in Stephen Colbert's chart, what do we find in his ninth? Neptune. Are Neptune's facts "true"? Stephen is himself expertly equipped to make that determination. Mars, the ruler of Neptune, is opposite, in Taurus, where it has clear aim. Jupiter, which has an affinity for the 9th, though in this case does not rule it, is in Taurus which lets it function as a ground. Mercury, quite at home in the third, gives them all expression.

So the question I put to you is this: Is Stephen Colbert's ninth house Neptune truthful?

Is Neptune ever truthful? When it is in opposition, does it not see what it can get away with? Can Neptune ever be truthful? Well, not really. Neptune in the 9th, all by itself, that's the very definition of **Truthiness**, don't you think?

So when did Stephen Colbert unleash this word onto the world? To my astonishment, it was on the very first broadcast of the *Colbert Report.* On the pilot episode. The one in which he would stake his claim, make his mark, give us the essence of himself, take it or leave it.

We all get flashes of intuition. Most of us are not well equipped to unpack them and so they pass us by. Colbert's stellium in Taurus in the third gives him the ability to exploit his intuitions and I would guess that over time he has learned to call on them, on command. And when he does, what he gets are the most intense Neptunian parodies.

Which begins to explain his ability with improv, which is how Stephen started his acting career, which only later became political. It also explains his dazzling performance at the White House Correspondents' Association Dinner on April 29, 2006, where he repeatedly lampooned and insulted the leaders of this country, who were seated, glaring, straight in front of him. The more they squirmed, the more Neptune reacted, and the funnier and more barbed Colbert got. If you ever wondered how Stephen got through that performance, look no further than his natal Taurus/Scorpio polarity. Not only could he not have done anything else, he was simply being true to himself.

Pity he will never be invited back. A man who has that kind of fearless power would be ideal as a leader.

Of what this native has shared with the world, this is the essence. Having studied the drawings of Anrias (*Man and the Zodiac*), I very much wanted to make Stephen's ascendant 20-ish degrees of Pisces, as Colbert has a notable "dolphin-like" appearance (sleek, streamlined), which is typical of one sort of Pisces rising. (The other sort is the whale, a mass of blubber, which reminds me of Garrison Keillor.) I will have to attribute his dark, "Piscean" appearance to the chart ruler, Saturn, which is in Pisces.

Saturn in Pisces, not really in the first, not really in the second, along with the Sun obscurely placed late in the 3rd, is why Colbert struggled to "find himself." He was further hindered by his Saturn-Uranus/Pluto opposition, which is to say the world, in general, keeps telling Stephen to "not be like that," whatever Stephen thinks "that" is this week. Which can be debilitating. Early in his stage career Colbert found he more enjoyed playing in empty houses than full ones.

The Saturn-Uranus opposition also happens to describe exactly the sort of TV persona that Colbert has created for himself. Saturn represents the old, Uranus the new and different. In opposition, we get a person who does not practice what he preaches, idealistic but oppressive, a person with few real friends, etc.

Which would be Colbert, except that Saturn-Uranus-Pluto being not quite here, not quite there, makes them just a bit remote in the chart. Which enables Colbert to deny that his TV persona is actually him. But as an alter ego, it's close enough and real enough that he wants to keep it away from his children. Look at his 5th house of children. It has Venus in Cancer in it: Intense love, intense protection.

There is one last detail, a sad one. Colbert is the youngest of eleven children. (Yikes! I am the eldest of nine. I know that kind of family.) When he was ten years old, the father of all eleven, James William Colbert Jr., was killed in a plane crash. The date was September 11, 1974, and if that sounds familiar, you're right. It was one year to the day after Salvador Allende, in Chile, was overthrown and killed. In a rectification based on accidents, September 11, 1974, should turn up in Colbert's chart. Anyone want to find it?

In sum, Stephen Colbert has taken a rather difficult chart, and a great deal of talent, and has reinvented himself as a cartoon character. It will be interesting to see what becomes of him over the coming years. — *October 18, 2011*

✤ Adam Savage, *Mythbuster*

ADAM Savage is co-host of Mythbusters, which is very likely my daughter's favorite TV show. Mythbusters is a science show on the Discovery channel.

Adam Whitney Savage was born on July 15,1967, in New York. As I have no idea what time he was born, I am going to discover it as I write these notes which you are now reading. Just as I discovered Stephen Colbert's birth time last week.

Merely being clever with his hands, as Savage is, can be explained by good aspects between Mars and the Sun, or Mars and Mercury, etc. These planets may end up tagged in the third house (a favorite of mine), or perhaps the 6th or maybe even the 5th or 12th, depending on the overall personality.

In Savage's case, this is not the entire story. Reading his Wiki page, it turns out that Savage has a specific ideology that guides him. As a result it seems he has confused his *mechanical ability* with a *belief system.* According to Wiki, Savage is an atheist who believes that he can, in his own words, *prove natural selection on the show* [Mythbusters]. He continues, *I'm sick of fifty percent of this country thinking creationism is reasonable. It's appalling.*

While I wish Mr. Savage every success in his project, I know his effort will end in failure. The world, in fact, has a metaphysical component. I myself have made use of it very nearly every day of my life. While this component is subtle and while it passes most people by and while we can all get along perfectly well without it, attempts to prove the existence of the physical world, as an entity in itself, will always fail, and for the very simple reason that the visible, physical world is the product of an invisible one.

When I got up this morning with no idea what I would write for my weekly feature and with a vague idea that I could "do a Mythbuster," I had no idea where that would lead me, or if I could delineate Savage's chart at

176

all. But now I know. Adam Savage has a defective 9th house. As I mentioned a week or two ago, no one gives up his father's religion, no one becomes an atheist, no one becomes militantly religious or *not*-religious (or even agnostic), without some 9th house kicker behind it. In all such cases that 9th house is never an empty house with a messed up ruler elsewhere in the chart. It's always a problem with planet(s) in the 9th itself. So now I will set up Savage's chart and walk me, as well as you, through it.

Looking at a chart drawn for noon on July 15, 1967 (New York), we see it will be tricky, as there is not one, but two good candidates for 9th house dysfunction.

The first is the Uranus-Pluto conjunction in Virgo. When that falls in the 9th, it's enough to power an entire generation of atheists, fundamentalists, and religious/scientific bigots of all shapes and sizes. Because the current religious/science conflict is really two sides of the same coin. Both are bigots. When bigots take the stage, those with more nuanced positions, such as myself, are blown off of it.

Which doesn't bother me (I have unique beliefs), but is a tragedy for those who need answers they will not get. Scientific bigots say the world is a cold, random place of Science, while religious bigots say there is a God that stands ready to punish, or reward, based on his personal whim. Both are simplistic, life-denying, cruel fantasies. You get the religion you pay for, and you're being cheated. If I were in front of an audience, I could dazzle. But I digress.

Uranus/Pluto in Virgo is a fascination with, and a belief in, details for their own sake. In Savage's case, Venus is also in Virgo, which gives a further love of details, which, given that Venus is debilitated in Virgo, Savage wants to apply universally, in other words, Venus wants to take those details and jump across the chart into its exalted sign of Pisces. Do you see how basic astrological fundamentals give you an essential grasp of the chart?

Given that the Uranus/Pluto conjunction is generational, then if they turn up in Savage's 9th house, they should connect him with others of like mind. In this regard we note that Savage is a regular speaker at James Randi's annual Skeptics conference. Randi is famous for his efforts to debunk what he calls the "paranormal." I personally believe Randi to be a reincarnation of a turncoat magus who was rather harshly treated (put to death) for breaking his oaths and is now seeking revenge. Randi is, on the one hand, too large a subject for this article, while on the other, no longer widely known, meaning I am unlikely to write an article expressly on him. I caution that I believe him to be exploiting people for his own private amusement, which is a dangerous thing. As is often said, revenge is best served cold, and Randi, who uses his considerable psychic powers to attack people, is best left alone.

THE alternative to Uranus/Pluto in the 9th is that we put Savage's Mars/South Node/Moon trio there and see what happens, but simply writing about Uranus-Pluto in the 9th is pushing me in that direction. It seems to me that Mars/S. Node/Moon in the 9th will not make for mechanical ability, which Savage clearly has in abundance.

So we now have a tentative chart for Adam Savage: **6:00 pm on July 15, 1967, New York.** Let's read this chart until contradictions between chart and Savage force us to throw it out wholesale, or until Savage and nuance leads us to tweak it. One or the other.

At 6:00 pm, the chart has Sagittarius rising. Sag rising is Enthusiastic! That's Savage. Eager to try anything, which he is. Ruler is Jupiter, in Leo, which means he is proud of his ability, and that he wants to be larger than life, the king of all. In the 8th house, he also wants to be profound in some way or another. It makes him a wannabe daredevil, as there is a distinct 8th house life-or-death aspect to his work on Mythbusters. So far, this looks like a good fit.

Jupiter is disposed by the Sun in Cancer, which is also in the 8th house, but you will note, not in the same sign as Jupiter. Savage will therefore profit from the resources of a partner, in fact needs a partner, which, so far as Mythbusters is concerned, is the person of Jamie Hyneman, eleven years senior, born September 25, 1956, in Marshall, Michigan. Mythbusters is in fact set in Hyneman's (not Savage's) shop. Hyneman is therefore "producing" Savage. Which is 8th house. For those of you looking to delineate chart subtleties, note that the conflict between chart ruler Jupiter, in Leo in the 8th, and the ruler, Sun in Cancer, also in the 8th, is one that takes time to resolve.

Mythbusters and the Hyneman/Savage partnership date from 2002, but the two men had previously worked together some years earlier. There should be some means to progress a chart to determine when a ruling planet like Jupiter "resolves," as it did in Savage's case, but I regret that in this case, without a better birth time and a first meeting chart, it will probably not be possible. Savage was 35 years old in 2002 when he and Hyneman started Mythbusters. In that same year, Savage married his wife, Julia.

SAVAGE and Hyneman are both convinced there is no God. I myself view God as a probability, but also as an unneeded distraction. When you're dead you will face a given scenario and it will make no difference if you are a craven believer or a raging atheist, but I am digressing again.

In Savage's chart, he believes in atheism because, Virgo on the 9th, he has the details that will prove it. These details, with Uranus and Pluto in the 9th itself, are widely shared among his peers, and with Venus in Virgo as well, they harmonize well. Venus in debility in Virgo, opposed to its proper home in Pisces, means that while Savage is probably wrong, he still feels he is a "modern", that he has repudiated an erroneous past. Note that each time we see a planet out of its element, in other words, in its debility or fall, the exact explanation changes from chart to chart, depending on the chart itself. As an astrologer, you have to know how to finesse these nuances.

For Savage we can go further. Venus in Virgo is disposed by Mercury, retrograde in Cancer. Mercury in Cancer is active, feels deeply and can be defensive. Retrograde, Mercury is usually wrong, but—for adverse aspects—has only a square to Saturn to annoy it. Savage can therefore largely convince himself that his beliefs are true and correct.

It sometimes happens that people take up public speaking in order to convince themselves of what they do not quite believe and I frankly have a hard time believing that atheists are all that happy with what they believe, because while we don't need a God to get ourselves from one life to the next, we do profit by knowing the process. Atheism repudiates that knowledge, while religions give only crude, fearful mechanisms. Neither are correct, both are harmful and should be ignored.

The post-death state is pretty much an autopilot process, but there are limits to it, and a disturbing number of people now arrive at death's door badly damaged psychologically, are unable to make use of it, and thus suffer horribly. Which is where ghosts come from, but again I digress. But look where Savage's Mercury goes:

In its turn, Mercury is disposed by the Moon, trine to it in intense Scorpio. This is a probing, searching, sexy nature. In the 11th house, it finds friends who agree with it. Since the Moon traces back to a debilitated Venus with strange beliefs, friends can be used to reaffirm what it wants to believe. We note its proximity to the south node, also in Scorpio, which, as with a debilitated Venus and a retrograde Mercury, confirms our belief that Savage has constructed a private fantasy. Well, why not? Many people do.

Pushing the Moon forward, we find it disposed by Mars in Libra. For itself, Mars is disposed, on the one hand, by Venus in Virgo, which makes a closed loop. Mars is also disposed by Saturn, which is exalted in Libra. As Saturn is itself debilitated in Aries, and as Mars disposes of Saturn, I will ignore the Mars/Venus relationship and concentrate instead on Mars/Saturn.

In Savage's chart, a debilitated Mars in Libra disposes of a debilitated Saturn in Aries. Mars in Libra is not confident of its own abilities. It would rather look across the chart, to Aries, which it rules, in order to find direction. Remember that the debilitated sign in question is Libra, which is the sign of the Other. And across the chart in Aries we find Saturn. Who represents someone who is older, authoritative, not active. In other words, Jamie Hyneman. You will note that Jamie's face has a reddish cast, red being the color of Aries, and that Hyneman shaves his head. Baldness, or lack of hair on the head, is said to happen with Aries when there is too much fire, which "burns the hair away." Saturn being incompatible with the fire of Aries, Jamie shaves his hair away.

HAVING, so far, found no reason to throw out the 6 pm chart and start over, we find Saturn near the 4th house cusp. Given that the 4th house is Savage's father and that Saturn is tied up with Mars in the 10th, we go back to Wiki to find out if Savage had serious Saturn/Mars conflicts with his father, which, if there was, would have left serious scars and would place Saturn in the 4th. Instead we learn that Savage's father gave his son an early break on Sesame Street, on which daddy worked as an animator. Saturn is thus not in the 4th. I advance the chart to 6:30. It puts Saturn definitely in the third, but it also changes the sign (Placidus cusps) on the 8th, from Cancer to Leo. This frees Jupiter in the 8th, but now intercepts and strands the Sun in the 7th. I thought about that. I also looked at the 6:15 pm chart. It also put Saturn in the 3rd, not the fourth, and kept the 6:00 pm intercepted Jupiter. At 6:00 and 6:15, Hyneman is Savage's "producer." At 6:30, with Leo on the cusp of the 8th, ruled by the Sun, and the Sun intercepted in Cancer in the 7th, Hyneman is now Savage's producer *and* his partner. At 6:30 pm, the Sun has rights in both houses, 7 and 8. This is clearly a better fit.

So now Savage's daddy is represented by an empty 4th house with Aries on the cusp. An empty 4th means that daddy was not important, one way or the other, in Savage's life. At Wiki I can find no more than a brief mention. Ruled by Mars in Libra, we would expect daddy to be involved with others (which he was), and in the 10th, we would expect daddy to make his son public in some way, which he did. That Mars is debilitated in Libra tells us daddy's efforts would fail in the end, which they did. This is all *ex post facto,* I am interpreting the chart to fit the life. The point is not to cheat in this way, but to show that you may have confidence in dispositors, in rulerships, in debilities and all the rest, and to use them in your work. Your "guesses" will more often be right than not.

Shifting the chart, from 6:00 pm to 6:30, you will note that Venus, which had been inside the 9th, is now just outside of it, late in the 8th. Which is, as I have mentioned before, a case of a planet wanting to be in the house with the same sign as the sign the planet is in. The effort to get into that house can make these planets "more eager" than planets which are actually in the house and so do not have to strain themselves. Venus wants to prove, in other words, that the quasi-religious, detailed beliefs that Adam Savage has, really are real and true. Again: A man who is quietly content with his beliefs (whatever they are) has no need to parade them before the public. An insecure man clamors to be heard.

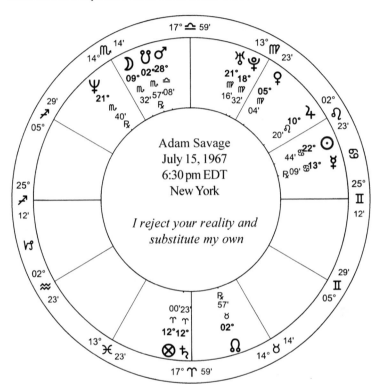

Adam Savage
July 15, 1967
6:30 pm EDT
New York

I reject your reality and substitute my own

On Mythbusters, Jamie Hyneman is known for his ingenuity, skill and craftsmanship. Savage, by contrast, is know for being crude and often wrong. Will Savage's chart tell us why? Of course:

Mars is the planet of energy. We find it debilitated in cardinal Libra, which means it needs someone to direct it. It is square to the Sun, also cardinal, giving both more energy than either can handle. It is also widely square to Mercury, the planet ruling the hands and fingers. The result is compulsively active fingers, as you would expect.

In Savage's chart, Mars is ruled more by Saturn, in Aries, than Venus in Virgo. Opposed by their signs, conjunct because of their mutual rulerships (Mars rules Saturn, Saturn rules Mars), the result is compulsively clunky, unwieldy Mars/Saturn, fast/slow, contraptions that only occasionally outshine those of Hyneman. Mars in the 10th, Savage has a compulsive need to show the results to the public. Look what I have made: Show and tell. Why so much compulsive? With four planets, and the nodes and the Part of Fortune, all in cardinals, one is always compulsive. With two of the four angles cardinal as well, visibly compulsive.

What if? What if Savage was goaded into finding his time of birth (it's at 125 Worth Street, downtown Manhattan, be sure and ask for the *long form),* just to prove me wrong and prove astrology to be utter bunk and rubbish? A tempting target for a Mythbuster, don't you think? Savage is, of course, proudly ignorant of astrology, so this would be an easy job for him. Merely cite my inane remarks and then display the **unadulterated** (NY State Seal clearly visible) long form of his birth certificate. Magnified so we can all read what it says. If Savage likes this challenge, and if his birth certificate is going to be on TV and I am therefore to be ridiculed, I claim the right to personally inspect the document beforehand. James Randi, whom I presume Savage idolizes, has pulled too many cheap tricks, and I have seen one or two on Mythbusters itself. I do not trust those who anoint themselves as "scientists." I've learned the hard way.

But what if I am right, that Savage was born after 6:15 pm but before 6:50 pm? A true believer, I expect Savage to find some way to privately rationalize it away and there would be no Mythbuster expose. Rationalization and denial has become the favorite excuses of weak and feeble "scientists." Those who are too timid to boldly go.

I myself would be amazed if I was right. I've been down in the trenches for 25-odd years. Astrology is really crazy. If I am wrong and it turns out that Savage was born at some other time, the analysis would be a wonderful learning experience, the sort I don't often get. I am essentially an empty-headed idiot, I am always eager to learn. As Savage himself says, *Failure is always an option.* For all of us.

And so it goes. Personally, I like Mythbusters, I like the banter between Adam and Jamie, I like the second string of Grant, Kari and Tory, I like the stunts they get up to. The Discovery channel has a policy prohibiting them from debunking the "paranormal" (whatever that is, the term is only used by those who are openly hostile), which keeps the Mythbusters from embarrassing themselves. A couple of weeks ago they started another new season. I wish them well. — *October 25, 2011*

❖Jeremy Clarkson, Top Gear

JEREMY CLARKSON is the well-known main presenter on BBC TV's Top Gear program. He was born April 11, 1960, in Doncaster, in Yorkshire. Yorkshire is the largest of the English counties and has a distinctive culture. Men from Yorkshire are known as Yorkshiremen. Their distinctive small dogs are known as Yorkies.

Clarkson's birth time is unknown and he seems to have escaped the attention of most astrologers. The most astrological mention I could find cited his Libra Moon, which was a surprise to me. I had rather guessed a Leo Moon. Clarkson himself has ridiculed astrology (well, who hasn't?). In a notable article on the Top Gear website, he proposed the seven characters in Winnie the Pooh as better human archetypes. It's vintage Clarkson and a howling good read.

For those of you who don't watch Top Gear on Monday evenings, Clarkson is a longtime journalist who stumbled into TV, and then stumbled into a serious program about cars. Which was the original Top Gear, a half hour show that ran from 1977 to 2001.

In 2002, the BBC revamped Top Gear into an hour long show and while Clarkson is but one of three presenters (the other two are Richard Hammond and James May), he clearly dominates. Over the years, and with Clarkson in the lead, the show has abandoned serious automotive review in favor of speed, fast cars, brazen comedy, and phenomenal film editing. Top Gear is by far the most intensely edited show I have ever seen.

For the past week I have been thinking about Clarkson's birth chart. Clarkson is self-centered, forceful, buffoonish, mechanically inept, travels well, dislikes common folk, loves the military, and has a family, about which he says very little. I wanted to make a fool of myself and guess at his chart and then go to his Wiki page and get the birth data, but when I did that, I found that what I had imagined bore no relationship to Clarkson's actual day of birth. I had imagined Sun in the first, Moon in the 5th,

183

Mercury in 12, Mars in the 3rd, Pluto in 6, Neptune in 8, etc. The usual scattered stuff.

When I set up his chart, I was surprised to discover a very well defined teeter-totter/see-saw, with a cluster of planets in Pisces and Aries, opposed by another cluster in Virgo and Libra, with Jupiter and Saturn making squares and trines and sextiles from Capricorn. There was no way to salvage my fancies. So I threw them out and started over.

THE most obvious thing to do was to put Clarkson's Mars-South Node-Mercury-Venus all in the third house. Mars in 3, that would be fast cars as well as a lead foot on the gas. Mercury in 3 is journalism, but in Pisces, inept when it comes to details, such as actually fixing a car. The third house is further reinforced by Venus in Aries, which is aggressive, as well as making him a good interviewer (fluent with words). I note Venus is in a sort of mutual reception with Mars. Venus rules Mars as Venus is exalted in Pisces, whereas Mars rules Venus, being the ruler of Aries. This strengthens an otherwise weak Venus.

The result, a 1:00 am-ish birth, was another Sagittarius rising. Like Adam Savage (last week), and Ron Paul, of a few weeks ago. If so, the chart ruler is again Jupiter, which for Clarkson is in the sign of Capricorn, its fall. Saturn in Capricorn as well keeps Jupiter in line, which in this case gives Clarkson a certain personal insecurity, a defensiveness that comes through quite strongly whenever he is challenged by either of his Top Gear co-presenters, James May in particular.

Clarkson has his Sun in Aries and his Moon in Libra, but, if born around 1 am, he is a full day before the exact full Moon. As I've developed Clarkson's chart, it can be read with the Sun in the third, or early in the fourth. Either way, the Moon will be in the ninth.

If Clarkson's Sun is in the third, we would have, as with Newton, the typical intellectual powerhouse, Sun in 3 opposing Moon in 9, the Sun more than compensating for Mercury's weak sign. But that's not Clarkson.

If Clarkson has his Sun in the 4th, he would be a homebody. The fourth being land, the Sun in the fourth ties one to the land, to ancestry, and, in Clarkson's case, to his country. An Aries Sun is already militaristic, so putting the Sun in the 4th neatly explains his love of the military. Clarkson likes military toys (tanks, big guns, etc.) and has often competed his cars against British military units. This is evidence, to me, of an astrological "smear" across both third and fourth houses. Across an angle, which I have not before seen. In support of this, note the ruler of Aries, Mars, is in the 3rd house of (what else?) cars.

But his Sun is not very far into the 4th, as his Moon is clearly not in the 10th. Moon in 10 gives an instinctive "feel" for the public. One has a "knack", which Clarkson, with his many controversial remarks, clearly does not. Also, the public opinion of a man with the Moon in the 10th "goes through phases." One day they are popular, the next day no one wants them. Waxes and wanes.

Clarkson's popularity is fairly stable. He says dumb things, he gets yelled at, he shrugs it off and continues, unbowed. Not a tenth house Moon. Which means the critical Sun-Moon polarity is not fully formed in Clarkson's chart. Sun and Moon oppose by sign, but not by house. This means his head and heart, while opposed, each go their own way.

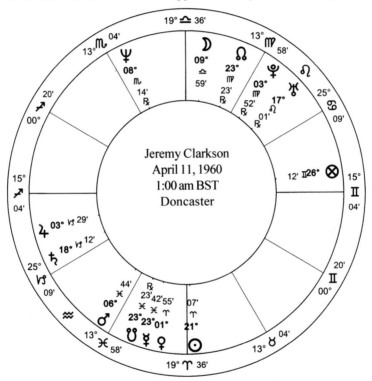

Instead Clarkson has a Moon-Venus opposition, which can make him feel unloved. Venus in 3, he likes his neighbors well enough, but Moon in 9, he is suspicious of outsiders.

Clarkson has his Moon square both Jupiter and Saturn, and very nearly exactly square their midpoint. Moon square Jupiter is emotional excess. Moon square Saturn is depression and moodiness. Both together would make him bipolar. If this is true, then Clarkson's upbeat TV persona is only half the story.

His Sun is trine Uranus, both in fire signs, which makes him even more impulsive. Mars trine Neptune (both in water) heightens his sense of instinct and emotion but puts it largely below his waking consciousness. Mars opposite Pluto is an aspect of a daredevil, but not the hair-raising life-or-death sort, as it falls not in 2/8, but 3 and 9.

One way this manifests in Clarkson's case is with duels (oppositions) of sheer speed. Sun-Moon-Mercury-Venus-Mars are personal planets. Uranus-Neptune-Pluto are generational. Third house is local and small scale. Ninth house is world-wide and large scale. Clarkson has repeatedly set himself seemingly impossible challenges. He drives a car (third house/Mars) in competition against high speed trains, small planes, jet-powered boats, and in atypical cases, a steam locomotive against vintage car and motorcycle, and a high speed boat against a bicycle and London transit. All of which are 9th and Pluto.

Clarkson will often drive from home (England) to someplace far away, such as Top Gear's numerous jaunts to the south of France, or from London to Oslo. Unlike his co-presenters, Clarkson is at home in many lands and is often well-prepared for what he will find there. This is a well-constructed ninth house.

A variation on this theme is driving cars where no cars have ever gone, such as through a southern African desert, over open sea ice to the North

Magnetic Pole, and from the middle of the Amazon jungle to the Pacific Ocean, crossing through elevations in the Andes so high they could not physically breathe. As well as routes that are physically unsafe, such as from northern Iraq to Jerusalem to find the infant Stig in a manger for a Christmas show a couple of years ago; or completely unlikely, as the trip from Saigon to Hanoi on motorbikes.

JEREMY Clarkson is, in short, a bundle of contradictions held together by petrol and bailing wire. He is a man in motion. Colourful. I hate to think what he will do when he retires. Perhaps he never will. —*November 1, 2011*

✤ Michael Bloomberg, Mayor of New York

FOR once I don't have to do a fancy rectification, because for Michael Bloomberg, three-term mayor of New York, I don't think I could. Mike was born February 14, 1942, in Brighton, MA, at 3:40 pm EWT.

With a reputed net worth of $19 billion, Michael is said to be the twelfth richest man in America. It is said he has made more than a billion dollars in the past year alone. While there is not necessarily a conflict with a rich man running a major city, there are lots of conflicts when that man is known to be making buckets of money while serving the public, as Bloomberg does, but I digress.

I would not have guessed this to be the chart of a fabulously rich man. It shows money, yes, but not of that sort. Checking his Wiki page, I find Bloomberg was born poor, so he is a self-made man, which is all the more impressive. Our first job is to use astrology to explain how Mike got so very rich.

Turning to Lois Rodden's *Money How To Find It With Astrology*, chapter 14, Business Wealth, Lois starts by saying tight aspects to Pluto gives the native power. The only tight aspect Bloomberg has with Pluto is opposite his Venus. Rodden says that Pluto aspects to the Moon or Venus put a focus on personal or family matters, rather than business per se. She goes on to cite Mars, Jupiter and Saturn, saying these should rule the angles and preferably be in them. Bloomberg lacks angular place-ments (Pluto is in the first but not in the same sign), but does have Mars ruling the 10th and Saturn ruling the 7th, the two planets conjunct in Taurus in the 11th.

In bold text, Lois says, **"The ruler of the MC in the first or second houses, or the ruler of the second house in the tenth or first house are high score indicators of mundane success. The ruler of the 8th house in the tenth or first houses are potent indicators."** (*Money*, pg. 148.)

The ruler of Bloomberg's MC, Mars, is in the 11th. The ruler of his second, the Sun, is in his eighth. The ruler of his 8th house, Saturn, is in

187

the 11th. If you like Uranus as the ruler of Aquarius, that's in the 11th as well. None of this makes for extraordinary wealth. One of the frustrating things about trying to sell you books is that I myself keep shooting them to pieces. Lois's book is very good and will teach you much. Pity it does not explain how the mayor got so rich.

It's easy enough to see that Michael likes money, in particular, Other People's Money, as he has Mercury, the Moon and the Sun all in Aquarius in the 8th, of other people's money. Wall Street is the land of other people's money, since, as it's well-known, finance doesn't actually make money. It manipulates the money of others for its own profit. For this reason you should beware of 8th house types, at least until you get the hang of them. That Michael would like money as his own is seen by the fact that his Sun in Aquarius is debilitated and would rather be on the other side of the chart, in Leo, in the second. The house of his own money.

On the other hand the Sun in Aquarius is self-effacing, and with the second house empty, Mike doesn't personally (2nd house) care for, or for that matter, actually need money. Money, for him, is a process (8th house, other people) as well as a means to some other end.

Mike made his fortune by providing information services to Wall Street, and this is also shown in his chart: Mercury, the ruler of Virgo and the third house cusp, is strongly placed in Aquarius on the 8th house cusp. Retrograde, the money would be made by indirect means. As it, in fact, was. That this would generate a great deal of energy is shown by the north node in Virgo in the third. Bloomberg's initial business was providing fancy computer terminals to Wall Street banks and brokerages. If I understand things correctly, these terminals were and are rented, and at high prices. Wall Street is money-drunk and always has been. They are accustomed to spending far too much on just about everything. Wastefulness is a matter of pride with them. Bloomberg profited from that.

Bloomberg's goal does not seem to be money per se, but rather currying favor with his "friends." With the inclusion of Venus, also in Aquarius, the four planets in Bloomberg's 8th house are all disposed, as well as squared by, Saturn in Taurus in the 11th. This is an uneasy relationship, made all the more so by Saturn being sandwiched between a debilitated Mars as well as Uranus. It's as if they're "nagging" him, as in *"what have you done for me lately?"* sort of thing. It is said that Bloomberg donates lavishly to a great many causes, which reminds us that idealism is also part of the 11th house. The traditional concept of great wealth, one shared by George H.W. Bush (Sr.) as well as Ron Paul, is that a rich man must help his lessers, and in ways that do not call attention to himself. Many rich people who follow this creed (Paul among them) also believe government should not give money to the poor, as this encourages sloth.

They presumably believe the need the poor have for "enhanced financial resources" to be within the means of wealthy donors. Which, regrettably, has never been true and never will. There are not only too many poor people, too much need, but also that simple donations are not as effective as actual programs. To reuse an old analogy, donating to the poor is like giving them fish. A government program could give them rod and tackle and teach them how to fish, in other words, the government can not only provide money, but also administration and infrastructure. Private individuals, no matter how generous, cannot. Another analogy are the many Carnegie libraries. A wealthy man can give libraries full of books, but only states can found and organize and run colleges and universities. There are things the state can do that cannot be done by individuals or corporations. Which is why we have government.

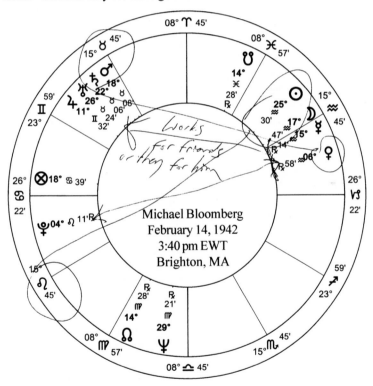

SO often we astrologers only look at a client's chart just before they arrive for a reading. I confess that I am the same, and while I can do a dang good job off the top of my head, when it comes time to write these delineations, I find that sketching the chart and then letting it sit a day greatly enhances my understanding of the individual. So it is with Michael Bloomberg. What makes Mike tick? Why was he driven to make so very much money, why does he give so much of it away, why was he compelled to run for mayor of New York, why has he declined the mayor's salary, and why, in this past week, has he ruined an outstanding career by brutally sweeping protesters from an insignificant plot of ground in lower Manhattan?

Answers to all of these questions can be found in the standoff between his 8th and 11th houses. Whether you use new rulers or old, in Mike's chart, the 8th house is ruled, is owned by, the 11th. In other words, Mike makes money, not for himself (Sun in the 8th, ruling the 2nd, which is empty), but for his friends. Sun-Moon-Mercury-Venus all in Aquarius, Mike is idealistic about money. He wants to put it to good uses. He wants to help humanity. While his Wiki page is silent about his high school and college days, Mike came of age in the maelstrom of the mid-1960's (he is 16 months younger than John Lennon, for example). If you have money, you're supposed to use it for the benefit of others. Not yourself.

Deep down, Michael Bloomberg believes this. In revealing the link between his 8th and 11th houses, astrology not only tells us so, it also tells us how the process works. Regrettably, it does not quite work perfectly.

Mike's eighth house cluster is ruled—traditionally—by Saturn. In money-loving Taurus, Saturn is needy and can never get enough. In the 11th of friends, Saturn is aloof and cold. True friends are few.

Giving the rulership of Aquarius to Uranus, we use other means and get nearly the same result. Uranus in Taurus wastes the seed it is given, so that no results are produced, money being like seed, Taurus being otherwise fertile. Uranus in the 11th, friends are erratic and, Taurus being an earth sign, tend to be brittle. The 11th house as ideals, Mike finds the causes to which he donates to be not the simple things he imagined them to be. Uranus makes them electric and complicated, rather than Taurean and simple.

This reaches another level of complexity when we note that the three planets in Taurus are themselves ruled by Venus in Aquarius in the 8th.

The first thing we note is that Venus in Aquarius is ruled by Saturn in Taurus, which is to say, the two planets are in mutual reception. Mutual reception is a *de facto* conjunction, pushing not only the two planets together, but also their houses — *not signs* (note that). So we have money (8th) for friends (11th), money for friends. Friends who never say "please" or "thank-you," as Saturn in Taurus is too crude for that. Saturn is direct in motion, which means it never has reason to reflect upon itself, or hesitate, or reconsider. It just goes on and on being needy, expecting Venus to provide. Now and forever.

For her part, Venus is in a very different frame of mind. **She is retrograde** as well as far behind the Sun. She has been thinking about this (Aquarius is a mental sign) and, further irked by the square between Aquarius and Taurus, the more she thinks, the less she likes and the further she drops behind, not only the Sun, but the Moon and Mercury as well. She sees herself approaching a backwards entry into Capricorn. Which, if she actually gets there, will be the end of her generosity. Capricorn is the sign of work, not of ideals. You get what you earn in Capricorn. As it turns out, she fell back another degree and then relented, going direct on the morning of February 22nd, eight days after Mr. Bloomberg was born. (And you thought ephemerides were just boring lists of numbers!)

Her decision to relent and not land in Capricorn was driven in part by Mars, also in Taurus. Venus is responsible for Mars, she is responsible for everything in Taurus, but Mars in Taurus is a dull, half-witted blunderbuss. Venus has to carry him as well, but if she slips back into Capricorn, Mars, exalted in that sign, immediately overwhelms her. Nor will Capricorn get her away from the needy Saturn. No. Aquarius may be bad, but Capricorn is worse. She's not going there.

WE come now to the disaster of last Tuesday morning, when police, and other forces, under the direct command of Mayor Michael Bloomberg, attacked and destroyed the Occupy Wall Street encampment in Zuccotti Park in lower Manhattan.

The proper analogy for what happened last week was not *"the failure of representative government"* since representation is merely a facade. Government has always been an entity unto itself, answerable only to itself, never to its citizens. Governments everywhere have always been this way and, one way or another, always will be.

The proper analogy is to a prison.

So far as New York City is concerned, Michael Bloomberg is the warden. He is a responsible warden, he cares deeply about the welfare of the prisoners entrusted to him. He sees to it that they are reasonably well fed, that they have heat in the winter and cool air in the summer, that there is work to keep their days busy. Is Michael's prison a pleasant place? Well, no, but then, prison is not supposed to be pleasant. The warden understands that from time to time, no matter how well he runs the facility, the prisoners will need to act out. He is prepared to tolerate this, to smile good-humoredly and to be patient. Children will misbehave, but they are still children, after all, and a prison is still a prison and must be run according to the rules. In America, the land of prisons, there are, in fact, prison uprisings every year or two. They have always been put down, they always will be. What happened in Zuccotti Park was not in any way unique.

But when his "children" do not get the hint, look what happens inside this particular warden's head. Bloomberg has sacrificed so much for their welfare. As warden, he has personally seen to it the prisoners of New York have the best that can be had. Remember that Michael Bloomberg has personally given many millions of dollars of his own money to charitable causes over the past 20 or 30 years, the majority of them in New York City itself. As its mayor, he has tried to arrange New York's government to be responsible to the needs of its "prisoners." Indeed, this was the entire reason he sought the office. To help his fellow man.

Michael Bloomberg, in short, has for many years offered the world his love, but in Zuccotti Park, his love was spurned. What happens when love is spurned? Typically, there is great anger. Which, if allowed to build, often produces great bursts of violence. Last week Michael Bloomberg lashed out and killed the one he loved.

Cancer rising, did he weep? Chart ruler Moon in indifferent Aquarius, waning, overwhelmed by the Sun, both of them fixed and stable, of course he did not. Michael never expresses his emotions. He is, rather like me (I have a fixed Moon, too), proud of his emotional stability. Proud that he never weeps. Moon in the 8th house of intensity, Michael knows there are far worse things than a 1:19 am wake-up call. Even if, so far as I can tell, he himself has never experienced it. (Aquarians use their minds to emulate. Scorpions drag themselves through the muck and experience the rawness first hand. Scorpions and Aquarians both admire, and mock, each other. Mercilessly.)

What is the astrological symbol of spurned love? Would that not be a retrograde Venus? Who spurned this love? Well, *they*—the nameless, faceless crowd—spurned it. What is the astrological symbol of the faceless crowd? That would be Aquarius, would it not? Presto: Venus retrograde in Aquarius.

But how is it possible that conditions from the middle of February, 1942, should relate to events of November, 2011? Would it not be true that Mr. Bloomberg has been down this path before, offering his love, love that was and still is ultimately spurned? Would this be this the first time he has struck out in response? I think not.

Attention now shifts to the protesters themselves. Did any of them think to go to Mr. Bloomberg and to personally *thank him* for his selfless, tireless work on their behalf? *Of course not!* Protesters, by definition, never, ever do any such thing. So far as Mr. Bloomberg is concerned, the protesters are like Larry Finkelstein, Dharma's father from *Dharma and Greg.* For Larry, protest is its own justification.

This puts Mayor Bloomberg in the role of Kitty Montgomery, Dharma's aristocratic, aloof, maladroit mother-in-law. But when times are hard — and they surely are hard now — there needs to be protest. When people are being crushed, their voices must be heard. I only wish the Occupy protests could be an enjoyable half-hour sit-com, rather than an unfolding national tragedy.

How these various individuals come to be in these places, how the great story plays out is a mystery that I fear no one will ever be able to solve. On the one hand, Michael Bloomberg is telling us, as clearly as he can, that *he* is not the problem, that *he* is already giving all that *he* can. He is the solution, at least in his own mind. In fact, as Mayor of New York, there is little he can do to help. The protesters have a national complaint. Theirs is not a city affair. Their complaint supersedes Bloomberg's duties and abilities.

On the other, the protestors are saying that they don't care. They just need more. More and more and more. Eighth house/Eleventh house. Retrograde Venus square Saturn in Taurus. It rarely gets more clear than this.

The fundamental problem is that Bloomberg is the wrong man in the wrong position. He needs to give, and he needs to have his gifts acknowledged. In this, he is intensely Jewish, which, in fact, is his religion. Past any other consideration, Jews are known by their generosity, by their ceaseless giving, but they are also qualified by the desire to have that generosity acknowledged. Which it never, ever has been.

One last detail. Thirty years ago I sold cameras at Harrods, in London. When I left England I settled in New York and soon found myself working for Nikon House, in Rockefeller Center, a location which has long since closed. I was hired because I needed a job and because I knew Nikons, having sold them in the UK. I lasted a year before HQ in Long Island ordered my boss, a man with the impossible name of Richard Clark, to fire me. (They had cause. Trust me. I can be one awful pest.) Years later he mentioned he had chosen me over a man who was independently rich and did not actually need the money. A man who knew Nikons far better than me. Richard was shrewd enough to realize the other candidate merely wanted toys to play with. Such, I believe, is the case with Michael Bloomberg. He is not a mayor so much as a nanny. Or a babysitter. Or a warden.

What New York needs is a mayor. An executive. Mike Bloomberg is not an executive. He hasn't the chart. Bloomberg is a well-wisher, a dilettante, *a philanthropist,* a man trying to please his own demons, a man without knowledge of or interest in the government he heads. He is, in the final analysis, a rich man playing with toys. And now, with fire.

And with that, my apologies to a man who has tried so very hard to be good: Behold the power of astrology.

Postscript
The following was originally part of this week's essay, but was not needed. It is an interesting piece on rays:

In the November 8th newsletter I sketched a new theory of astrology. Astrology is a complex set of earth-based energies. Not from the sky. Towards the end I took a swipe at the new age/Theosophical/Alice Bailey doctrine of the Seven Rays.

Esotericists say that our Sun is a second ray star, one qualified by Love-Wisdom, and, so far as the stars in our neighborhood are concerned, this is presumably true. In a group that includes Alpha Centauri, Sirius, Polaris, Regulus, Spica and all the rest, our Sun is second ray. But it's not true so far as we on Earth are concerned. The Tibetans are being cute, they are giving us half the story. So far as the Earth-Sun relationship is concerned, the Sun is first ray. Will, or Power.

Look up in the night sky, the Moon has always attracted man's love and affection, his very emotional nature. On a crude level — which is all that the mass of men can comprehend — the Moon is second ray. But this brings up a host of problems, because the Moon, as both esotericists and scientists well-know, is dead. We are in love with a corpse, which is our primary source of what we call "love." What kind of "love" could this be? Well, malefic, of course. Unhappily like the last scene in Alfred Hitchcock's Psycho, where we creep up the stairs to the room in the attic and spin the chair around to find a badly decomposed corpse. That's our Moon.

So, being fair as well as realistic, how advanced, how loving, how caring, can we on Earth be with that kind of deathly radiation pouring down upon us? The evasive Tibetan merely says the Moon is a channel for some nicer energy, and no doubt he would like that to be true, but at best it would be like running your fresh water supply through your bathroom toilet. Get the drift? Which presumes the Earth itself is all that much better. Some of us doubt that.

But the Moon has another function as well. It is a limit, beyond which physical earth creatures cannot go. Nor can we reliably send metal boxes further out. Did you know that few Martian space probes survive the journey? The ones that do never produce the results for which they were designed. And there is a flip side to this limit as well: It keeps the manifest evil of the Earth away from the other planets. I will not sugarcoat this. On no other known planet are living creatures routinely killed for no reason whatsoever. That no other planet has living creatures is not the point. It is that the Earth kills. If humans were able to land on Mars and build a city, Mars would not harm them, but given enough time, the Earth-creatures would set upon each other. Rather like the teenage boys in *Lord of the Flies.*

The New Age was an attempt to fuse laboriously crafted Piscean ideals with Aquarian energy and practicality. It is the pet project of the witless Masters and, along with the Church itself, is trotted out every 25,800 years, as you may discover for yourself by a close reading of the character of Lot in the Book of Genesis. (When reading the Wiki page, combine the "herds of sheep" with the unleavened bread served to the two angels at their "last supper" and draw the obvious conclusion: Lot was the very last Pope of that Age.) But just as every sign repudiates the sign that came before it, every great Age repudiates the previous Age, so the grand project always fails, *always will fail,* condemning the Earth to another 25,800 year round of misery. This project most recently failed in the 20th century. Only a few years prior to my own arrival.

Which, bluntly put, means Heaven on Earth cannot ever arrive. We simply do not have the necessary materials. It is like trying to sculpt in marble when the only stone you have is shot full of fissures and the only tools you have are made of wood. Yet humans aspire anyway. From time to time great and noble and wonderful things are achieved — in sand, not marble—before being swept away by the ceaseless tides of the Earth and Moon.

The reason humans endlessly aspire for greatness and godliness (for lack of a better word) is because human souls, unlike human flesh, are not of this earth. Souls were formed and came from elsewhere. It was quite clearly better than here, which explains our longing to go back, but where this is I know not.

We are here until we individually wake up and figure a way out of this maze. Whereupon, when we die, we no longer need to reincarnate. We go elsewhere and perhaps are happy. Perhaps. Some day I may entertain you with excerpts from my **Book of the Church of Guaranteed Salvation.** The sub-title is *What You Need to Know the First Five Minutes After You 're Dead.* Someday. — *November 22, 2011*

✣ **Steve Jobs**, Apple Computers

THIS week I take up the chart of the late Steve Jobs, cofounder, chairman, and chief executive officer of Apple Computers, who died on October 5, 2011, at the young age of 56. Not being enamored of Apples and i-things, I was surprised to learn that Jobs was not a computer programmer, but rather a designer. You should know that I am not an expert on astrology software programs, but that Hank Friedman is.

Steve Jobs was born on February 24,1955, at 7:15 pm, in San Francisco. He was known for fanatic attention to detail, and a severely formal sense of design. His chart presents few problems in delineation and is a good example of tracing rulerships around the chart.

Jobs had fussy Virgo rising. The ruler, Mercury, is retrograde in Aquarius in the 5th house. Aquarius is a strong placement for Jobs' chart ruler. Mutable Virgo gives a love of details, Aquarius, a fixed sign, gives stability, and as a "universal" sign, also gives breadth of outlook. Mercury retrograde, it tends to "chew the cud," going over and over things until they are, with a nod to the ascendant, *perfect* in every detail. Mercury in the 5th house, there is great creativity.

The 5th house has Capricorn on the cusp and Venus hard on it. The lower form of Venus in Capricorn is tasteless and would just as soon make scribbles. The higher form of Venus in Capricorn is elegant and refined. It likes the old masters. The classical forms. What granny liked, whatever is old, whatever that was. Mikhail Gorbachev, the last Soviet leader, has Venus in Capricorn and has always dressed very well. From the pictures I've seen, Jobs was the opposite. For a long time he dressed like a slob. Then he found black, the color of Saturn, and adopted it as a uniform.

In its turn, Venus is ruled by Saturn in Scorpio in the 3rd. The third is the house of every day life, Scorpio is intensity, Saturn is NO! which means, in sum, that Jobs could never be satisfied.

Note what I am doing here. I am not blindly reading my astrology books. I am using *simple keywords* to *build an interpretation.* I don't really know where I am going until I have all the keywords, all the pieces, strung out in front of me. Looking ahead, I see Mars out there. He's going to be important, too. I look at all the pieces and then I have the whole story.

Steve's Virgo ascendant (keyword: detail) takes me to its ruler, Mercury (dexterous), which I find retrograde (re-do) in Aquarius (universal) in the 5th (creative). I find Venus (beauty) in Capricorn (severe) on the 5th house cusp (creative), which is ruled by Saturn (NO!) in Scorpio (intense) in the third (every day life). Noting degree positions, I find Venus tightly trine to the ascendant and Saturn tightly sextile both of them. Mercury is a wide inconjunction to the ascendant and square to Saturn. *Aspects reinforce rulerships.* Already a picture is building of a very unpleasant person. Which confirms what I have read.

In its turn, Saturn is ruled by Mars, which I find in Aries in the life-or-death 8th house. This is a man who will bet his life, a man who knows what the stakes truly are, a man who will not settle for second best, as well as a man who may well pass away at a young age. Mars in Aries, the sign of the sword, says he would die by knife, or, as it turned out, by surgery. Steve Jobs, like many others, died as a result of inept surgery, specifically long-term consequences from the pancreatic surgery of July, 2004.

Before I take up Steve Jobs' death, I want to highlight one or two other factors in his chart. The seventh house is Pisces, ruled by Jupiter. I find Jupiter in Jobs' 11th house, of friends. This indicates a partner chosen from among friends. Since friends are not lovers, when the 7th ruler is in the 11th, the native has difficulty distinguishing between friends and lovers. Jupiter, the ruling planet, says this friend will be someone "larger than life." As this is not, by definition, a peer to peer relationship, there can be hesitation about marriage. The specially selected Jupiterian friend may feel the native (Jobs himself) to be beneath her and thus not give consent. This amounts to an aphorism, and this is how aphorisms are made.

When the ruler of the 7th house is found in the 11th, any opposition to that ruler indicates problems with children, since children are ruled by the 5th house. Such as we find with Jobs. Venus is tightly opposed Jupiter, at 21° Capricorn.

Jobs had a child by Chris Ann Brennan, with whom he lived with for many years but whom he never married. Jobs denied paternity, claiming he was sterile, rendering mother and child destitute. This was at a time when he was becoming rapidly wealthy. This plays out explicitly in his chart:

Pisces on the 7th house cusp, ruled by Jupiter in Cancer, both signs being fertile, indicates a wife who is fertile, although Jupiter being retrograde, she might be slow to figure that out. Jobs' excuse was that he was "sterile." This belief is shown by Capricorn on the 5th house cusp, the house of children. If Cancer is the most fertile sign, then Capricorn, the opposite sign, is the least. Therefore a 5th house Capricorn would seem to be an indicator of few or no children.

This was reinforced by the ruler of Capricorn, Saturn, which was in fertile Scorpio. Saturn in Scorpio would make Scorpio not fertile, or at the very least, less fertile. In the third house of the mind, Jobs would be aware of this, and this is before I note that Mercury in Aquarius (waking consciousness), is square to the house cusp itself.

It gets more grubby. Lisa Nicole Brennan-Jobs, the daughter, is represented by Venus in Capricorn, just as one would expect. Opposite Jupiter (the mother), this would indicate the mother did not want or did not expect the child, whom the mother would see as a burden. For Steve Jobs there was yet another factor:

Venus rules his 2nd house, of money. The child would therefore have claim to Jobs' money. Jobs did not want that. With his Mars in Aries in the 8th, Jobs wanted other people's money. Opposite Neptune in the 2nd, he was presumably paranoid his money would be stolen. How much easier to disown the child and claim he was sterile. No one ever said this was nice.

The seventh house produces the first significant relationship, which seems to have been with Chris Brennan. The 9th house produces the second (the 11th house the third, etc.). Jobs' 9th has Taurus on the cusp. It is ruled by Venus. The second child — from whatever wife — is ruled by the 7th house, the third by the 9th, etc. So when the ruler of the 7th is in the 11th, marriage results not from the first great relationship, but the second. In this case, the second child, from the second mother, flipped the Jupiter-Venus opposition to something that more favored marriage and children and settling down. Sometimes astrology really is just that black and white.

IN a night chart, like that of Steve Jobs (Sun in houses 2 through 6), Mars is the sect ruler of the water signs and therefore has co-rulership of the Sun in Pisces in the 6th. The 6th is the house of doctors. Since the 6th house is normally the territory of Virgo, when the opposite sign of Pisces is found in the 6th, I would judge that Jobs had sympathetic, well-meaning, but befuddled and incompetent doctors. Normally I would read the sign on the cusp (a much more hopeful Aquarius), but the Sun in Pisces gives the house a focal point and so the Sun in Pisces will overwhelm Aquarius on the cusp.

Pisces is ruled by Jupiter, which is in Cancer. Jobs suffered, and ultimately died, from pancreatic cancer. Turning to Cornell, I find the pancreas to be co-ruled by Cancer and Virgo. Virgo, of course, being Job's ascendant, was ruled by a retrograde Mercury, while retrograde Jupiter in Cancer ruled his Sun. Note that Mercury is square Saturn, its ruler, and that Cancer is ruled by the Moon, which is in Aries, a fire sign that makes it hot. Jupiter is also exactly opposite the other benefic, Venus, which is in the sign of Jupiter's debility, Capricorn. Some authors say that Uranus is a malefic (which I would agree with), so its presence in Cancer would not be welcome. Finally we see the south node in Cancer. I agree with Judith Hill, that the south node functions as an energy drain.

We thus see that Jobs had a weakness in Cancer and his pancreas. Cornell says that pancreatic cancer is caused by afflictions to Jupiter. Which Steve Jobs had.

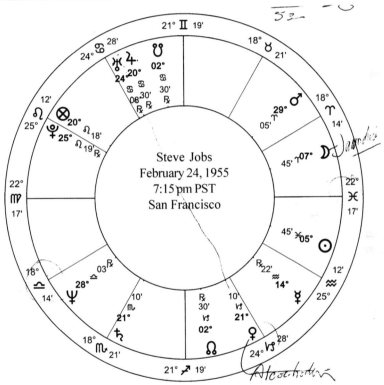

As an aside, while I don't often feature Cornell's *Encyclopaedia of Medical Astrology* in the newsletter (much too hard to transcribe), you will note that I do not set him up as a straw man to blow him down. Cornell is simply too awesome for that, and if any of you are seriously studying medieval medical astrology, you will find his book to be the best text ever written. Out of print for a decade, I initially reprinted it in hardcover in

2003, with a retail price of $89.95. I sold it directly for $74.95. It is now in a good sturdy paperback edition (970-ish pages) that sells for $69.95. I sell it directly for $49.95. (Cheaper than Amazon, by the way.) Fifty bucks is pretty much the going price for a serious gift. But I digress.

STEVE JOBS seems to have been faddish about his health and his diet. When health problems arose, he did one thing, he did another, he tried everything, and then in the end he seems to have given up and gone straight to surgery. In other words, Mars in Aries in the 8th had the last word. In this, it was backed up by the Moon, also in Aries. Aside from its ruler, Mars, Steve's Moon had little support. It had no close aspects. The Wiki page says that after the surgery, Steve did not have chemo nor radiation, presumably at his express request. Aries will have none of that. Aries wants action, not drugs.

Since we are now discussing the death of Steve Jobs, a simple reading of classical astrology says that death ensues when a malefic planet arrives at the 8th house cusp. Placidus is the usual house system. Let's test that.

With a 7:15 pm birth, Steve's 8th house has 18 Aries on the cusp. So let's look for aspects.

Starting with transits. On the day Jobs died, Mercury was at 17 Libra, and Saturn at 19 Libra. Their midpoint tightly sandwiches the second house cusp, directly opposite. This is malefic, but since transits to house cusps happen all the time, it can only be a straw in the wind. **Not a deciding factor,** so don't worry about simple transits to your 8th house. Transiting Saturn had previously been through Job's 8th house 30 years before. Transiting Pluto made a station opposite the 8th house cusp in 1979. Transiting Mars, yet another malefic, sailed through the 8th house some two dozen times in Steve's life, conjuncting itself every time it did. Not one of these were fatal. Relax! It takes a lot more than a transit to kill you.

Solar arcs for October 5, 2011, tell us more (Naibod system). Looking for 18 degrees, we find the solar arc ascendant to be 18 Scorpio, Saturn was at 17 Capricorn, Venus at 17 Pisces, and Jupiter at 16 Virgo. Of these, Saturn is square to the 8th house cusp and must be considered malefic. The others are inconjuncts, which in classical astrology are said to be ineffective ("turned away," per Valens). Thus the benefics, Jupiter and Venus, were unable to assist. Note the solar arc ascendant, 18 Scorpio, is ruled by the ruler of the 8th house, Mars.

What I wanted to find were hard aspects, presumably progressions or solar arcs, to the Sun, Moon and chart ruler, which here is Mercury. Which I do not find. In the progressed chart set for the day Jobs died, I find progressed Mars 1°30' from the *progressed* 8th house cusp, a progressed to progressed aspect, which are often revealing. Which, as the original birth time of 7:15 pm sounds a bit approximate, is within a reasonable rectification. A birth time at 7:07:38 pm puts progressed Mars exactly on his progressed (Placidus) 8th house cusp at the time of death.

But still I wasn't satisfied, and so consulted Abu Ali Al-Khayyat, *The Judgements of Nativities.* Here I am indebted to Meegan, who, having lost her husband at an early age, was determined to find out why. She sifted through the mass of early texts (including Valens, by the way) until she found James Holden's translation of Abu Ali Al-Khayyat, which she says is a good start. I am hopeful she will write a book and if no one else will publish it, I will.

While I do not pretend to be competent with Khayyat's text, here is the approximate method:

We first determine the *hyleg,* or *life giver.* In a nocturnal chart, the Sun is never hyleg, so that is eliminated.

Next we go to the Moon. We find it to be in a masculine sign without aspects from the rest of the chart, which by definition means not aspected by its ruler, term, triplicity or anything else. So the Moon is not hyleg.

Next we go to the ascendant. At 7:15, the ascending degree is 22°17' of Virgo. The ruler is Mercury, which is not in aspect. The term ruler is Saturn, which is in tight sextile. This makes the ascendant the hyleg.

It also makes Saturn the *alcochoden,* which is to say, the *giver of years,* the exact number of which is found in a table (based on a specific formula which I confess I have forgotten). Saturn in angles gives 57 (great), in succeedent houses 2, 5, 8, 11, 43.5 (medium), and in cadent houses 30 (least). With Saturn in the third, Jobs gets the least, or 30 years. To this we *subtract* the least years of malefics if they are in hard aspect, and *add* the least years of the benefics, if we find them in good aspect. As it happens, both Venus and Jupiter are tightly aspected (sextile and trine) which adds 12 years for Jupiter and 8 for Venus. We now have a 50 year life for Steve Jobs.

If I understand the theory correctly, the 50th year will not be the year of death, but its earliest opportunity, based on the next appropriate trigger event. This would presumably be a solar arc direction or progressed aspect, itself being triggered by an ordinary transit. For the actual death date of October 5, 2011, we seem to have found a lot of deadly solar arcs. We get another if we tweak the birth time by seven minutes.

You will note that in July 2004, when Jobs had his first major surgery (from which he seems to have never fully recovered), he was 49 years and six months old. That he lived an additional seven years might be because there were no significant death factors in his chart, or might be because, as a very wealthy man, he could afford a great deal of medicine. Or a combination.

Presuming I understand Abu Ali Al-Khayyat correctly (and I expect

I will hear from Megan about this), it would seem that Steve Jobs was, astrologically speaking, unlikely to live a long life.

What of the liver transplant? Two factors. One, most modern drugs are toxic and must be removed by the liver, putting a strain on that organ. Second, according to Carter (*Encyclopaedia of Psychological Astrology*), 7° Aries, the position of Jobs' Moon, is a marker for jaundice, which is a liver ailment. Which would indicate a weak liver.

At a notable conference in September, 2008, Jobs ended his presentation with a slide giving his blood pressure: 110/70. Which is quite good — better than mine, but then, my heart is stressed, whereas Steve's was not. This tells me that of the many alternatives that Steve tried, astrology was not one of them. Which is a pity, as **astro-medicine is superior to all other treatments.** Astrology not only tells you what specific parts of your body are strong or weak, it will also tell you how long you will live, if you are brave enough to find out. As Benson Bobrick wrote in his book, *The Fated Sky*, ancient rulers commonly knew both the approximate date of their deaths, as well as the means of their passing, both supplied by their trusted soothsayers, I mean, astrologers. When you suspect every shadow that flits about the palace, such knowledge can be priceless.

IF the 8th house tells us *when* we die, the 4th house (the "end of the matter") tells us *how.* Jobs' last words were "OH WOW OH WOW OH WOW." (Given in all caps in his obituary.) This is not hard to decipher.

Sagittarius on Jobs' 4th house says that death would be an adventure. The kind of adventure is shown by Jupiter, the ruler of Sag. We find it retrograde in Cancer, meaning something very personal, which, retrograde, had been overlooked or forgotten, and in (or, more exactly, wanting to be in) the 11th house of friends.

It would therefore seem that at the time of his death Steve found himself in the company of a larger than life friend (Jupiter), who was most likely accompanied by others of similar stature. I wasn't there, of course, but it sounds similar to what I have experienced, on several occasions, when I led unhappy discarnates (*explicitly:* individuals who had been dead, anywhere from a month, to a century or so, *none* of whom I ever met while alive) to their "great friend." (Which is the term I usually employ. It is deliberately vague.) Who then have an OH WOW experience and instantly disappear from the "Earth plane." This is in fact a wonderful, joyous moment. In my experience it will bring sudden, unexpected tears to the eyes of everyone lucky enough to be in the room, followed by a great sense of peace. If this is in fact how Steve Jobs died, then after years of suffering and pain, he had a most outstanding transition, a most wonderful death. We should all be so lucky. — *November 29, 2011*

⚜ Dave's own fudge recipe

MY mother made fudge, and whatever a mother or father does, their children believe that they can do, too. My mother made bread two or three times a week. So today I make bread. I always have, though I only do it once every other week.

I did not attempt fudge until after I had left home and was in college. I had a two-volume paperback edition of *Joy of Cooking* and followed the recipe. Except that I did not have baking chocolate. I had cocoa, as I love hot cocoa (try it with a dash of instant coffee crystals). But not to worry. In the reference section of *Joy* are equivalents. For two ounces of grated chocolate, *Joy* says you can use 6 tablespoons of cocoa, and 2 tablespoons of "fat." Unsalted butter, if you please!

Now I think that when you substitute cocoa for chocolate you get lousy results. If it was today, I'd say, I'm not poor, I will get the right ingredients and do a good job. Back in the 1970's I was young and poor and stupid and could still make mistakes. And as a result of having been cheap and ignorant when I was younger, now when I go into a chocolate shop and sample the best fudge in the house, I invariably find it of poor quality. Nothing like mine.

It wasn't until I made a batch for an old girlfriend and saw her reaction that I discovered how good mine was. A tiny piece is all you need. Eat a bunch and you'll get "high" from the chocolate. I always do.

The recipe, straight from *Joy*:

1 cup, minus 1 tablespoon, rich milk. I have been known to use half whole milk and half half'n'half.

2 cups sugar

1/8th teaspoon salt

6 tablespoons cocoa (Hershey's is good) and 2 tablespoons unsalted butter

You are expected to know your basic candy making: Heavy pot, careful attention to the heat so as not to burn, no stirring while the mixture

203

heats—or cools, the "quilting" pattern that signifies the exact temperature (I never use a thermometer), the soft ball stage, etc. As there is a great deal of fat, you should wait for a firm ball. Remove from heat and let cool. Do not stir. Add another 4 tablespoons of butter and 1-2 teaspoons of vanilla. When the fudge is cool enough to stick your finger in it, you must beat and beat and beat before it loses its sheen and solidifies. Sometimes it never does, there is so much fat. I think that while you're reading these notes, I am going to make a batch. Cheers! — *November 29, 2011*

✣Bibliography

Books mentioned in this book. Some mentions are oblique:—
Abu 'Ali Al-Khayyat (*trans:* James Holden) *The Judgments of Nativities*, AFA, 2009
Al Biruni (trans: R. Ramsay Wright) *The Book of Instruction*, Astrology Classics, 2006
Anrias, David, *Man and the Zodiac*, Astrology Classics, 2010
Appleby, Derek, *Horary Astrology*, Astrology Classics, 2005
Bills, Rex, *The Rulership Book*, AFA, 1971
Blaschke, Robert, *A Handbook for the Self Employed Astrologer*, Earthwalk School, 2002
Blagrave, Joseph, *Astrological Practice of Physick*, Astrology Classics, 2010
Bobrick, Benson, *The Fated Sky*, Simon and Schuster, 2005
Patty Tobin Brittain, *Planetary Powers: The Morin Method*, AFA, 2011
Canfield, Thomas, *Yankee Doodle Discord*, ACS Publications, 2010
Carter, Charles, *An Encyclopædia of Psychological Astrology*, Astrology Classics, 2003
Carter, Charles, *The Principles of Astrology*, Astrology Classics, 2009
Carter, Charles, *Symbolic Directions in Modern Astrology*, Astrology Classics, 2010
Clement, Stephanie, *Aspect Patterns*, Llewellyn, 2007
Cornelius, Geoffrey, *The Moment of Astrology*, Wessex Astrologer, 2003
Cornell, H.L., *The Encyclopædia of Medical Astrology*, Astrology Classics, 2003
Culpeper, Nicholas, *Astrological Judgement of Diseases from the Decumbiture of the Sick, and,
        Urinalia*, Astrology Classics, 2003
deVore, Nicholas, *Encyclopedia of Astrology*, Astrology Classics, 2005
Farnell, Kim, *Flirting with the Zodiac*, Wessex Astrologer, 2007
Frawley, John, *The Horary Textbook*, Apprentice Books, 2005
Goldstein-Jacobson, Ivy, *Simplified Horary Astrology*, 1960
Hunter, M. Kelley, *Black Moon Lilith*, AFA, 2010
Hunter, M. Kelley, *Living Lilith*, Wessex Astrologer, 2009
Jones, Marc Edmund, *Guide to Horoscope Interpretation*, Quest, 1981
Lehman, J. Lee, *Book of Rulerships*, Schiffer, 1992
Lilly, William, *Christian Astrology, Books 1 and 2*, Astrology Classics, 2004
Lilly, William, *Christian Astrology, Book 3*, Astrology Classics, 2005
Michelsen, Neil F., *Tables of Planetary Phenomena, 3rd edition*, Starcrafts Publishing, 2007
Morin, Jean-Baptiste (*trans:* Richard Baldwin), *Astrologia Gallica Book 21*, AFA, 1974
Louis, Anthony, *Horary Astrology Plain and Simple*, Llewellyn, 1998
Oken, Alan, *Alan Oken's Complete Astrology*, Bantam, 1980
Raman, B.V., *Astrology in Predicting Weather and Earthquakes*, UBSPD, 2011
Robson, Vivian, *Astrology and Sex*, Astrology Classics, 2004
Robson, Vivian, *A Beginner's Guide to Practical Astrology*, Astrology Classics, 2010
Robson, Vivian, *Electional Astrology*, Astrology Classics, 2005
Robson, Vivian, *The Fixed Stars and Constellations in Astrology*, Astrology Classics, 2005
Robson, Vivian, *A Student's Text-Book of Astrology*, Astrology Classics, 2010
Rodden, Lois, *Money How to Find It with Astrology*, AFA, 1994
Roell, David, *Skeet Shooting for Astrologers*, Astrology Classics, 2011
Rombauer and Becker, *Joy of Cooking*, New American Library, 1974
Sakoian and Acker, *The Astrologer's Handbook*, Quill, 2001
Sellar, Wanda, *The Consultation Chart*, Wessex Astrologer, 2000
Saunders, Richard, *The Astrological Judgement and Practice of Physick*, Astrology Classics, 2003
Sepharial, *The Manual of Astrology, The Standard Work*, Astrology Classics, 2010

Better books make better astrologers.
Here are some of our other titles:

AstroAmerica's Daily Ephemeris, 2010-2020
AstroAmerica's Daily Ephemeris, 2000-2020
 - both for Midnight. Compiled and formatted by David R. Roell

Al Biruni: **The Book of Instructions in the Elements of the Art of Astrology,** *1029 AD, translated by R. Ramsay Wright*

David Anrias: **Man and the Zodiac**

Derek Appleby: **Horary Astrology: The Art of Astrological Divination**

E.H. Bailey: **The Prenatal Epoch**

Joseph Blagrave: **Astrological Practice of Physick**

Luke Broughton: **The Elements of Astrology, 1898**

C.E.O. Carter:
The Astrology of Accidents
An Encyclopaedia of Psychological Astrology
Essays on the Foundations of Astrology
The Principles of Astrology, *Intermediate no. 1*
Some Principles of Horoscopic Delineation, *Intermediate no. 2*
Symbolic Directions in Modern Astrology
The Zodiac and the Soul

Charubel and Sepharial: **Degrees of the Zodiac Symbolized,** *1898*

H.L. Cornell: **Encyclopaedia of Medical Astrology**

Nicholas Culpeper: **Astrological Judgement of Diseases from the Decumbiture of the Sick,** *1655, and,* **Urinalia,** *1658*

Dorotheus of Sidon: **Carmen Astrologicum,** *c. 50 AD, translated by David Pingree*

Nicholas deVore: **Encyclopedia of Astrology**

Firmicus Maternus: **Ancient Astrology Theory and Practice: Matheseos Libri VIII,** *c. 350 AD, translated by Jean Rhys Bram*

Margaret Hone: **The Modern Text-Book of Astrology**

Alan Leo:
The Progressed Horoscope, *1905*
The Key to Your Own Nativity, *1910*
Dictionary of Astrology, *edited by Vivian Robson, 1929*

William Lilly
Christian Astrology, books 1 and 2, *1647*
 The Introduction to Astrology, Resolution of all manner of questions.
Christian Astrology, book 3, *1647*
 Easie and plaine method teaching how to judge upon nativities.

George J. McCormack: **A Text-Book of Long Range Weather Forecasting**
 With Foreword by David R. Roell, Astrology At Our Feet

Jean-Baptiste Morin: **The Cabal of the Twelve Houses Astrological**
  translated by George Wharton, edited by D.R. Roell

Claudius Ptolemy: **Tetrabiblos**, *c. 140 AD, translated by J.M. Ashmand*

Vivian Robson:
Astrology and Sex
Electional Astrology
Fixed Stars and Constellations in Astrology
A Beginner's Guide to Practical Astrology
A Student's Text-Book of Astrology, *Vivian Robson Memorial Edition*

Diana Roche: **The Sabian Symbols, A Screen of Prophecy**

David Roell: **Skeet Shooting for Astrologers**

Richard Saunders: **The Astrological Judgement and Practice of**
  Physick, *1677*

Sepharial:
The Manual of Astrology, the Standard Work
Primary Directions, a definitive study
Sepharial On Money. *In one volume, complete texts:*
  • **Law of Values**
  • **Silver Key**
  • **Arcana, or Stock and Share Key** — *first time in print!*

Zane Stein: **Essence and Application, A View from Chiron**

James Wilson, Esq.: **Dictionary of Astrology**

H.S. Green, Raphael and C.E.O. Carter
Mundane Astrology: *3 Books, complete in one volume.*

If not available from your local bookseller, order directly from:
The Astrology Center of America
207 Victory Lane
Bel Air, MD 21014

on the web at:
http://www.astroamerica.com

CPSIA information can be obtained at www.ICGtesting.com
Printed in the USA
BVOW040027190712

295607BV00002B/10/P